Teamwork in Multipr

Also available from Lyceum Books, Inc.:

Case Management: An Introduction to Concepts and Skills,
by Arthur Frankel and Sheldon Gelman

Modern Social Work Theory: A Critical Introduction, 2E,
by Malcolm Payne, foreword by Stephen C. Anderson

Cross-cultural Practice: Social Work with Diverse Populations,
by Karen Harper and Jim Lantz

*Clinical Assessment for Social Workers: Quantitative and
Qualitative Methods,* by Cathleen Jordan and Cynthia Franklin

Policy Analysis and Research Technology,
by Thomas Meenaghan and Keith Kilty

*Structuring Change: Effective Practice for Common
Client Problems,* edited by Kevin Corcoran

Working with Children and Their Families, 2E,
by Karen Harper-Dorton and Martin Herbert

Strengthening Refugee Families, by Daniel Scheinfeld
and Lorraine Wallach

Collaboration Skills for Educators and Nonprofit Leaders,
by Hank Rubin

Managed Care in Human Services, edited by Stephen Wernet

School Social Work: Practice, Research and Policy Perspectives,
4E, by Robert Constable, Shirley McDonald and John Flynn

Teamwork in Multiprofessional Care

Malcolm Payne

BOOKS, INC.

5758 S. Blackstone Ave.
Chicago, Illinois 60637

© Malcolm Payne, Lyceum Books, Inc., 2000

Published by
LYCEUM BOOKS, INC.
5758 S. Blackstone Ave.
Chicago, Illinois 60637
773+643–1903 (Fax)
773+643–1902 (Phone)
lyceum@lyceumbooks.com
http://www.lyceumbooks.com

ISBN 0–925065–36–6

Printed in Malaysia

CIP information is available from the Library of Congress.

Contents

List of Figures   viii

List of Tables   ix

Foreword by Thomas Meenaghan   xi

Preface and Acknowledgements   xiii

1   Open Teamwork   **1**
    Teamwork: three paradoxes   1
    Open teamwork: a manifesto   3
    Fine words defined   5
    The structure of the book   21
    Activities   22

2   Working Together: Policy and Concepts   **25**
    Working together: policy and practice guidance   25
    Teamwork developments   29
    Teamwork in care services   36
    Activities   43

3   Assessing and Reviewing Open Teams   **46**
    Assessing open teams: why, when and how   46
    Reviewing   49
    Team characteristics   51
    Problem assessment   55
    Task-focused   55
    Group or relationship dynamics   59
    Activities   62

4   Open Team Development   **68**
    Introduction   68
    Ideas about team development   69
    Practical teambuilding   76
    Practical networking   96
    Conclusion   101
    Activities   102

5   **Individuals and the Open Team**   **113**
     Introduction   113
     The individual   114
     Interpersonal factors and roles   117
     The individual and the open team identity   124
     Potential professions in a team and network   133
     Conclusion   136
     Activities   136

6   **Power Issues in Open Teamwork**   **141**
     The power principle in open teamwork   141
     Conflict   148
     Promoting participation   156
     Communication   159
     Movement and change   163
     Conclusion   166
     Activities   166

7   **Open Teamwork: Structure and Context**   **168**
     Teamwork structures in organisations   170
     Teamwork and field organisations   175
     Multiprofessional contexts   180
     Community networking contexts   187
     Institutional contexts   189
     Conclusion   194
     Activities   195

8   **Teamwork and Management: Team Leaders and Others** **201**
     Ideas on leadership   202
     Leading and managing in teams   204
     Support to teams and networks   208
     Problems in open team management and leadership   210
     Followership   213
     Conclusion   215
     Activities   216

9   **Four Teamwork Crunches**   **219**
     Child Protection   221
     Community care and health care   228
     Community mental health settings   234
     Criminal justice and public safety   239

Appendix on Team Development Activities **243**
    Briefing and debriefing 244
    Icebreaking 245
    Rounds 245
    Snowballing 246
    Brainstorming and filtering 246

Further Reading **248**
    Multiprofessional work in health and social care 248
    Practical books on team development 249

Bibliography 251

Author Index 263

Subject Index 265

List of Figures

1.1a   The traditional team in the community   3
1.1b   The open team – going out and drawing in   4
1.2   Network map   12
1.3   Seed's style of network diagram   19

3.1a   The Johari window   61
3.1b   The Johari window used for information sharing   61
3.1c   The Johari window used for problem-solving   61
3.2   The network star   63
3.3a   Network diagram   65
3.3b   Network diagram with weights   65

4.1   Scales of three features of teamworking organisation   73
4.2   Aims, requirements and stages in supervision   79
4.3   Forcefield analysis   111

5.1   Three interlocking networks in multiprofessional
        teamwork   127
5.2a   Concentric open team analysis   128
5.2b   Network open team analysis   129
5.3   Interpersonal professional roles as sets in fields   131
5.4   Network analysis of some agency relations   135

7.1a   Link pin structure: teams in a hierarchy   171
7.1b   Matrix structure   173
7.1c   Systems analysis of an organisation   174
7.2   The tension grid   197
7.3   Models of collaboration   199

9.1   Sources of poor practice in multiprofessional
        teamwork   237

List of Tables

1.1   Definitions of teams and teamwork   6

3.1   Assessing teams   50
3.2   Characteristics of teams   52
3.3   Team characteristics questionnaire   56

4.1   Webb and Hobdell's taxonomy of teams   72
4.2   Aids, hindrances and organisational strategies for
      women's personal development   77
4.3   Network assessment   98
4.4   Scale: helpful and unhelpful aspects of team
      relationships   104
4.5   Rating scale: motivation and satisfaction in the team   106

5.1   Personal factors in team membership   115
5.2   Benne and Skeats'group roles   118
5.3   Belbin's team role   120
5.4   How I work in my team rating scale   138

6.1   Strategies for dealing with conflict   149
6.2   Ground rules for team behaviour   151
6.3   Limiting conflict behaviour   152
6.4   Active listening   160
6.5   Being open in meetings   162
6.6   Fallacies which lead to powerlessness over making
      changes   164

7.1   Potential areas of difference between professions
      (with GPs and social workers as examples)   200

8.1   Support in the team   218

About the Author

Malcolm Payne is Professor and Head of Applied Community Studies at the Manchester Metropolitan University, having worked in probation, social services and the local and national voluntary sector in community work and mental health. He is the author of a number of books including the bestselling *Modern Social Work Theory* (second edition).

Foreword

Malcolm Payne's most recent book, *Teamwork in Multiprofessional Care*, is a timely and scholarly work. Unlike most graduate professional education programs, it recognizes the crucial role of teams in contemporary professional practice. Because it fills this knowledge gap between graduate curricula and the demands of actual practice, this book is a welcome addition to the literature.

From a conceptual perspective, the book clearly reflects an appreciation of how teams and groups have to adapt to both evolving internal group processes and dynamics as well as to external forces. This approach to teams is securely grounded in systems theory and organizational dynamics as well as organizational realties. To these sound conceptual underpinnings, the author adds persuasive and effective discussions of force field analysis and the interrelations between policy and practice.

From a basic practice perspective, *Teamwork in Multiprofessional Care* clearly recognizes the centrality of the problem-solving model. The book stresses assessment, and a focus on task completion is present throughout. In addition, Payne does not dichotomize personality and individuality considerations from social structure and power considerations. Rather, he interweaves a broad range of concepts into a coherent picture of practice that stresses role and role performance.

The book is rich in case material and reflects unusual breadth in its conceptual discussion. It is well written and integrates a broad range of practice material, and it stands alone in its ability to articulate the importance of professional teams and how normatively they could and should behave.

THOMAS MEENAGHAN
New York University

Preface and Acknowledgements

I have been working in teams for nearly 30 years and writing about teams and teamwork for 20. In 1982, Macmillan published my short text for social workers, *Working in Teams*, which has remained in print and in use ever since. It was based on my experience in the early days of social services departments, in the probation service and in teaching and training various professional groups and middle managers in the social services. Since then, I have had much more experience of a wider range of teams, particularly in the voluntary sector and in the mental health world. I have undertaken many consultancies, trained teams in a wide range of services and settings and provided training on multiprofessional teamwork and teamwork in community care. This new book builds on all of that experience.

It is, however, not a new edition, because the world of teamwork has changed out of all recognition, as have the services in which it takes place. The new world of purchaser–provider splits, demands for coordination and efficiency in health and social care, needs for partnership, partnership with service users, patients and clients creates a completely new context. Ideas have moved on, too. Team roles, self-managing teams, team coaching, team briefing... all these and more have entered the lexicon. Multiprofessional teamwork has also participated in substantial developments in health and social care. So the focus of this book is completely different.

First, it is wholly concerned with setting teamwork skills in a multiprofessional setting where efficient coordination of services and responsibility is vital, whether it is in health and social care, community justice, education or housing. All these services contribute to the modern community's health and social care. We must learn to participate with them all and more besides. Second, it directs teamwork towards promoting partnerships with service users, patients and clients, and it does so through incorporating ideas of networking which have been a crucial development of the 1980s and 90s. This leads teamwork to be more outward-looking, rather than concerned with group navel-gazing.

Some features of the book remain the same, however. First, it is not a 'management book' although managers may well use it; it is written for all members of teams. I argue in Chapter 5 that we all play many roles in teams and networks, and in Chapter 8 that everyone takes leadership roles from time to time in different contexts. Therefore, I think that everyone should have an awareness of and commitment to making a contribution in teams and networks to their management. Although this is not a management book, I have continued to try to bring together the strands of work on teams which come from management training and development and the strands which are influenced by professional developments in health and social care. Networking has been added to these aspects of teamwork. I have also focused, as in my previous work, on practical ways of developing teamwork around the actual daily tasks that readers will be carrying out. I focus on doing the work better, not group dynamics, although of course better teamwork does involve better group dynamics to some extent. But my view is and always has been that however interesting it is to study how we relate to others in groups, teams of professionals are there to do a job and teamwork aims to help them do it better.

I should like to acknowledge the advice given by Gurid Aga Askeland, an experienced teacher of groupwork, social services management and teamwork who commented on an early draft of the text, by an anonymous reviewer, and by Margaret Reith for her advice and suggestions from the point of view of a skilled multiprofessional worker in health care and in forensic mental health. She also drew my attention to the source of the criminal justice case study in Chapter 9. I am grateful for the help of all the contributors to Chapter 9 for their case studies. Beverley Burke and Jane Dalrymple would like to thank Brendan Kelly and Michelle Hyams-Ssekasi for their advice and comments on their contribution to Chapter 9. None of these contributors and helpers is in any way responsible for any failings in the book.

MALCOLM PAYNE

1

Open Teamwork

Teamwork: three paradoxes

Teamwork in multiprofessional care faces three paradoxes. First, if we concentrate on building team relationships, so that we work together better, we may become inward-looking and obsessed by the group or our own behaviour in it. Yet in care services, we must build relationships with professionals in other agencies and teams: we must look outward. Second, many people value teams as a source of mutual support in the face of external pressures and in particular the demands of the agencies and institutions in which we work. Yet managers see teamwork as the instrument for carrying out the organisation's objectives. Also, many people fear that working in a team will limit their personal and professional freedom. So, does teamwork support or oppress us? Third, thinking about teamwork causes us to focus on our colleagues and our interactions at work. Yet modern care services should be responsive to service users' needs. The policy trend is to involve them in decisions which affect them and the services that they receive. Being too team focused may mean excluding service users.

Care services are different now, compared with the past, although cooperation under the old regime did not come easily, either. Organisational reforms have fragmented what used to be a more uniform system of provision. At one time most health and social services organised and provided services directly. Now, health service and community care reforms have created a purchaser–provider split in which one group of staff commissions or purchases services from another. In education, schools have opted out from local authority management, so counselling, pastoral and welfare services may be provided in different ways to different schools. GPs have greater independence to employ their own practice nurses, rather than relying on a system of health visitor and district nurse provision provided by a

1

health authority. Many care services are partly privatised, so that residential and nursing home care, domiciliary care and day provision may be in public, voluntary or private sectors. Locality commissioning and primary care groups (PCGs) managing local community health services mean responsiveness to locally defined needs, rather than a comprehensive uniform care system. The probation service offers a range of different community justice alternatives in partnership with voluntary, private and other public providers. Its relationships with other parts of the criminal justice system become daily more complex. Everywhere, then, care service relationships are more complex and varied than they used to be. This may, perhaps, make them more responsive to local conditions, but it may also make them more difficult to follow, both for professionals and for service users. Enhancing cooperation and coordination may become more difficult.

These conflicting aims have, perhaps, been the reason workers in the caring services sometimes view teamwork with a jaundiced eye. Teamwork involves too many inconsistencies and difficulties: let's get on with our own job, they say. Nevertheless, frequent government reports and professional guidance seek cooperation, coordination and partnership between and within professional groups, between agencies and between individuals in the care services. People's lives and well-being are at risk – young children, elderly people, people with mental illnesses, physical disabilities or learning difficulties. Protection of vulnerable people, public safety, personal, family and community fulfilment: all these are at issue. In an increasingly diverse community, minorities of all kinds feel excluded and they need special action to make sure they receive relevant and appropriate services. Many clients, patients and users of care services have long histories of suffering oppression and injustice on top of their health or social problem. Sometimes, we find it hard to recognise this, and miss seeing how this disadvantages whole social groups in getting the right services for them. It makes it difficult for us to serve them properly, and draw them into participating with us in providing for their needs. Why should they believe we will be any different from the bad experiences they have had with services in the past? Everywhere, we are urged to get communication and relationships right. Managers and planners need to ensure that services use resources well, both personnel and budgets. Personally, too, workers want the satisfaction of cooperating with congenial colleagues in positive relationships to worthwhile ends.

Open teamwork: a manifesto

So we still need teamwork, but how can we deal with the conflicts that it presents us with? This book presents and argues for *open teamwork*. This approach combines the traditional, but still developing, view of teamwork with the concept of networking. Open teamwork argues that teams cannot just be about interpersonal group relations among professionals working together. Figure 1.1a shows what might be an 'ideal' traditional team, with good reciprocal interpersonal relationships. These allow the team members to operate consistently in the community around them.

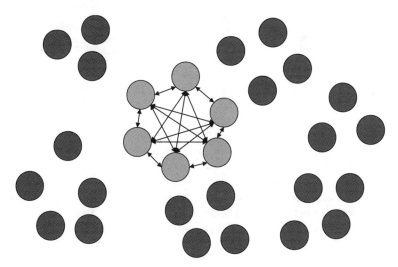

Figure 1.1a   The traditional team in the community

Figure 1.1b, however, shows more open teamwork, which is more appropriate to the modern situation. Here the close relationships in the team are the basis for team members going outwards to community, user or professional networks that they have contact with. As well as going outwards, they also draw those networks in to the team's work. This 'going out and drawing in' is a crucial aspect of modern teamwork. Group processes are still important because they provide a secure centre for developing openness. However, the team must also be a centre of relationships within wider multiprofessional, service user and community networks. So, professionals must foster close, positive relationships within their own work groups so that they may

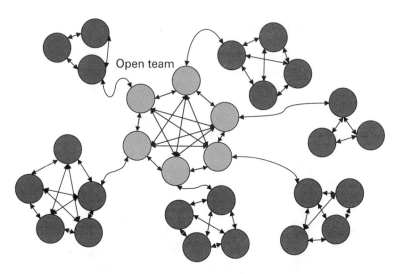

Figure 1.1b   The open team – going out and drawing in

build them into cooperative, multiprofessional networks and empowering, participative service networks. They must build effective relationships in the network so that they can contribute effectively to the team.

Teams are integral to the network. The team *is* an aspect of the network; the network *is* an extension of the team. Teamwork and networking are not different: they require similar skills and commitments to relationships. Knowledge about and skills in networking help to develop teamwork and teamwork skills can improve networking. Open teamwork requires the study and development of skills in both group- and teambuilding and in linking and networking. Both together help to fertilise teamworking with networking and vice versa.

Teamwork aims to stimulate group cohesion and cooperation towards professional and service objectives. *Multiprofessional care* uses teamwork to bridge divisions and conflicts between and within professional groups in care services, so stimulating more effective and coordinated use of resources. *Networking* seeks to extend the professional links created by teamwork into interpersonal and community links. These should involve and empower clients, patients and service users to use and develop services meeting their individual and collective needs. *Open teamwork* extends group cohesion and cooperation within agency and professional groups by looking outwards to participation by other agencies and professional groups. It also seeks involvement and empowerment of service users, making care services truly multiprofessional and fully participative and empowering. When I talk about 'the open team' and 'open teamwork' in this book, I mean the professional *and* multiprofessional teams *and* the network of people we link with in the community and team-working and networking together as an integrated form of practice.

Fine words defined

These are fine words: what do they mean? And where do they come from?

Team and teamwork

The meaning of 'team' and 'teamwork' is controversial. It is a useful part of any team development activity that participants review what they mean, and understand the differences in meaning which exist within their group. See the exercises at the end of this chapter for activities which may help you to work on this issue.

Table 1.1 gives examples of previous attempts to define a team.

Some of these definitions imply that 'teamwork' is uncontested, but this is not so. 'Team' and 'teamwork' represent aspirations towards cooperation, collaboration and coordination; they are 'hurrah'-words. A group of people are often labelled as a team because they, or their organisation or their manager, hope they will work well together or wish they would. The aspiration is of some perfect, seamless robe of shared endeavour, when different people, from different organisa-tions, act in different ways according to different knowledge bases, cultural traditions and objectives. This is a very common assumption in management texts about teamwork. There is often an explicit aim to develop or build a non-team group of people, often called a work group (Payne, 1982), towards more cooperative working. Another example is my early account of social services area teams (Payne, 1979), where I described traditional, transitional (that is, between traditional and community) and community teams. As in these cases, there is often an underlying moral assumption that independence is bad, perfect collaboration is good and every group should progress

Table 1.1   Definitions of teams and teamwork

Definition	Source
A common objective, differential professional contributions, and a system of communication will be considered necessary for an interprofessional team to exist.	Kane, 1975b: 5
A team is a group of people each of whom possesses particular expertise; each of whom is responsible for making individual decisions; who together hold a common purpose; who meet together to communicate, collaborate, and consolidate knowledge, from which plans are made, actions determined and future decisions influenced.	Brill, 1976: 22
A group who share a common health goal and common objectives, determined by community needs, to the achievement of which each member of the team contributes, in accordance with his or her competences and skill and in coordination with the functions of others.	WHO, 1984: 13
A number of persons in concerted action... a common task and complementary contributions – are essential to the concept of a team.	Adair, 1986: 8, 95
People who depend on each other to some extent to get their work done.	Gawlinski and Graessle, 1988: 4
Teamworking: a form of work organisation in which tasks are assigned to the group as a whole rather than to specific individuals or roles. In addition, the group assumes responsibility for making decisions relating to its work within defined boundaries.	Marchington, 1992: 32
A team is 'two or more people who must coordinate their activities to accomplish a common goal' (Plovnick *et al.*, 1975). The common goal and the required coordination make them a team. It is not enough for people to want to coordinate because it would be nice. Coordination must be required to accomplish the task in order to be a team.	Shonk, 1992: 1
A team is a small number of people with complementary skills who are committed to a common purpose, performance goals, and approach for which they hold themselves mutually accountable.	Katzenbach and Smith, 1993: 45

Table 1.1 (cont'd)

Definition	Source
A group of people who make different contributions towards the achievement of a common goal.	Pritchard and Pritchard, 1994: 13
Teams are entities composed of professionals from varying disciplines and organisations. They bring a diversity of skills backgrounds and training to the [child protection] investigation, and the result is stronger than the individuals acting alone. Teams share a common mission, and the members identify themselves as part of a collective effort to protect children.	Pence and Wilson, 1994: 14
Teams are organised task groups composed of persons from differing professions or of differing specialists from the same profession who work together using structured activities, processes and procedures. Teams are defined as organisational work groups or administrative groups consisting of staff members whose work is generally sanctioned by a sponsoring agency... devoted to accomplishing social service tasks... In addition to focusing on their tasks, successful teams attend to their process... the work of teams is intended to benefit clients... and to have broader benefits for the clients' family members, team members and leaders, the social service organisation, and the wider society.	Fatout and Rose, 1995: 46
A group of individuals who share work activities and the responsibility for specific outcomes.	McIntosh-Fletcher, 1996: 1–2
Those groups that constitute a system whose parts interrelate and whose members share a common goal.	Syer and Connolly, 1996: 7
A team, has five basic characteristics... the sharing of a common interest; to have a common aim and set of values; to have common objectives and/or tasks; for members to have designated roles and/or tasks; the feeling of membership and loyalty to the group.	Redman, 1996: 13
Three strands constantly intertwine in teams and teaming: commonality of objective or purpose; belonging and being part of something successful; synergy – achieving more collectively than can be achieved by individuals acting outside a team environment.	Colenso, 1997: 11

from one to the other. If we move from non-teams called things such as work groups towards 'real' or 'good' teams, there must be 'sort-of-teams' in progress. Are these teams or are they not?

To take a step further, what kind of team are we talking about? Payne (not me) and Scott (1982) distinguish between football, tennis and athletics teams. Each aims to win matches. With football teams everyone is on the field of play together and team members interact with each other throughout and they win or lose collectively. Analogies in the care services would be the team of doctors and nurses carrying out an operation, or a group of care staff running a residential home or day centre. Tennis teams play separate matches and individuals have to win their own match. However, they all play tennis. In the care services, a group of GPs working from a health centre or an area social work team are like this. An athletics team is like a tennis team in that they all play separately, but here they all do completely different things. This is like a multiprofessional team working to treat people in a geriatric or psychiatric service which covers both hospital and community health and social services. Clearly each different sort of team would need a different approach to teamwork. This leads to the situational view that the characteristics of teamwork depend on the factors affecting the social situation in which the teamwork takes place.

This analogy, which is commonplace in teamwork writing (see, for example, West, 1994), has been applied to multiprofessional teams. Horwitz (1970) made an important distinction between *coordinate* and *integrative* teams, that is, athletics and football teams. Øvretveit (1997) makes a similar distinction, between *coordinated professional* and *collective responsibility teams*, building on his research into health care teams in the UK. A coordinate/coordinated professional team has separate professionals with their own roles, accountable within their professional hierarchies, who refer work to each other and are influenced by each others' ideas. Horwitz emphasises the team leader, who may allocate work to other members of the team who are subordinate, common in the traditional medical team. An integrative/collective responsibility team shares responsibility and work roles, often with a coordinator or single manager responsible for work across the different professions.

Multiprofessional work

Many different terms are used to reflect the cooperative work of different professional groups. These are often used interchangeably in everyday talk and even in the literature. However, different terms have different implications.

Words with a '*multi*' prefix imply several different professional groups working together. However, this does not imply that they adapt aspects of their professional role, their skill or knowledge base, or their agency responsibilities to fit in with the roles, knowledge and skills or responsibilities of other groups. The concern is with collaboration or cooperation within their roles, rather than seeking to cross boundaries. Pappas (1994: 65–70), among other writers, therefore argues that separation of roles leads to parallel decision-making and seems to regard this as a step towards the integration that interdisciplinary work seeks. An '*inter*' prefix does imply the adaptation of roles, knowledge, skills and responsibilities to adjust to those of other professional groups or agencies.

'*Professional*' suggests a concern for different professional groups and functions and activities which are associated with those groups. '*Disciplinary*' suggests a concern with the knowledge and skills underlying particular professional roles. '*Agency*' suggests a concern for responsibilities associated with the roles of different agencies within the overall structure of services.

So, multiprofessional, multidisciplinary and multiagency work imply, respectively, that several professional groups, various knowledge and skill bases and different agencies are drawn together in a structure to provide services. Interprofessional, interdisciplinary and interagency work imply, respectively, that professional groups make adaptations in their role to take account of and interact with the roles of others, they similarly adjust those knowledge and skill bases and vary agency responsibilities.

Garner and Orelove (1994) distinguish between multi-, inter- and transdisciplinary work. Transdisciplinary teamwork requires the transfer of information, knowledge and skills across disciplinary boundaries and ultimately professionals taking on roles usually associated with another occupational group. 'Role release' is an important concept, meaning that team members allow aspects of their primary function to be undertaken by team members from other occupational groups. The origins lie in nursing, specifically an American project for 'atypical infants and their families' (Orelove, 1994: 37–40).

Multiprofessional work requires open teamwork at different stages of any activity. There are examples of teamwork in:

- *policy and service development and planning*, for example in community care (Payne, 1995);

- *prevention*, for example in crime prevention (Morgan, 1991);

- *investigation and assessment*, for example in child protection (Lloyd and Burman, 1996) or in admitting mentally ill people to mental hospital compulsorily (DoH/Welsh Office, 1993: 3–19);

- *treatment and care*, for example in residential care (Clough, 1982) or pre-school care (David, 1994);

- *evaluation and review*, for example in child abuse (Durfee and Tilton-Durfee, 1995), research (Holdsworth *et al.*, 1995) and in inspection of services (Clough, 1994b: 135).

Some guidance and policy development focuses on only one or some of these stages. More generally, multiprofessional work is promoted throughout service planning and provision.

Networks and networking

Four sources provide the origins of ideas of networks and networking. First, the concept of network is mathematical, and we may describe networks through mathematical models, although this is unnecessary for our purposes. Some of the ideas can help to understand more sociological ideas about networks. Second, a body of sociological work on networks covers social relations between family members, within communities and among organisations. This has produced a research methodology as well as evidence about links between people. Third, this has been extended into an application concerned with networks among people with social needs, elderly people, for example, and gives rise to policy and service provision to promote networking. Fourth, more broadly still, within public policy, and management (particularly feminist) studies, the idea of networking to develop 'policy networks' and to promote opportunities in marketing and for personal development has a wide currency. I shall look at each of these briefly, but clearly the most important for our purposes is the third. All these areas of knowledge, however, can inform our practice when we come to do things in multiprofessional teams, because we have to develop networks of relationships in our teams. Also, open teamwork means extending those multiprofessional networks beyond organisational boundaries and formal collaborative systems.

The mathematics of networking give us some basic ideas to understand networks. I have selected (Scott, 1991; Wasserman and Faust, 1994) concepts which recur in teamwork and networking writing, usually without explicit connection with mathematical ideas. Starting from the maths is useful, I find, because it gives us a clarity about the ideas we are using. It comes from graph theory, invented by Euler (1707–83). The myth is that he tried to solve a classic problem of the citizens of Königsberg, which is built on two islands in a river, with several bridges between them and the two riversides. The problem was how to walk over each bridge only once and get back to the starting point. He solved this by treating land masses as points on a map and bridges as lines symbolising links between the land masses. He could then work out a path round the whole system.

The ideas that come from this are, first, networking is about simplifying complexity by focusing on the important things and, second, the ideas of *points* as individuals or groups of people (in *social* network theory, 'actors') and *lines* as the connections between them. Social network ideas focus on *relational ties*, rather than the *characteristics* of the individuals (Knoke and Kuklinski, 1982: 9–21), and this emphasises how these ideas are a social rather than psychological form of explanation and analysis. Some people dislike the way networking treats people as points and relationships as lines: it seems impersonal. But hang on to the idea that this is a simplification to help us understand complexity.

Graph theory then goes on to how *connected* a system is. For example, there may be many possible lines between a set of points: the points are more connected if all or most of them are used, less connected if few or none of them are used. Seed (1990: 38–9) and many anthropologists call this *density*. We might assume that the more dense a social network is (around someone who needs care, for example) the better it would be. Connections may also be weighted. *Weights* might be about efficiency, for example, the shortest journey between two houses or the speed of a telephone call rather than a home visit. This may be important for disabled people who cannot move very quickly or for workers doing their job efficiently. In care services, we often weight connections by their quality, such as how

people evaluate each other. Do they like each other? Are they friends
or relations? Are their contacts frequent? Do they transfer material
resources by lending or borrowing? Do they belong to the same
organisations or have the same social experiences? Notice how, as
with 'close–distant', we often use a physical metaphor which points
up the way we think physically about mental or emotional issues.

Figure 1.2 offers a map of a network, a pattern of points and lines
showing connectedness and figures showing the weight of the
connections. The higher the weight, the closer the connection, either
in strength of emotion or in travelling distance. The map exists in a
field, that is, the total geographical area or the total possible points
and relationships that we might consider. Points cluster in groups, so
we can identify *boundaries* around parts of the map. These might be
significant. For example, this network map covers the relationships of
our *focus*, an elderly person Mrs Anderson (point A). The bounded
group (in maths, 'set') of points B is separate from group C. This
might be in distance, or if we are looking at closeness of relationship
simply that people who live in the same town form different friendship networks. One connection, between A and D, forms a *bridge*
between two different groups. The weight shows us that it is close. If
this is a distance map and we want to increase the number of relationships for Mrs Anderson, we might want to find other people who are

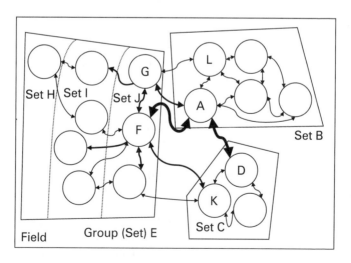

Figure 1.2   Network map

close by. If we want to improve the quality of her relationships, we might focus on strengthening the weight of some connections. If, as community workers, we wanted to strengthen networks in the town we might build on the connections between A and D to increase the number of bridges between B and C.

I have so far neglected one part of Figure 1.2. Group E represents a multiprofessional team. Mrs Anderson has close relationships with team member F (Freda – perhaps a social worker) and a less close relationship with G (perhaps her GP). The others rely on these relationships as a bridge. The boundaries forming sets H, I and J here are *concentric*, that is, each is successively inside the others.

The team will have connections in other parts of Mrs Anderson's networks, but I have not drawn these, because from her point of view (remember, she is the focal point) they are unknown or unimportant (remember, networks are always a simplification to understand something specific). If Freda wants to strengthen Mrs Anderson's network, she might have to draw in some of these additional connections. This might redraw the network from two focal points, those of Mrs Anderson and Freda herself. Freda's focus might be an intervention network – all the connections she might intervene with to affect Mrs Anderson's network, for example, D–K and A–L. To intervene, of course, she would have to know far more about the connections and about the people represented. Understanding networks does not mean ignoring relationships and personalities. They are a crucial part of *networking*, that is, intervening in networks to improve the quality or extent of connections between people in a network.

The preceding paragraphs introduce enough of the mathematical ideas to make sense of the sociology of networks and, building on this, the use of networks and networking in research, policy and practice in social services. Network ideas come from two different sources (Scott, 1991: 7). Social psychology developed a series of concepts from gestalt psychology, leading to sociometry, which influenced Lewin's field theory and led to the study of group dynamics. Structural–functional sociology influenced human relations management theory and, through social anthropology, studies of community relations in tribal and village societies. Group dynamics and human relations management both had an impact on teamwork ideas – more in Chapter 2. Both these sets of ideas had an impact on each other and led to the possibility of using networks in studying all social relations, both at general social levels and in everyday life.

Important landmarks of the development of these ideas are
as follows:

- Köhler's gestalt psychology which stresses how thoughts and
  perceptions are structured in organised patterns. These affect the
  whole personality and a person's ways of thinking.

- Lewin's 'field theory' is about how human groups interact with the
  environment in a system of relationships which could be studied
  mathematically.

- Moreno's therapeutically based theory of sociometry says that psychological well-being is related to patterns of relationships
  and feelings about others. These may be studied through maps
  of personal choices and liking for others studied in sociometry.
  Such patterns are the basis for larger social collectivities such as
  the economy or the state. Stability in wider social relationships
  comes from the smaller-scale patterns of relationships between
  individuals.

- Cartwright and Harary applied graph theory to representing interpersonal relationships in groups mathematically. They emphasised
  the importance of balance in interpersonal and group relations,
  rather than within individuals.

- Management studies by Mayo (see Chapter 2) took up anthropological ideas from Radcliffe-Brown to study the structure of relationships in local communities and industrial settings.

- The 'Manchester' anthropologists (Scott, 1991: 27) wanted to
  emphasise how structural aspects of society such as power and conflict maintained and transformed social relationships. Barnes studied how kinship, friendship and neighbourhood relations played a
  part in community integration, unrelated to economic or political
  structures. Bott used networks to understand the different forms of
  kinship relationships. Nadel (1957: 12) proposed theories about
  how society formed 'an overall system, network or pattern' of
  social relations. Mitchell distinguished two important types of
  action in networks: 'communication' which transferred information, established social norms and consensus and 'instrumental',
  where people acted with a purpose to transfer resources in the form
  of goods or services.

- Studies by the 'Harvard structuralists' Granovetter and Lee (Scott, 1991: 34) showed that information diffusion through relationships was more important in social activities than rational choices in some social relations. Granovetter showed how 'weak ties' were important to gaining new information when searching for jobs, since we share the same 'stale' information with people with whom we have strong ties. Lee showed that several out-of-the-ordinary contacts were needed to achieve contact with an abortionist. In both cases, thinking about social networks illuminated the range of different, overlapping social structures we are involved in.

All these ideas allow sociologists to say something about aspects of relationships among people. Wasserman and Faust (1994), for example, focus on the structure and properties of relationships, roles and positions and interaction within groups. Structure includes issues such as who is central, what groups and subgroups are present, who feels attached to them, and how strong and reachable they are to others in the network (see Chapters 3 and 4). Roles and position focus on what part people play in different networks and the kinds of ties which exist between people (see Chapter 5). Interaction looks at the size and characteristics of groups and how they fit together in larger organisations (see Chapters 6, 7 and 8). We need all these concepts and focuses to work on improving professional and multiprofessional teamwork and to extend it into the wider network.

The third group of contributors to network ideas is an example of how these ideas have been implemented in research in social policy and in the practice of networking. These two aspects are partly connected, because, particularly around mental health services and community care for adults, much of the policy work which has been done is concerned to understand how social networks contribute to social care, or might be recruited to do so.

An important broad contribution of network ideas to social policy lies in the analysis of the general processes by which we make policy. Benson (1982: 148) defines policy networks as a 'complex of organisations connected to each other by resource dependencies and distinguished from other... complexes by breaks in the structure of resource dependencies'. This means that connections with and conflicts between organisations that we try to work with can arise from being dependent on, or independent of, each other for resources. Conflict can be reduced by increasing resource dependency. Also, where there is independence in resources, it is easier for conflicts and poor collaboration to arise. Trevillion (1988) sees networks as systems of exchange, rather than as formal structures. He makes the point that we have to move from seeking reciprocity in an exchange to being mutually dependent in order to improve the functioning of a network. Rhodes (1986) examines the range of networks which depend on one another in forming policy: these include interests, membership, vertical interdependence (for example between central and local government), horizontal interdependence (for example between public, private and voluntary sectors) and the distribution of resources. There are policy communities of networks of organisations in constant touch with one another, such as health authorities and local authorities in each area. Issue networks are concerned with particular subjects, such as mental health and child protection. Professional networks are concerned with promoting the interests of professions, such as doctors, nurses and social workers' associations. These groups form different interests in the formation of social policy. Streeck and Schmitter (1985) argue that the mass of 'associations' involved in policy development form another social order to balance the interaction of community, market and the state or the bureaucracy in forming policy. The networks involved in policy communities form the context within which coordination activities between organisations and collaboration between professionals take place (see Chapter 2).

Ideas about professional collaboration have developed almost independently of policy developments about coordination, but have interacted with them. See Chapters 2 and 7 for more information about how multiprofessional work developed. A multiprofessional group of mental health workers associated with Caplan (Caplan, 1974; Caplan and Caplan, 1993; Caplan and Killilea, 1976) made the crucial contribution to connecting professional teamwork with networking. They used *consultation* from professionals to assist, support and train other professionals, carers and people in the community to help others. The consultant offers 'helpful clarification, diagnostic formulations, or advice on treatment; but the consultee will be free to accept or reject all or part of his help' (Caplan and Caplan, 1993: 11–12). Collins and Pancoast (1976) describe a particularly striking experimental project. They followed up mentally ill people who had been successfully discharged from hospital to identify informal community helpers who were unknown to professional services. These people, in turn, were provided with consultation to enable them to use their natural skills and established community contacts to help others.

Surveying a range of previous work, including Caplan's early contributions, Maguire (1991: xiii) identifies the following features of social networks which provide support:

- They are relationships among defined sets of people.
- They are enduring.
- They provide encouragement, care and direction.

In health and social care, Berkman (1985) shows that social support reduces the likelihood of dying or falling ill by providing care to people, advising people on getting help, modelling good self-care and providing interpersonal relationships, which helps reduce the effect of any disposition to illness. Maguire (1991: xv–xix) summarises the benefits of strengthening social support networks as improving services users' sense of self, providing more frequent encouragement and positive feedback than can be obtained from professionals, protection against stress, additional knowledge skills and resources and opportunities to socialise.

Maguire (1991: 26–33) identifies three ways for professionals to work on networking:

- *Network interventions.* This develops from a family therapy approach of bringing together family or community contacts and working in groups to improve relationships.

- *Case management*, called 'care management' in British community care practice. It involves coordinating a range of services so that they are appropriate to the service user's needs.

- *System development.* This involves trying to build up the number and quality of the links in service users' support systems.

Wenger's (1994) approach to network analysis in community care is based on research with elderly peoples' networks. It is mainly concerned with deciding what type of network an elderly person has; we can transfer the ideas to other user groups. The analysis deals with three factors: whether close relatives live nearby, the proportions of family, friends and neighbours involved in a network and the amount of interaction between an old person and their various contacts. Wenger's work identified five types of network:

- *Family-dependent networks.* Most contacts were with close family members, with few contacts with neighbours and friends.

- *Locally integrated networks* included family, neighbours and friends, and many friends were neighbours.

- *Local self-contained networks* involved arms-length relationships and infrequent contact. Although a relative lived nearby, most of the little contact they had was with neighbours.

- *Wider community-focused networks.* People in this category often had few family members living locally but kept active contact with family living at a distance. They were actively involved in community life, had many friends but few contacts among neighbours.

- *Private restricted networks* often arose where an elderly person lived alone or with a spouse and had few other family or neighbourhood contacts. They often had a 'difficult' personality.

Workers testing the typology found it easy to use, but could not always devise specific interventions to respond to the different types of network. However, they were able to respond to evidence that people with private restricted networks did badly in residential care, that neighbours in locally integrated networks were often highly stressed and that carers in wider community-focused and private restricted networks were often isolated and unsupported.

Seed's (1990) social work network analysis originated in several pieces of research. He developed a standard set of diagrams to display networks around service users (see Figure 1.3 for an example), using these for assessment, planning and monitoring and reviewing services. He proposes that thinking in this way helps to understand and build on the networks of people in residential and day care. It also helps planning for people who are moving between settings, such as discharge from hospital.

Trevillion's (1992) work applied many of these ideas to social work, particularly community social work and community care practice. He makes the important distinction (Trevillion, 1992: 12–13) between thinking about networks as frames of reference and as personal networks. The frame of reference may be an identifiable social institution, such as an agency, a group with a social problem, such as unemployed people, or a geographical area, such as a housing estate. We see ourselves as working within that frame for a wide range of different activities. Seeing it as a network enables us to focus on how the needs

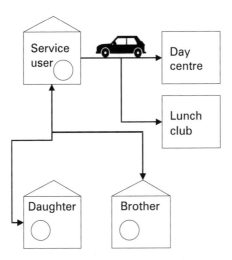

Figure 1.3   Seed's style of network diagram

and interests of stakeholders in that frame of reference interlock with each other. Personal networks are associated with an individual, family or group of people. Working with these networks involves developing links within the network and creating links to other people outside it. He identifies five uses of networking, as follows:

- Enabling better interpersonal relationships can increase caring, trust and develop people's self-image and the identity of their network as a set of important links.

- Enabling a sense of community identity can enhance mutual support and make wider choices of lifestyle and service available.

- Enabling joint work and the collective ownership of tasks helps overcome mutual suspicion.

- Enabling better communication through a variety of means improves information and links between people.

- Enabling 'action-sets' allows people to put together groups to help achieve some community or personal outcome.

Looking at these ideas, we can see that they can apply to anyone in a community setting, but they also connect to many important ideas in teamwork. The open teamwork approach proposes joining the frame of reference network (our agencies) with the personal networks of families and communities we work with.

All these pieces of research and analysis offer concepts which can help us grasp what we should do in networking within and beyond our team. We can identify which kind of network we are working with, possible alternatives to work towards and ways of analysing and describing what we are doing. Open teamwork means sharing this knowledge and understanding, first with other colleagues in the professional and multiprofessional teams. This helps us arrive at a shared understanding about how we are going to practise so that we can be consistent in the way we operate with people outside our agencies. However, open teamwork also means sharing our ideas and concepts within the wider network of people in the community, not in glorious technicolour, but enough for them to see that we do understand the connections among the different services and methods of practice. Also, they can begin to understand and use our knowledge as well: we should not be keeping the skills of networking to the professionals, but sharing it within the community.

We now turn to the fourth set of networking ideas, that which comes from management and feminist ideas. These suggest that we make decisions in organisations more effectively if they are based on a wide range of connections within the organisation and the environment which affects the organisations. As individuals, we can get our work done more easily if we have many connections within the networks of an organisation and its environment. It is a good way of improving organisations and good for people's personal development in organisations to improve their networks. Feminist ideas suggest that organisations are dominated by men who have networks which exclude women: this makes it difficult for women to gain influence and to work effectively. This causes a problem because, it is claimed, men are typically not very good at networking, that is making new connections and building up a pattern of links, so they stay with their existing contacts, which excludes women even more. Ways round this are for women to focus on networking, perhaps especially with other women, because they can use their particular skills to balance other disadvantages they have in male-dominated environments. This approach is associated with the idea of *mentoring*. This means subordinates finding superiors who they feel are sympathetic. They develop an explicit relationship in which the superior makes a special effort to support the subordinate's personal development, and help to integrate and advance them in the organisation. Some organisations plan mentoring systems as part of personal development and training programmes, but this may negate the element of personal relationship and choice implied in the original concept.

Some issues are particularly gender-related, relevant to ethnic divisions or to other social divisions deriving from disability or sexuality, for example. For example, Werbner (1988) studied female and immigrant relationships around working for Pakistani women in Manchester. Teams will need to be particularly alert where they are working on issues which might concern particular gender, ethnic or other divisions. They need to seek links with relevant networks, because existing networks and team relationships are likely to be weak.

The structure of the book

This chapter has been concerned with explaining the complex terminology of the ideas we will be dealing with in this book. I have also presented the idea of open teamwork. The book builds on this beginning. Its view is, first, that we have to understand the complexities of teamwork and the relationships that it implies. Being questioning is important, because we may take for granted that teamwork is a good, to be pursued at all costs. I shall go on emphasising that we have to make choices about how much to do and how to approach it. One aim of the book is to help make these choices.

Although any work group or manager thinking about teamwork could use much of the book, it focuses on multiprofessional work in care services. In Chapter 2, I examine more fully what 'multiprofessional' and related concepts mean. I also introduce the development of teamwork ideas in management and in care services. 'Care services' have no obvious boundary. The centre of care provision lies in the health and social services, but it brings in criminal justice, especially community justice services, education, housing, particularly social housing, the police service and social security. Not all aspects of these agencies and professionals within them are relevant. However, they interact in some of their work, and official guidance on important care services draws them in.

The following four chapters examine successively the practicalities of professional practice within teams and networks. I look at ways of assessing and reviewing teamwork and networks (Chapter 3); ways of developing them through teambuilding and networking (Chapter 4);

ways of thinking how an individual fits into a team and network structure (Chapter 5) and issues we have to face when working in this way, which I think derive mainly from problems about the use of power (Chapter 6). The last third of the book looks at fitting teamwork and networking into the organisations within which we work. This includes understanding organisational structure and training in teamwork and networking (Chapter 7) and how these relate to management, leadership and 'followership' (Chapter 8). Chapter 9 rounds this off by giving some extended case studies of teamwork and networking within common multiprofessional situations.

Each chapter moves broadly from the conceptual to the practical, but with different balances of conceptual and practical material. Each chapter also contains some activities which teams can use to work on together to stimulate and build open teamwork. The activities are relevant to the material covered in their chapter, but might be used more widely or adapted. They are only examples, and can be changed to take in the activities that the team wants. Activities need to be part of a planned programme, so that they arise out of an agenda which the team has. Also, when finished, activities need to be reconnected to a plan of action, if they are not to be just games-playing.

Activities

See the Appendix for basic team development activities.

What is a team (or is it a network)?

A useful beginning activity for any exploration of teamwork is finding out different team members' views of what teamwork is and how they value it.

Stage 1:   Brainstorm *or* snowball for single words that describe a team.

Stage 2:   Create a statement, using all the words, which satisfactorily describes the work group's view of 'what is a team?' If you cannot use all the words or they are repetitive, decide which is the most important and why some are less good.

Stage 3: Brainstrom *or* snowball for single words that describe a network.

Stage 4: Create a statement, using all the words, which satisfactorily describes the work group's view of 'what is a network?' If you cannot use all the words or they are repetitive, decide which is the most important and why some are less good.

Stage 5: Compare the statements and prepare an ageed statement showing what the difference is between a team and a network.

Stage 6: Decide, based on the statements, in what ways the work group is a team and in what ways a network. Are different aspects of work represented as teams and network?

Alternative: Use some or all of the statements in Table 1.1 as the basis for a discussion about the best definition of a team. Then proceed with Stage 3 onwards.

Teams in my life

(derived from Douglas *et al.*, 1988)

Stage 1: Ask each participant, working alone, to identify some work and some non-work teams of which they are, or have been within the last five years, a member.

Stage 2: Ask pairs to work on classifying them into football, tennis and athletics type teams.

Stage 3: Public report back, asking for any difficulties in allocation. Are there teams which you cannot classify in this way?

Alternative: Ask for the teams and classify them as they are given without disclosing the basis on which you do this. Get team members to work out the differences, before giving the labels and explaining them. Ask if they disagree with any of your classifications and why.

Stage 4: Prepare a questionnaire and ask members to complete it individually listing their primary work group or team, case conferences and reviews, divisional or area management meetings, management committees, policy development groups, trade union and professional association groups, user or consumer groups, professional interest groups, special interest groups, staff development and supervision groups and others. Ask people to classify groups as teams, networks or neither.

Stage 5: Ask each participant to identify their primary work group, their most interesting group and their most worrying group and say why. Record what people see as their primary work group, what interests and worries them.

Stage 6: Debrief. From this develop a discussion about difficulties in identifying and classifying groups.

Context: policy networks

This activity is useful for identifying organisations which are important in affecting the context in which a multiprofessional team or community or service user group works. Also, where the team or group faces the need to make policy changes, it can provide a useful analysis for seeking changes.

Stage 1: After defining the issue and an intended outcome on which the team wishes to work (you may need a separate activity for this), brainstorm organisations with influence on that issue in a series of categories: international and national, regional and local, professional and trade union, specialist issue-related.

Stage 2: Filter the organisations into those likely to be opposed to the team's preferred outcome and those likely to be supportive.

Stage 3: For each organisation, identify resource connections with other organisations which would support the team's preferred outcome and oppose it (for example, pairs of team members could research each organisation).

Stage 4: Identify individuals likely to represent each organisation on the issue, and identify ways of making contact with and influencing those individuals.

Stage 5: Identify individuals' likely links (including resource links) with other organisations and how they would support or obstruct the team's preferred outcome.

2

Working Together: Policy and Concepts

Working together: policy and practice guidance

In Chapter 1, we looked briefly at how pressures in care services have led to a focus on teamwork to help carry out policy in practice. We also saw that ways of doing teamwork are problematic. As a foundation for examining teamwork and networking, this chapter looks at policy and practice on coordination in health and social provision, in this section. It then goes on to explore developments in teamwork ideas generally and in the final section in care services.

Open teamwork means that we have to understand the policy and professional context, because we must help others understand it. Doctors need to understand how nurses see teamwork, health visitors and social workers the policy and legal requirements imposed on each other, probation, prison and police officers what to expect of each other. The understandings derive from all of the sources explored in this chapter: legal, organisational and policy contexts and professional traditions, experiences and understandings.

Teamwork, cooperation and coordination are about the division of labour in any activity and in society in general: more about this in Chapter 4. Once we divide tasks in complex societies among people or organisations, it is always possible that actions pursuing any goal may not be perfectly coordinated and structured. Going further, any complex activity carried out in and on behalf of an organisation will involve dividing the job and putting together the people who are contributing to it in an organised way.

Government is no exception to the need to coordinate divided activities. Large government organisations pursue quite complex policy objectives which have political origins, and thus may be often the result of compromises between disputed and confused aims. Such organisations therefore have different, possibly conflicting, focuses and priorities. Provision develops from Acts of Parliament passed at different times to meet different political exigencies.

Services based in government or coming from legislation and government policy might, therefore, always present problems of coordinating policy and objectives. Health and social services, education, housing, social security, community justice and the police all represent major arms of government. Each pursues its own objectives and priorities, perceived by the public as separate, each employing different occupational and professional groups. Power struggles about objectives, roles and responsibilities are major impediments to collaboration.

There are also different structures of provision: more about this in Chapter 7. One important division is between central and local government services. Even at these different levels, different types of organisation exist. For example, there are different types of local authority. Unitary authorities have wide responsibilities, but in some areas a county authority is responsible for strategic planning, social services and education, while a more local body deals with housing and local planning. At an even lower level, parish or town councils provide an involving consultative process for planning and take on some local responsibilities for welfare or community development. In regions, there may be coordinating bodies for specialised services such as police, fire and civil defence and increasingly also for economic development as well. These may become the basis for more regional government. In Northern Ireland, Scotland and Wales there have been separate government departments and, at the time of writing, separate representative assemblies are being set up. There is a European level of representation and decision-making. At the national level, some services are managed directly by government departments. Increasingly, after the privatisation policies of the Conservative government of the 1980s and 90s, these are managed partly separately from the government department. The Health Service always had rather separate management arrangements, which have become more complex in the 1990s.

Conflicts and uncertainties about government policy and provision are legion, therefore, and government has always sought to find ways of overcoming the problems caused by lack of coordination and pursuing objectives consistently.

General development of coordination policy

Different words are used, often interchangeably, to describe coordination, collaboration and teamwork. I offer some common conventions in the next paragraph.

'*Coordination*' is mainly used to describe the need to achieve better relationships between the objectives and organisation of different agencies. '*Collaboration*' is mainly used to describe people working together between different agencies and services to improve coordination in practice. '*Teamwork*' is mainly used to describe collaboration between people in regular working relationships concerned with the same group of clients. Often they are people from different professions or people with different tasks within an agency work group. '*Partnership*' is mainly used to describe collaboration where there is a long-term agreement about coordination and planning to achieve it. It is also often used to describe collaboration between different sectors of provision, for example, the probation service and voluntary and private services in the community justice field. Another usage is to describe collaboration between professionals and service users, as in the requirement for partnership between parents and professionals under the Children Act 1989. Both these uses of partnership connect with the management literature, which (see below) discusses partnerships between companies and their suppliers or customers. Very often, however, professional/service user collaboration is called '*participation*' or '*involvement*' as in the policy documents about the NHS and Community Care Act 1990. This implies a subordinate position for the service user: they are being 'participants' in something professional that already exists.

Loxley (1997: 95–105) identifies 25 different Acts and government documents published between 1970 and 1990 and 10 national professional coordinating bodies concerned in some way with cooperation between health and social services. There are many more in other related welfare areas. Indeed, it is hard to find a policy or guidance document that does not promote coordination of services and collaboration of workers. These were influential in establishing political and managerial goals to coordinate services, and pressure on workers to demonstrate collaboration. These political and professional pressures to coordinate services and promote collaboration between professionals and other workers form the context within which ideas about teamwork and multiprofessional collaboration have developed.

Theories of collaboration

Loxley (1997: 25, 34–40) identifies three social theories which underlie collaboration activities in health and social care: general systems theory, social exchange theory and cooperation theory.

The crucial contributions of general systems theory are of seeing organisations as wholes, made up of interlocking parts (subsystems) which are interdependent with each other. You can influence one part and this will influence all the other parts through the complex of inter-locking factors (equifinality). Also, the complexity means that one action might have many different results (multifinality). Systems and subsystems interact with and adapt to each other.

Social exchange theory comes particularly from anthropological studies, but has wide application in sociology and economics. The basis of the theory is that reciprocity strongly influences many rela-tions in society. I behave towards you as I expect you to behave towards me, or according to how you have behaved in the past. The exchange may be delayed. For example, I felt obliged to care for my elderly mother at least in part because of her care for me 30 years before when I was a child. The exchange may also be indirect. Many volunteers, for example, help in social care because they feel that society has benefited them and they must make some return. Exchange relationships may be complex. We calculate costs and benefits, power differences and we negotiate expectations and roles and relationships. To make a success of social exchanges, we need to know how to get involved. We also need the skills to make our contri-bution. We saw in Chapter 1 that some network theory is also based on social exchange theory and that this has been criticised because it only takes you so far in understanding cooperative links: you also have to look at interdependence, particularly resource dependency.

Cooperation theory (Axelrod, 1984) helps with this. It uses game theory, a mathematical theory which calculates the best strategy where there are conflicts of interest and a variety of options. Generally, better results are achieved where people cooperate rather than behaving indi-vidualistically. There has to be reciprocity in the relationships between participants and their relationships must be durable. Participants also need the capacity to make others involved realise that it is to their disad-vantage if they fail to cooperate – provocability. According to Loxley (1997: 39) this echoes evidence from the health care field, where coop-eration is better where relationships are durable and trust relies on a history and evidence of reliability. Each must also have roughly equal power to be provocable – that is, to damage the overall gain unless both cooperate. Failing to be strong in your own profession, therefore, undermines cooperative work. Bywaters (1986) argues in relation to medical social work in hospitals that both parties must reciprocate and be provocable, and cooperation must not be unconditional. Such arguments often run counter to political assumptions of the value of cooperation. For example, suppose the government requires social services departments (SSDs) to provide move-on accommodation to elderly people to clear hospital beds. This makes SSD cooperation unconditional and allows the health service and its employees greater power than SSD staff in decision-making. However, this is doomed to failure if this means that health care staff do not plan carefully for discharge, cooperating with SSD staff, because many discharges will fail. Similarly, if the pressure on SSDs means that no preventive work is done, admissions to hospital will rise. It is much better to provide incentives to cooperation which equalise power and let negotiation take its course.

Loxley (1997: 39–40) also makes the point that cooperation between parties for the benefit of a third party will not, according to this theory, be effective unless the third party also has a powerful part in the negotiation. Thus, professionals will negotiate for their own interests and not for those of service users, unless the service user has an active part in the process. This is another strong argument for developing service user involvement in professional processes.

All these theories share the characteristic that they focus on networks rather than small groups. Systems theory focuses on interacting groups within an organisation, exchange theory on reciprocity within all sorts of social networks and cooperation theory on relationships between interested stakeholders. This makes a strong case for including a network focus on any activity which is intended to develop cooperation policies. We cannot develop cooperation solely through promoting close interpersonal relationships in a team of professionals. Instead, we must look more widely at the stakes that each group has within the whole pattern of service provision and the exchanges that result from the interaction of their interests. That is the main direction of the discussion of teamwork in this book.

Teamwork developments

Ideas about teamwork originate from research and professional practice experience in many fields. This review starts from general management theories and research. It then explores, selectively, some ideas and literature that may be found in various fields of public service. Material from care services is reserved for the next section on 'teamwork in care services'.

Managing through teamwork – origins

Teamwork in management derives from the 'human relations' school of management theory, which developed in the 1930s and first flowered in the 1950s. This was a response to 'Taylorism', scientific, rational management science. The human relations school argues that to achieve successful results in managing an organisation you must be concerned for the motivation, aspirations and personal needs of workers. The rational management view focuses on organisational structure, time and motion study and things like procedures and the flow of resources. It rather takes for granted that human beings will fit in with the machines, either on the production line or in the office.

Early writing and research from the human relations school emphasises the work group as an important basis for motivation and organisation. In the famous Hawthorne research, management changes in a factory seemed to lead to improvements in production whatever was done. It turned out that the improvements came from the social consequences of taking an interest in groups of workers. Mayo (1933, quoted in Dyer, 1987: 8–9) says:

> The original provisions were effective largely because the experimental room was in [the] charge of an interested and sympathetic chief observer... He helped the group to feel that its duty was to set its own conditions of work... The group unquestionably develops a sense of participation in the critical determinations and becomes something of a social unit.

This emphasis on the success gained from improving group and social relations and an open democratic style of leadership strongly influenced human relations management ideas. Various writers contributed other important ideas to this basic view which led to an explosion of interest in teamwork in the 1960s. McGregor (1960) suggested that there were two views of employees. People who took a 'Theory X' (rational management) view thought that workers were unwilling to work, and needed a structure of rules and regulations, constant pressure and financial and other incentives to make them achieve what managers wanted. 'Theory Y' suggested that workers wanted to work and were motivated by having an interest in what they were doing, supportive social relationships in work and encouragement and involvement. McGregor (1960: 228–9) argued that unity of purpose among groups of workers was a crucial way of improving performance. However, in many organisations people worked individualistically and had most work communications with their superiors or subordinates rather than their colleagues. Recent comment suggests that workers like Theory Y management and most senior managers like to think that their organisation runs like that, but that to retain financial and procedural control, middle managers are forced to use Theory X procedures. The argument is that you have to change the whole organisation from top to bottom to make it a Theory Y organisation.

At more or less the same time, Likert (1961) argued that managers should be 'linking pins' between interlocking groups within an organisation (see Figure 7.1a for an example) and promoted participative group management rather than individualised supervision. Blake and Mouton (1964), again in the same period, considered that workers should concentrate on both the task to be achieved and the process of social relations within which they must work. They created a 'managerial grid' (see Figure 2.1), a graph of two nine-point scales in which low management emphasis on both task and social relations aligned with point 1 on the task and social relations scales was called 1,1 management, low focus on task, but high focus on social relations would be 1, 9 management and so on. They sought not a balance (5, 5 management, say) but attempts to achieve both the best task performance and social relations (9, 9 management), which would then support each other to the greatest possible extent. The practical importance of this formulation is its emphasis not on creating a *balance* between concern for the task and concern for personnel, but the value of giving a high degree of attention to *both* if we are to achieve effective teamwork.

Other writers on teamwork take this idea further. Adair (1986), in a well-known text, focuses on the importance of:

- Task
- Group
- Individual

in the life of the team.

These three aspects of team life, in Adair's view, interlock. That is, how one is supported or developed influences how the others function. Thus, as with Blake and Mouton's managerial grid analysis, the implication for practice is that focusing on one may damage the functioning of the others. Teams must have a ready concern for each.

This has implications for the whole team, not only for a team manager or leader, Take the example of a 'conference groupie' who is always going off on conferences for their personal development. By concentrating on their own individual needs, without concern for the task or for others' opportunities, they are unbalancing their contribution to the team. Equally, someone who gets on with the job day in and day out, but does not seek to develop themselves by taking up training or contributing to team developments, may be more than meeting the requirements of the task, but is not helping the team or agency to develop their work.

The focus on human relations management thinking, however, led to an emphasis on how the 'group', and to some extent the individual, had been neglected in favour of emphasising the task in scientific management thinking. The developments of the 1960s and 70s, therefore, focused on the need for the work group's contribution to the well-being of individuals and the task to be recognised.

All this work led to management efforts to improve group relations in work. This was further stimulated by the development of group psychology and a variety of group relations therapies, such as T-groups and encounter groups in the 1960s. Into the 1970s these ideas had a strong impact on health and social care. Work on intergroup relations, power and influence in small groups seemed to emphasise the importance of participative and democratic styles of leadership in groups (see Chapter 8). Therefore, improving group relations in teams became an important aspect of management development.

This led to a concern with *teambuilding*, which is usually interpreted as developing the relationships within the team so that there is more and better interpersonal interaction. An important influence is the work of Schein, a social psychologist who devised the idea of 'process consultation' (summarised ultimately in Schein, 1988; updated in Schein, 1999) as part of 'organisation development' (OD). Schein argues that an external consultant is needed to intervene in a work group's 'group dynamics' to achieve the best basis for effective work. OD places this in the context of participation in designing effective structures for group relations within organisations. Organisations should shift from a hierarchical structure, where more senior groups direct subordinate groups, towards a systems view, where relationships between groups are more various and equal. This approach has been applied in health and social care (Goodstein, 1978). The methods used have links with consultation as a way of extending expertise within the network (see Chapter 1).

These management ideas gained influence in the care system, reinforced by the interpersonal, social and psychological focus of much of the work and the training of the participant workers, which made them responsive to human relations management ideas. However, much of the work discussed above is concerned either with teams of equal managers of different aspects or divisions of industrial or commercial organisations, or with groups of industrial or office workers with routine jobs. It is not clear that we can directly apply it to more complex relationships between semi-autonomous professionals in organisations with more multifarious public service objectives and intricate relationships with other services and service users. This issue constantly arises in discussing teamwork. See, for example, the discussion of team roles in Chapter 5.

Managing through teamwork – recent developments

Interest in the management field began to shift, for various reasons. Influences include: two bouts of economic recession in the early and late 1980s; a political shift towards conservative values in much of Europe and the USA; the 'information revolution'; the global economy in which there was competition for industry and commerce in the developed world; and the success of the Japanese economy compared with Europe and the USA. Recession led to the need for closure or reductions in the size of large industrial and commercial organisations. This and competition seemed to need a more directive form of management, and this was reinforced by political moves against the power of trade unions and representative structures in industry generally. More individualistic values were ascendant. Japanese industry, with its more hierarchical, individualistic, paternalistic management structures, became a model for study since Japan had a very successful developing economy at the time. These achievements were thought to originate from the cultural approach to management (Wilson, 1995: 16–20).

One development which fed into new ideas on teamwork was the quality management movement of the 1980s. This shifted the focus of management thinking from organisational change and new product and service development towards improving standards of work and quality of existing products and services. Partly this came about because industrial production was mechanised, reducing the need for managing assembly-line workers, and service industries became more important. Many quality assurance developments came from the concern to examine Japanese management methods. Concepts grew out of the quality movement such as quality circles, in which groups of workers came together to make *and implement* suggestions which would improve the efficiency of their work or the quality of outcomes (Bradley and Hill, 1983). More generally, some proponents of total quality management (TQM) focus on involving employees in ensuring that everything they do and achieve is the best quality, often using group- and teamwork. However, other views of TQM derive from operations management in factories which concentrates on finding bad spots in the chain of production. These take a more rational management approach (Marchington, 1992: 92–6).

Several management developments of the 1980s were concerned with communication with employees. In the more 'top-down' management approach fashionable in the period, there was a growing concern to motivate employees and gain their commitment to management objectives. One way of doing this was through 'employee involvement', various forms of communication downwards (Marchington, 1992). Joint consultation on management objectives was valued in some large companies, newsletters and corporate videos also proliferated. Communication ideas included ideas such as *team briefing* (McGeogh, 1995), in which reports and instructions from managers were communicated through the organisation in a planned series of regular meetings. Another idea was *coaching* (Deeprose, 1995), an idea familiar to health and social care professions because it is similar to professional supervision which is commonplace in therapeutic and social work services. The role of a manager is conceived not solely as giving instructions and checking that they are carried out to the necessary quality, but helping staff by advising them on ways of doing things, being with them and planning a programme of teaching new skills. Applied to teams (Harrington-Mackin, 1996: 184–98) it involves tasks like helping the team set aims, training people to do tasks, building relationships among team members, motivating and encouraging the team and monitoring and feeding back on their achievements and performance.

The Japanese example, however, eventually led to a greater interest in teamwork again, but from a different perspective from that of earlier work which concentrated on improving interpersonal relationships and group functioning. The new perspective was to create *self-directed* (Ray and Bronstein, 1995; Wilson, 1996) or *self-managed* (Leigh and Maynard, 1995; Wilson, 1995) *high-achieving* teams. This came from Japanese use of employees in flexible work roles. Responsibility for an area of work was passed to a team with a definition of the outcome required and the resources available. They were jointly responsible for planning and managing their work to produce the outcome. This approach was particularly useful with task forces, project teams and quality circles (Colenso, 1997), where the group took continuous responsibility for achievement. This form of management went well with the 1980s delayering of organisations, which removed supervisory middle management. It also appeared to work well in creative tasks where knowledge, imagination and use of new technologies were relevant. It is related to the idea of empowerment in management, which means enabling and training staff to make their own decisions without constant supervision (Wilson, 1996). A crucial issue with self-management is *accountability* to the organisation, to each other and to service users. In traditional teams, a manager or team leader is responsible to a more senior manager. With a self-managed team, making people accountable seems more difficult.

Directly relevant to the networking focus of this book, a recent management development is work on partnerships. The argument here is that merely building up effectiveness in your own organisation brings limited gains. You achieve much more if you develop partnerships with your suppliers and with the people who distribute and use your products or services. There is an analogy with transdisciplinary teamwork in health care 'crossing the boundaries', mentioned in Chapter 1. Marriotti's (1996) book *The Power of Partnerships* is an example. He suggests that effective organisations need effective relationships with suppliers and consumers. In care services, 'supplier' translates into the agencies and professionals who refer clients and patients to us, 'distributors' into service providers who are part of a package of services for people in the community and 'consumers' into clients, patients and service users. Effective relationships with all these groups are likely to improve how we do our work and the responsiveness with which we deal with services users' needs. Another example of this trend towards concern for 'partnerships' which had a direct impact on my ideas when I was planning this book,

concerned with physical resources like hospitals and residential care homes. Professionals were left to get on with providing their services. There was also consensus across the political parties that the services were desirable and should be developed within the state.

However, the global concern from conservative politics in the 1980s to constrain or reduce public expenditure led to political intervention in management to reduce inefficiencies. More important, these policies came from an ideology to reduce the power of and expenditure on state services, and the influence of professions in state provision. Better services were equated with a market or at least quasi-market which, through competition, would produce economic efficiencies. When the Labour government was elected in 1997, it sought to demonstrate its greater effectiveness in managing services, particularly those where it had a political advantage, being more trusted than the Conservatives to maintain their quality. The priorities were health and education. Leaving multiprofessional teamwork to develop and overcome coordination problems was clearly inefficient in meeting political aims. Services were to become 'user driven' rather than 'provider driven'.

The first of these concerns is a modern concern with strategy. It proposes that policy must be effectively implemented and achieve policy goals, not merely work towards them. Guidance and research are used to support legislative and managerial control to achieve policy aims; to keep services 'on target' to achieve the outcomes which will support the political 'message'. Auditing and regulation are used to evaluate achievements and return deviant developments towards policy goals.

The second is a response to concern about professionalisation, leading to professional divisions and jealousies and inefficiencies which come from services divided along professional lines.

The third is particularly concerned to recognise the disillusion with professional expertise among many members of the public. Also, there was frequent criticism and scandal about the quality of services. The dislike of bureaucracy, a less deferential view of people in authority and a consequent attack on state or government management of people's lives is an aspect of the populist political movements of the 1990s. Consumer movements within the commercial and retail sectors led the way and this was applied to public services. However, there are differences. Consumerism in the private sector is concerned with preventing ill-effects from unsafe technology or materials and unreasonable pressure through advertising and misleading labelling.

In the public sector the concern is with proper systems of rationing and decision-making. Also, government can regulate the private sector by right through legislation. Setting up separate aspects of the public sector to control each other is more difficult.

This difficulty has led to various ways of getting consumer influence on public services. For example, surveys of consumer opinion apply pressure to improve services in ways the public prefers. Setting up standards of service and generally providing information help members of the public to see what they should be getting and allow them to ask for what they want. This is the approach of citizens' charters. Requiring partnership with service users is another way of enforcing public influence on professionals. This may be strengthened by ideas such as advocacy services, which improve the capacity of service users to take part.

In the 1990s there was a rising concern, influenced by European Union policy, for people whose economic and social circumstances exclude them from participation in society. Many public services are directly focused on providing for them. We must avoid excluding them from influence on those services too. This is for two reasons. First, democratic societies give people rights for involvement in decision-making. This is a right for public services, whereas private and commercial services may legitimately exclude people from decision-making. Second, participation in public services, particularly if advocacy strengthens it, can give people experience and confidence in having influence, which can then strengthen their involvement in other aspects of society. Public services have more responsibilities in this educational task than private services which have to make profits to survive. Open teamwork might be a way of achieving that aim.

Origins of multiprofessional teamwork

The idea of multiprofessional teamwork comes from health care. Pietroni (1994) describes the development of hospitals, particularly in the nineteenth century, where groups of medical practitioners worked together. As populations grew and large-scale wars with many casualties led to larger units the model of management became 'militarised', with an authoritarian chain of command within nursing, learned from the hospitals of the Crimea, the Boer War and the First World War. The operating theatre, with a surgeon commanding a team of people who undertook lesser medical tasks or managed equipment, became a model for other teams. In consequence, the ward round became a parade ground of the medical hierarchy and their nurse handmaidens, with almoners (medical social workers) as the quartermasters making sure outside provisions, such as housing and social security, were made available when required. This model transferred into the National Health Service (NHS), when it was set up during the late 1940s.

Services grew in complexity and size, and ideas of teamwork were used to coordinate and manage groups of similar professionals in general practice, child protection, hospital and residential care and psychiatric care. Some of the trends are considered in Chapter 7. As these services developed, coordination between them became more important. Other related services, in criminal justice, education and housing, followed similar trends of complexity, professionalisation and demands for coordination.

Movements to provide services in voluntary and private sectors also encouraged the development of coordination and collaboration policies. Voluntary sector services provided a counterpoint and alternative to many of these public services, and professionals transferred to and fro. However, in the 1960s a small pre-existing group of workers and agencies concerned with coordination of agencies in councils for voluntary service and volunteer bureaux gained greater strength and wider availability. Their development was an important recommendation of the Wolfenden Committee (1978) on the voluntary sector.

A fairly simple concept of health care provision based on hospitals, with medical leadership, has shifted, with the growth of broader public provision in a whole range of fields, to a complex pattern of services all with some interrelation. There are four patterns of coordination which have grown up organically, each with problems and advantages:

● *Keyworker coordination.* Here, one profession mainly based in one agency is responsible for the service to a service user, but needs to refer to or call on the involvement of others. This is the main pattern of most agencies in their daily work, for example where the GP provides most treatment but calls in other professionals to provide some aspect of the services. Other examples are the police officer who mainly deals with matters which come to the police service, but occasionally needs to pass them on to other agencies and the area team social worker who responds to most enquiries, but refers on or advises clients where to go for things they need. Because this is such a general pattern, an assumption of autonomous service builds up which, combined with separate professional training, establishes conventional divisions between professionals. The assumption of service and professional autonomy which comes out of this may obstruct closer working relationships and regular sharing of work. Cooperation and teamwork are always peripheral to the main workload. Senior staff or managers from agencies involved might meet at times to coordinate their approach to problems which arise.

- *Strategic coordination.* Here, agencies recognise some overall gain in coordination of the direction of work and planning. This is what leads to umbrella organisations in the voluntary and private sectors and corporate management in local authorities. However, coordination at this level is usually about service development and funding. It does not mean that professionals involved in the services resulting will necessarily work together.

- *Informal collaboration.* As professionals work together a great deal, they form informal collaborations across agencies, especially if there are shared interests like a service user group in common, for example, working with people with learning disabilities, or in a local area, for example, where many local authority services share the same office in a small town and get to know local GPs and community health services well. The problem is that without strategic decisions and management structures which support such collaboration, it is hard to progress beyond informal local agreements and cooperation. It may also be hard to get over personality clashes and structural or financial obstructions.

- *Multiprofessional services.* These often arise in situations where to achieve the task adequately professions, even if they are from different agencies and professional backgrounds, have to work together. There may be severe risks, where teams deal with child protection investigation and treatment and mentally disordered offenders. As Shepherd (1995: 122–3, emphasis original) comments:

> Getting teams to work together effectively is difficult, but unfortunately there is no other solution. The care of individuals with serious mental illness *and* a potential for serious violence is simply too complicated to be

carried out by one individual. Effective teamwork is the only means by which the range of necessary skills to address they can bring the problems together. Similarly, good teamwork is the only way that they can share crucial information and made available in a crisis and that they can achieve some semblance of continuity of care.

We can identify, then, six purposes for multiprofessional work:

- bringing together skills;
- sharing information;
- achieving continuity of care;
- apportioning and ensuring responsibility and accountability;
- coordination in planning resources;
- coordination in delivering resources for professionals to apply for the benefit of service users.

Many important areas of multiprofessional work have arisen out of professional developments: hospital care, primary health care, social services area teams, community social work, mental health community care and residential care are the main examples: see Chapter 7 for more detailed analysis of their contribution to teamwork practice. Others have arisen from various institutional arrangements: cooperation between probation and prison services in community justice and provision for disabled children, children with learning difficulties or emotional and behavioural disorders and other education welfare provisions from the social work, psychological and other services built up within the education system are examples. Governments and others have tried to coordinate these in various ways at different times, but the issue of coordination has particularly arisen recently around three areas of work.

First, concern about child protection has grown. This has required cooperation between a range of services which deal with children and their professionals, in particular hospital paediatric, community child health, education and social services. General practice has also become a major participant. As concern has risen, Britain has adopted an exceptionally (compared with some other European countries) legally based form of intervention and this has drawn in police and courts systems. Coordination of services and shared decision-making have become crucial and most of the services described above have become involved, at least in assessment if not in treatment.

Second, the aspect of community care concerned with psychiatric care has become more complex as there has been a move from hospital to community care. Where serious mental illness is allied with social disruption, violence or offending, police and other justice systems have been drawn into the networks of provision. The model of networks of services spreading out from hospitals into community services run by health trusts first developed with care for people with learning disabilities. SSDs and voluntary sector organisations, especially in the social housing field, were drawn in. These services also pull in education departments because of the need for psychological and special education provision for young people with learning disabilities. Coordination and shared decision-making have become complex, and multiprofessional teams drawing on some of these agencies were set up. A similar pattern has developed later for mental illness services, as the large hospitals for these groups have also run down.

Third, broader community care policy has led to attempts to heal a division between housing, health and social services in providing for long-term care for other adults, particularly elderly people. This is almost a separate system, because within the health service and to some extent SSDs the psychiatric system is largely separated. Also, education departments are not really involved in networks for this group, although of course lifelong education provision has much to offer elderly people to help stimulate them and extend their social networks.

All these areas have peculiar characteristics. Although there is a strong element of health service provision, it is not substantially medically led. This is partly because care not medical treatment is the issue, so the professional focus is on nursing or social work. Also, medical leadership is limited because legal responsibilities for child protection lie with SSDs. For mentally ill people and people with learning disabilities it is divided, with a substantial element of legal responsibility with SSDs or education departments. In community care, responsibility for provision is divided between SSDs and health care, and providers cover an even wider range of organisations, but SSDs take the lead in planning. Medical responsibility is largely for diagnosis and acute treatment, while long-term care does not require medical leadership to the same degree as acute services.

Consequently, the traditional medical team described by Pietroni (1994), already adapted by developments in professions allied to medicine, in these major multiprofessional areas has been displaced by a more complex set of relationships. Leadership may be in different places at different times: medical at diagnosis, nursing when there is physical care to be provided, social services when a package of services must be offered and perhaps in housing or education departments for service provision.

Øvretveit (1997) helpfully describes these as a series of pathways through services often being concurrently provided in different places or by different people, with the pathways coming together at case conferences or where work is handed over. At these points where pathways transfer or merge, shifts may take place in the focus of services, in leadership and in the formation of the team.

Similar histories of multiprofessional work may be identified in other countries. In the USA, for example, longstanding concern for professional cooperation with doctors and other professionals in health care (Kane, 1980: 138) shifted in the 1970s towards multi-professional teamwork first in community mental health centres. As in Britain, this was a movement to strengthen community services as psychiatric hospitals reduced their role. A similar development then affected the related community health centres, where family and personal medical services were provided, involving also community nursing, social work and other professions allied to medicine.

We can thus identify a range of areas in which cooperation policy and multiprofessional practice have led to teamwork. I have also argued that such theory, policy and practice in modern services require a networking focus outside the professional team and involving the service user. This arises because of social change and rising expectations, and because political impetus to respond to consumer movements has led to an outward-looking response. Also, theoretical developments focus on systems; social exchange and cooperation theory assume a wider focus. They suggest the need to involve service users if cooperation is to be effective within the politics of interaction among professionals.

Activities

See the Appendix for basic team development activities.

Our policy network

This activity aims to help teams look at the policy which affects teamwork in the particular network they work in.

Stage 1:	Pairs of team or network members, including service users, research legislation, government guidance and agency policy which affect their work.
Stage 2:	Report back, creating a complete listing.
Additional stage:	A team project to put together a library or information pack about teamwork guidance may be helpful.
Stage 3:	Brainstorm the range of professionals and agencies which the team works with.
Stage 4:	Pairs research legislation, government guidance and agency policy which affect each of those professions and agencies in their work with your team.
Stage 5:	Report back, creating a complete listing.
Stage 6:	Discuss differences and plan whether inconsistencies or lack of knowledge needs to be brought to the attention of your own or other professions and agencies. Do service users also need to understand differences? How might they be informed?

Professional teamwork styles

This activity aims to help identify issues in working with other professionals which arise from different professional histories and teamwork styles (see also, 'Evaluating the occupational groups in the team', Chapter 7).

Stage 1:	Brainstorm different professionals that the team and network work with. Identify settings in which this takes place.
Stage 2:	Pairs research the history of teamwork for that profession and research into teamwork attitudes of that profession.

Stage 3:   Report back, creating an analysis of the research and information, and snowball comparisons of the research and information with members of that profession in your network. Give an example of behaviour or practice which is similar to the research and an example which is different.

Additional stage: Role play a situation in one of the settings identified in Stage 1 which demonstrates the differences and similarities between the research and local experience, and/or between the situation now and how you would like it to be.

Additional stage: A team project to put together a library or information pack about professional teamwork styles may be helpful.

Stage 4:   Brainstorm and plan a strategy for changing or managing relationships with other professionals in more helpful ways.

3

Assessing and Reviewing Open Teams

Assessing open teams: why, when and how

Why assess?

Assessing teams is important from several points of view. When we apply or are moved to a new job it often means joining a team, and we need to look from the outside. A team leader needs to look at how a team is working as a team, and how individuals are developing and managing their work. Teams as groups might also want to examine and do something about the way they work. Before doing anything about teambuilding, we need to understand how the team is now.

At different times, therefore, different people may wish to assess a team from different points of view. The aim of this chapter is to offer perspectives and methods which people in different positions might adapt to their purposes. One difficulty is that assessing in any situation implies an element of standing outside, or on the margins, while of course working with a team and network implies being an insider. Team members involved in assessing therefore need to think out quite carefully what being an insider means and how this affects their assessment. It is often possible for teams and networks to assess their work jointly; other aspects of assessment require a more individual and personal focus. Thinking out a programme of assessment will often involve both elements. Often it is a team leader or someone with a particular specialist responsibility who will take on the role of introducing and building up some team or network assessment, as part of their role. However, I would not wish to exclude the possibility that on a particular issue or in a particular situation another member of the team might take up an aspect of the leadership in proposing or

46

organising an assessment process. Often, they might do so as part of a team decision. In one instance, for example, I worked with a team who used a student on a basic social work course who also had considerable management experience as the agent for planning a team assessment programme.

Similarly with networks. When we move into a new case, work with a new community group, or take up work in a new team, we may want to assess the networks involved. More commonly, we set off on our tasks, and only sometimes feel the need to use network ideas, or we are suddenly brought up short by the need to understand them better, so we start looking for information which allows us to map them. Sometimes, we decide to work on networks, and set out on them as a formal part of our assessment. This is a well-established way of doing family therapy, for example.

Open teamwork means focusing on *both* the team and the network. A modern health or social care team does not get its success only from the immediate group. It only works if it is effective in linking with surrounding professionals and the network of its service users. It will fail to protect and fail to get the best out of the system for its clients and patients unless it both works together *and* networks well. Chapter 2 shows that open teamwork looks at the organisational context which sets barriers to coordination and also applies pressures to collaborate. It is the same with assessment. We need to *think team* and *think network* simultaneously in all we do, not one or the other.

When to assess

There are particular points in any professional work that we need to consider when assessing team and network.

- *Starting points*. A new job, a new posting or a new case should cause us to ask: who will I be working with? who might be involved? what possible links are there?

- *Change points*. Where we or a service user need to make some changes we need to ask: who might be involved? would strengthening the network or building the team help?

- *Difficult points*. Where what we are trying to do seems not to be working we need to ask: would it be better if we involved others? are we involving people inappropriately?

- *End points.* Where a piece of work is finishing, we need to make sure everyone knows what is happening, secure relationships for further contacts and make sure everyone involved is thanked and feels good about the experience.

In all these circumstances, we need to think about team and network and find a way of understanding and analysing it.

How to assess

There are several basic approaches to open team assessment, covered in more detail later in the chapter.

With *reviewing*, we progress through a range of issues about open teamwork perhaps to identify issues to work on more. Although it is comprehensive and avoids focusing on problems rather than strengths, it may feel like time-wasting to go through things that seem satisfactory anyway. Even if network diagrams might help to understand a service user's situation, for example, it is probably not necessary in every case, only when it may be important. Also, reviewing may not be incisive enough: it may not get to the most important issues.

One way of reviewing is to look at *characteristics* of effective teams, to see whether your open team has them. It is more prescriptive than reviewing, because it often includes assumptions about teams coming from the nature of an 'ideal', usually collaborative, team. It may focus only on the professional or multiprofessional team rather than on the open team.

Problem assessment assumes that there will be problems in how the open team functions which need to be corrected: teams may be stressful as well as helpful (Thompson *et al.*, 1996). Some people find this negative and feel it criticises others: it can get personal. It also means starting on difficult, and perhaps intractable, issues. Issues that engage and motivate people may be better.

Working in a *task-focused* way builds on some specific task in the team. Perhaps new legislation and policy or new organisational structures require you to think again. Or, the network may need to sort out support in the home for someone coming out of hospital quickly. Focusing on the specific task may be immediately practical, makes sense to people and can be motivating. Doing the work on this issue allows group relationships to improve through working on the task. However, it may miss important things not relevant to this particular task.

Group dynamics or relationships approaches focus on understanding group relations and interpersonal relations within the open team. Doing this can be very interesting, enjoyable and makes people feel good about their work together. On the other hand, some people pragmatically want to get on with things and dislike navel-gazing. Other people love it so much it distracts them from meeting the open team's tasks. Also, if there are poor relationships to start with, it may reveal all sorts of difficulties which being out in the open makes worse.

Reviewing

In an earlier book (Payne, 1982: 30–3), I suggested a set of questions about a team to see what its style of operating is. A team or individual can then compare it with their own preferences. Over the years, I have adapted them into an activity with scales which allowed people to describe their own team or their own preferences. Then, as my ideas have changed towards open teamwork, I added to the scales to look not only at how we do things in a team, but also how adequately these connect with wider networks – see Table 3.1. For example, I started with asking whether a team had goals and how they were agreed. Moving towards open teamwork, I added other sorts of questions. Here are some examples: how are these goals communicated to other professionals and service users? how are other professionals and service users involved in creating the goals? how are the goals adapted by team experience? You need to add these 'other colleague' and 'service users' questions to everything you do, if you are aiming at open teamwork.

Evidence, as with other ways of assessing discussed in this chapter, is a crucial aspect of any review. No team member's view should be accepted without evidence, found from examples of practice or documents available to the team. Where the answer is a matter of judgement, different members of the team may feel differently.

In such cases, questionnaires may be devised to be completed privately and collated. Some questionnaires might well use rating scales as in Table 3.1. Team members' ratings for all the items, provided anonymously, can be totalled to give a picture of the team members' view. In this way, teams can get a view of each member's

Table 3.1   Assessing teams

More managed	Rating	More collaborative	Open team: users and other professionals
Goals defined as required	3 2 1 0 1 2 3	Goals clearly planned	understand goals
Participation in defining goals	3 2 1 0 1 2 3	Goals planned together	involved in goal planning
Good relations with superiors	3 2 1 0 1 2 3	Clearly defined relations with superiors	understand management structures well
Work allocation and priorities organised by manager	3 2 1 0 1 2 3	Members involved in planning priorities and workload	understand workload and priority systems
Clear relationships with wider agency	3 2 1 0 1 2 3	Complex and constantly renewed relationships with wider agency	understand team's relations with wider agency
Manager is leader for most activities	3 2 1 0 1 2 3	Leadership complex, and well-understood	understand how leadership is organised
Unpopular new policies introduced through discussion, planning and training	3 2 1 0 1 2 3	Members involved in developing response to new policies	understand how to influence team's response to issues
Regular group meetings work efficiently: purposeful and pleasant	3 2 1 0 1 2 3	Regular, effective group meetings jointly planned and managed	understand how to feed into team processes
Disagreements well-managed	3 2 1 0 1 2 3	Disagreements openly discussed and dealt with	understand how to raise problems and participate in responding
Team members are supportive to others	3 2 1 0 1 2 3	Systems for mutual support well-known and jointly planned	understand how to gain and give support in the team
Clear process for planning personal development	3 2 1 0 1 2 3	Team members plan all and carry out some personal development jointly	contribute to planning for and participate in personal development
Regular review of team systems	3 2 1 0 1 2 3	Participation in review of teamworking	contribute to reviews of teamworking
Layout of office planned to promote effective working	3 2 1 0 1 2 3	Members understand and participate in planning office layout	contribute to planning flow of work and layout of office

Source: adapted and developed from Payne (1982: 30–3)

particular attitude. Alternatively, each item can be totalled and averaged across the responses to give overall judgement of each item from all members of the team. With ratings like this, the eventual discussion should take into account where there are extremes of *division*, where there are *minorities* and where items are *out of alignment* with the general view of all the items. These offer a point for teambuilding to start where there are agreed problems. Identify where there are disagreements along ethnic and gender splits in the team, because conventional attitudes make it easy to miss their importance (see Chapter 6). For example, perhaps some team members express a view that communication is open and all women in the team disagree. This raises the issue of whether communication is dominated by men; similarly if minority ethnic group members feel excluded.

Team characteristics

The team characteristics approach to assessing teams starts from the assumption that there are typical features of a 'good' or 'effective' team. You compare your team with these features, and try to fulfil any that are missing. Table 3.2 lists my analysis of characteristics that are commonly cited. In some cases, I have summarised the general import of a characteristic in the first column although mostly I have quoted the formulation of a writer as typical of the presentation of the characteristic. I have collapsed some sets of characteristics and summarised, sometimes heavily, some descriptions, but by looking at the references you can see the range of points made by each author. However, the purpose of this presentation is to reveal the extent of agreement and the outlying points. For example, only a few writers mention effective external relations but this is important in *open* teamwork. You might also use this list of characteristics, or the particular formulations that are relevant to your team or attractive to its members, in one of the activities at the end of the chapter.

Each formulation reflects the focus and argument of the author and to some extent the concerns of the period (see Chapter 2). Likert (1961), writing early in an influential 'human relations' text for example, focuses on how good interpersonal relations in a group help members influence each other more successfully and this results in more flexible working. He calls this the principle of 'interaction influence'. This suggests that we need not fear being open to influence. It will not lead to others having power over us, but to more influence

Table 3.2   Characteristics of teams

Characteristic	Alternative formulations
Clear and common purpose (Colenso, 1997: 11*; Owen, 1996: 27–9; Parker, 1990: 33)	Clearly states mission and goals (Chang, 1995b: 6); goals clearly understood and members are loyal to objectives stimulating achievement but not anxiety (Likert, 1961: 166–9); know your objectives (Lundy, 1994); group task well-understood and accepted (McGregor, 1960: 232–5); commitment to team goals, rewards based on contribution and peer recognition (Quick, 1992); clear objectives and agreed goals (Woodcock, 1989)
Sense of belonging (Owen, 1996)	Belonging to something successful (Colenso, 1997); group loyalty, group expresses values of members (Likert, 1961); hard work to make the team best (Owen, 1996); sense of ownership (Maddux, 1996); belonging needs satisfied, more chance of achievement through the group (Quick, 1992)
Synergy[†] – team is more than the sum of its parts (Colenso, 1997)	Developing a feeling of teamness – synergistic (Owen, 1996)
Openness	Communicates openly (Chang, 1995b); full, frank communication of important matters (Likert, 1961); trust, open and honest communication, conflict seen as normal (Maddux, 1996); open communication (Parker, 1990); open and honest information sharing (Quick, 1992: 4–5); openness and confrontation (Woodcock, 1989)
Cooperation and mutual support; informal atmosphere	Supports leadership and each other; develops team climate; resolves disagreements (Chang, 1995b); well-established relaxed working relationships, cooperative atmosphere, high mutual expectations, each helps others, wish to influence and be influenced (Likert, 1961); welcomes new teammates enthusiastically and supports them (Lundy, 1994); informal atmosphere, there is disagreement but no 'tyranny of the minority', criticism frequent and comfortable (McGregor, 1960); interdependence (Maddux, 1996); informality, civilised disagreement, consensus decisions; shared leadership (Parker, 1990); trusting, collaborative, respectful, supportive team relationships, conflict on issues, not persons, natural and helpful (Quick, 1992); cooperation and conflict, support and trust (Woodcock, 1989)
Clarifies roles and responsibilities (Chang, 1995b)	Know what is expected of you in your position, understand the relationship of your position to others (Lundy, 1994); clear assignments made and accepted (McGregor, 1960); clear roles and work assignments (Parker, 1990)

Table 3.2 (cont'd)

Characteristic	Alternative formulations
Sound procedures (Woodcock, 1989)	Well-organised (Chang, 1995b); know the rules, make principled decisions and long-term strategies which always benefit the team (Lundy, 1994); members listen, discussion not jumpy (McGregor, 1960)
Appropriate leadership (Woodcock, 1989)	A carefully selected leader creates support and cooperative relationships (Likert, 1961); chair does not dominate (McGregor, 1960)
Regular reviews (Woodcock, 1989)	Focuses on results; makes objective decisions; evaluates own effectiveness (Chang, 1995b); assess individual and team strengths regularly (Lundy, 1994); self-assessment (Parker, 1990)
Individual development (Woodcock, 1989)	Builds on individual strengths (Chang, 1995b); all members help to develop others (Likert, 1961); practice to get things right, maintain self-discipline, get and develop the best talent, coach and guide constructively, help less effective improve or withdraw gracefully (Lundy, 1994); members contribute unique talent and knowledge, develop skills (Maddux, 1986)
Participation in good group relations	Members skilled in interpersonal roles, good group and leader mutual influence (Likert, 1961); much participative discussion, decisions made by consensus, group self-conscious about group process (McGregor, 1960); members participate in decisions (Maddux, 1986); participation (Parker, 1990); open, non-threatening, non-competitive, participative atmosphere, consensus decisions (Quick, 1992); sound intergroup relations (Woodcock, 1989)
Develops effective external relations	Builds effective links with relevant external groups (Likert, 1961); develops key external relations, builds credibility with other stakeholders (Parker, 1990)
Operates creatively (Chang, 1995b)	Supportive atmosphere stimulates creativity, flexibility enhanced by mutual influence (Likert, 1961); efficient resource use, creativity by identifying more options and solution-oriented approach (Quick, 1992)

* The page reference is given on the first appearance of an author's analysis in this table.

† Technically, synergy is the capacity for self-creation and is an outcome of non-summativity, a system being more than the sum of its parts, but the two terms are sometimes conflated.

being used in the situation altogether. Some later lists, for example Parker's (1990) analysis, rely explicitly on the earlier analyses of Likert (1961) and McGregor (1960), the classic writers in the field. Generally, though, the later formulations are much briefer and focus on a cooperative team climate or synergy and common goals. Some writers lean more towards considering how people should be or behave to have a cooperative group, some towards communication and decision-making processes. The former emphasis focuses on achieving good relationships and implies that they bring their own rewards in personal satisfaction and successful working. The latter represents a more modern concern with developing easily learned skills to achieve the agreed outcomes. Lundy (1994) uses a sports analogy and Owen (1996) draws on high-speed formation flying teams.

Most writers agree on common purpose, informal and consensual atmosphere, with a high degree of participation in decision-making as the main things to look for. Most also stress maintaining and considering individual development and motivation. Management and decision-making writers stress clarifying roles, well-organised procedures and regular evaluations and reviews of team functioning; writers about teams as groups emphasise interpersonal interaction. Synergy and non-summativity (explained in the table notes) are complex, but thinking about what being together brings to and takes away from team members' performances can help to get into what feels good and bad about a team for its members.

Because these analyses come from the teamwork literature, they tend to focus on the group, but open teamworkers need to look at them in a different way. Group and network are inseparable parts of the same whole which must both be present.

The team might begin by reviewing each team characteristic from Table 3.2. A summary with questions and evidence to use appears in Table 3.3.

In each case, the team might formulate some questions about the extent to which their own team fulfils this characteristic. It might also wish to examine whether this is a characteristic that they want to fulfil. For example, some might feel more at home with informal communication than others. Then, in each case, evidence is needed to justify answers to the questions. See the activity at the end of the chapter.

Problem assessment

A common approach to team assessment is to examine the problems that a team has. This carries all the disadvantages of the negativity which goes with looking at bad points rather than good ones. However, it may be a useful way of focusing on the most important. It is, in this way, a specific form of reviewing. We sometimes take networks for granted, and it can be useful to look at links with other agencies, or between the people involved in a particular case (see the 'network star' activity).

Some writers, again, present analyses of the sort of problems which might assail teams. Some have questionnaires which suggest problem areas to be tackled. Most track the particular writer's approach to teamwork and include assumptions about how teams *ought* to be. Working on problems should really start from team members' own assumptions. Members can look at each characteristic to identify how they want their team or network to be.

Alternatively, another common practice is to undertake a SWOT analysis. This involves considering the internal **S**trengths and **W**eaknesses and the external **O**pportunities and **T**hreats which might impinge on your work. This may focus on general teamworking, or around a particular issue or change that the team is facing. SWOT analyses are often usefully done through snowballing (see Appendix). Sometimes, drawing a Johari window may help (see Figure 3.1) with S, W, O, T each having a pane. Teams may also work on SWOT activities by dividing the team or network into groups, each taking one of S, W, O and T.

Task-focused

Many teams or individuals feel uncomfortable with a focus on themselves. Instead, they want to develop their team- or network by doing things that focus directly on their own work. The approach here is to work on the priorities, tasks and skills that the team uses.

At the assessment stage of this, the important thing is reconsider team members' judgements about what is happening, rather than plan for the future. For example, we often have a twisted view of our priorities. Parsloe (1981) evaluates a range of priority scaling and workload management systems. Another way of looking at priorities which some agencies have tried is to put aspects of work or legal

Table 3.3 Team characteristics questionnaire

Characteristic	Questions	Open teamwork issues	Evidence
Clear and common purpose	Are there stated purposes? Are they clear? Are they agreed?	Are they communicated to colleagues and service users? Does the network participate in agreeing them?	Documented statement. Records of debate
Sense of belonging	Do members feel the team is successful? Are there agreed values? Do people feel good about the team?	Do colleagues and service users feel good about cooperation and understand and participate in agreeing values?	Questionnaires. Rating scales
Synergy	Are joint activities undertaken? Are there clear team achievements?	Also with colleagues and service users?	Questionnaires. Rating scales. Evidence of activities
Openness	Do all members of the team speak in meetings? Are difficult matters raised? Can people be constructively critical of others? Are plans and organisation policies discussed in advance of implementation?	Similarly from colleagues and service users?	Examples of practice. Documents
Cooperation and mutual support; informal atmosphere	Are first names or titles used? Is there good induction? Do people work together? Do they discuss practice? Can they criticise each other and the organisation constructively?	Similarly with colleagues and service users. Are links within networks researched, explicit and evaluated?	Examples of practice. Audio and video tapes
Clarifies roles and responsibilities	Are there defined roles and responsibilities? Are they clear? Up-to-date? Are jobs allocated on the basis of them?	Do colleagues and service users understand them in general and in specific cases? Do they have clear roles with fit?	Examples of practice. Meeting minutes

responsibilities into hierarchies: it becomes more important to do x rather than y. A useful activity for a team may be looking at the reality of the caseload according to these systems and pointing out inconsistencies and aspects of work which are missing or not given what you think is the proper priority. You can then try to change policy based on the firm evidence of your assessment of your caseload, or at least be more aware of and work around some of the pressure which your agency has not taken into account. This can be particularly good for looking at different policies in agencies contributing staff to a multiprofessional team, and will be particularly apparent to service users and people outside the team, who can be involved, through inconsistencies in how we deal with them. Ways of looking at this include diaries of time spent on various activities, expenditure surveys, where items get dealt with on agendas of meetings, how much time we talk about things at meetings and so on.

A particularly useful way of approaching such an activity is to look at the *flow* of work into, within and out of an agency or among members of network working on a particular case (see the activities). Flow analysis (and diagrams) are a different way of analysing networks from those we have considered so far, because it, realistically, sees network relationships as succeeding one another. Relationships in networks are not all simultaneous or consistently maintained. Flow analysis can help identify discontinuities in the flow of work or the flow of contributions to a particular case. Plans for the future may thus be based on a more accurate assessment of what we are doing now.

Another approach to task-focused assessment is to concentrate on the network. A popular beginning is team projects to build up a resource bank of information about the agency, if it is a complex one, the community or networks of agencies and people in them to make contact with. This kind of activity often shows up where there are poor relationships or attitudes that 'this is my resource and you can't use it' or 'I don't want you spoiling my carefully built-up relationships with…' As you find out about these, you can then decide how to take on the problem. Sometimes they reveal a view that someone is not competent in particular fields, and this might involve training or careful work allocation; or it may be prejudice or self-interest. Other open team projects are equally useful, for example writing an information leaflet, policy or practice guidelines, taking part in a local public event or building up a new self-help group can involve professional and multiprofessional teams and will, inevitably in open teamwork, involve members of the public and service users. You can get more sophisticated. For example, two colleagues, after an episode of sexual abuse in a residential setting, developed a policy on touch, working with groups of residents, staff and outside agencies such as voluntary groups to contribute to it. This is an example of working with the open team of service users and with a multiprofessional and multiagency focus.

Group or relationship dynamics

Assessment of group or relationship dynamics assumes the importance of interpersonal and group relationships as the most important focus of improving open teamwork. Most group and relationship dynamics assessments involve communication, relationship networks, decision-making and conflicts. Assessment can be based on diagrams of communication networks, friendship or contact networks, or who works together most. Both quantity and quality can be dealt with in the diagrams. Relevant activities are suggested at the end of the chapter.

The assumption of 'group dynamics' ideas is that a group performs hidden emotional functions for its members which are unrelated to its task. These emotional aspects of working in a group may get in the way of rational functioning to pursue the team's objectives; of course, they may also help. Another assumption of such approaches is that insight into these emotional needs will help people behave in ways which will assist the team's purposes. All of this, which comes from psychodynamic and other therapeutic theories, leads to activities usually separate from daily team activities often facilitated by an outsider. Sometimes people feel they have not really done any team development until they have looked at such issues in this way. In reality, most agencies just do not have the training budgets to do this kind of work. It also requires a shared perception that this is worthwhile and commitment to act on the learning from it. Otherwise people who reject the assumptions are only half-hearted participants and can obstruct the learning. Also, insight may not help people behave better towards one another: it may make things worse and raise resentments. This sometimes happens where facilitation is not handled well or there is not enough time to deal with the issues which come out. Open teamwork emphasises building network relation-ships, even in a group. Concentrating on creating a group feeling of inclusiveness, also creates somewhere feelings of exclusion among others. There are theoretical objections to the focus on emotions and hidden behavioural drives, rather than rational thinking and planning with a task focus. Some would argue that looking at feelings encourages time-wasting 'navel-gazing' and that these issues can never be assessed clearly. Focusing on thinking and planning can be much more explicit. On the other hand, attitude scales may help to clarify and organise information about feelings and attitudes, and an alternative view is that feelings are important and should not be ignored. Team assessment requires thinking out these issues, perhaps in the team, before plunging in.

While, in general, my preference is for more rational, more task-focused and more network-oriented methods, within that two aspects of activity should be included which derive from understandings gained from group relations work:

- *Process* is as important as content, and must be considered every time you take part in an activity as an open team. You must always think not only what you did, or are going to do, but also how you did it, or are going to do it better in the future; hence the importance of briefing and debriefing.

- *Feelings* as well as thinking, or emotions as well as rational planning must always be taken into account in assessing or planning, because they are always there.

Merry and Allerhand (1977: 131–7) argue that the quality of decisions improves if teams have more information and expertise to take them. Implementing a decision works better if appropriate people are involved in making it. Effective decision-making tries to improve the quality of the decision and its implementation. Teams need to assess how important the decision is to people who might be involved: if it is important they will need to be involved. If not, it may be enough to improve our information and expertise. Where expertise and involvement are required, participation and problem-solving may become quite complex.

A useful technique for looking at group dynamics is the Johari window, based on an idea by Joe Luft and Harry Ingham (hence the name). The window, in Figure 3.1a, is a matrix. It can be used simply for sharing information about the team (see Figure 3.1b for examples) or its work, or about a problem situation (see Figure 3.1c). It can also be used in a more complex way to work on conflicts between subgroups. The open area includes things known to you, or about the problem and that others also know about. These are apparently

	Known to self	Not known to self
Known to others	Open area	Blind area
Not known to others	Hidden area	Unknown area

Figure 3.1a   The Johari window

	Known to self	Not known to self
Known to others	Poor liaison with GPs	GP complained about case
Not known to others	Father was a GP	GP's marriage in trouble

Figure 3.1b   The Johari window used for information sharing

	Known to self	Not known to self
Known to others	I prefer child care work	Others want more child care experience
Not known to others	I want promotion	New child care specialist post postponed

Figure 3.1c   The Johari window used for problem-solving

shared, but may have been forgotten. They might include skills, experience, points of view. The unknown area is things that neither you nor others know about you or about the problem. In a problem-solving exercise you might write here the things you do not know or things you need to understand or find out about. The blind area covers things others know, but you do not. The hidden area includes things you know but you think others might not. The ways of using the window, and the more complex intergroup use of it for mirroring values are given in the activities at the end of the chapter.

People sometimes avoid looking at conflicts because this brings them back into 'relationship problem' territory and may seem too difficult. However, not all conflicts are interpersonal. Many are conflicts about resources, or inconsistencies in policies. A study of your agency's procedures for conflicts and inconsistencies can be a very team-enhancing activity and produce evidence that can lead instantly to effective change. Involving service users is valuable, especially for example residents in care homes who are usually intimately involved with the way things work. Carers and service users of a community care package can also bring good insights into how things connect with each other.

We shall see in the next chapter on team development that looking at roles and relationships can sometimes reveal relationship problems which arise from group dynamics. The next chapter also looks at tackling the feeling and process aspects of open teamwork alongside the planning and thinking aspects.

Activities

See the Appendix for basic team development activities.

The team and its setting

This activity, which is particularly useful for residential and day care teams, is a good starting point for teambuilding, because it makes clear differences of view about who is in or out of the team and what is or is not the team's territory (for example, some people exclude the garden, or the office, or the team leader's office). It also raises useful discussion points about who is always in the office or the kitchen, or out somewhere, so it is good for challenging people's self-perception.

Stage 1:   Each team member privately writes a list of team members.

Stage 2:   Lists are compared and different assumptions about who is included or not included are raised.

Alternative: If there is agreement, the team should work specifically on management, non-professionals, administrative and clerical staff and links with main colleagues outside the team.

Stage 3:   Each team member privately draws a map of the team territory.

Stage 4:   Each team member is asked to put each team member where they usually are.

Stage 5:   The team can compare and discuss.

The network star

This activity uses copies of Figure 3.2.

Figure 3.2   The network star

Stage 1: For a team: extend the points of the star with links to colleagues and services which deal with each aspect of service users' lives. For a service user network: extend the points of the star to links in each aspect of the user's life. Note in each case that one link may lead on to another (for example the area social services team links with the consultant psychiatrist through the community psychiatric nurse).

Stage 2: Snowball or brainstorm an evaluation of missing links in each area of life. Also look at where links are through another person or agency: should they be direct?

Stage 3: Draw a new star of the links to be made and work out a plan to make them.

Stage 4: As links are made transfer the planned links to the original diagram.

Network diagrams

This activity makes use of a variety of networks which a team may be part of, or looks at different kinds of link between members. It may also be used by and about a team involved with a particular case, where it will also involve colleagues and service users in the process.

Stage 1: Ask each participant to list other team members and rate how much they speak with *or* work with each person. You can also ask where this happens, for example, in meetings, in working together, socially, or rate each category separately.

Extra stage: Ask each participant to rate on a five-point scale how supportive they find each other person, using each of the aspects of support in Figure 8.1. You can do this for any type of behaviour, such as aggression or negativity. Positive features usually lead to more constructive discussion.

Stage 2: Using the data, each person can draw a network diagram of their own links. As in the example of Figure 3.3a, you can use simple links or as in Figure 3.3b, you can weight the links with figures or by the weight of lines.

Stage 3: Snowball a discussion of different perceptions of links, to arrive at an agreed network diagram on that aspect of the network.

Stage 4: Plan which networks need strengthening and how that will be done.

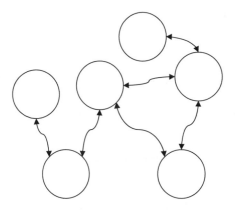

Figure 3.3a   Network diagram

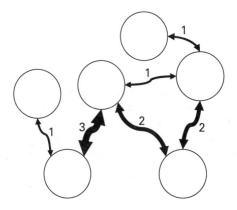

Figure 3.3b   Network diagram with weights

The Johari window

Conventional use: for sharing information in a team or network that does not know each other well. It can be restricted to particular areas of knowledge:

Stage 1:   Team or network members are asked to make a list of their strengths or capacities and liabilities or weaknesses *that they are willing to share with others.*

Stage 2:   Each member lists all other team members and for each lists their strengths and weaknesses *that they are willing to disclose.*

Stage 3:   Lists are handed in to the leader.

Stage 4:   Each member makes a Johari window for themselves.

Stage 5:   The leader reads out the lists *without attribution.* Each member puts things known to them about themselves in the open window, things unknown to them in the blind window. They then write down things not known to anyone else in the hidden window. In the unknown area they write down questions that they might wish to raise. The window is their private property, not to be shared.

Stage 6:   A round of 'what we have gained from the activity'. A more general discussion may include people reporting hidden things and asking questions, but they are not obliged to do so.

Sorting out a problem

Stage 1:   All team or network members write down everything they know and can do about a problem or issue.

Stage 2:   Each member draws a window and writes down what they think is known to themselves and others (open) about the problem and what they can do and what they think they know or can do that is not known to others (hidden). They then write down their questions in the unknown area.

Stage 3:   The leader asks each person to read their open points and lists them, then their hidden points and lists them. Members complete their window by noting things they did not know in the unknown area.

Stage 4:   The team or network discusses what they have learned, the range of options and skills available, and their questions.

Mirroring about conflicts

For example, you can look at mirroring between professional groups, men/women, different ethnic groups, different agencies (derived from McIntosh-Fletcher, 1996: 114–21). This activity should be used with caution, because it may disclose unknown conflicts in a distressing way. Participants should be briefed and debriefed covering the activity's aims and members' expectations, as discussed in the Appendix on Team Development Activities.

Stage 1: The groups to be considered are clearly identified and people are explicitly identified with their group. Each subgroup draws a window and writes one statement including positives and negatives of 'how we see ourselves' with evidence of each point drawn from experience in daily work in the hidden area.

Stage 2: Each subgroup writes one statement including positives and negatives of 'how we see them' with evidence of each point drawn from experience in daily work for each of the subgroups in the open area.

Stage 3: Each subgroup writes one statement including positives and negatives of 'how we think they see us' with evidence of each point drawn from experience in daily work for each of the subgroups in the 'blind' area.

Stage 4: Each subgroup writes questions about subgroup perceptions in the 'unknown' area.

Stage 5: The subgroup windows are handed in to the leader, who produces a window of points from each window, without attributing views to any subgroup (so the views of each subgroup about themselves are included in their list).

Stage 6: Each subgroup compares their perception of themselves with others' and produces a plan to build on the positives and work to reduce the negatives.

Stage 7: The whole group discusses the plans made.

4

Open Team Development

Introduction

Improving how open teams work means understanding how they develop. Then we can find ways to build up their capacity to contribute to the care system. Fortunately, although much of the writing and research on this kind of development is about teams, we can apply most of the techniques to networking. Partly, this is because there is no clear boundary between a network and a team: they are ends of a continuum. Also, much practical development involves building links from new or strengthening existing ones, so many available ideas focus on this.

The next section looks at ideas about team development. This leads on to two sections about teambuilding and network development. In these, I look at the arguments for and against different teambuilding approaches, and practical methods of teambuilding and networking to contribute to developing open teams. Then, in Chapter 5, I move on to discuss how individuals might themselves work within open teams.

As with team assessment, discussed in Chapter 3, open team development involves different levels of action: in the networks involved with individual cases, in teams or part of them or in the organisation as a whole. The purposes of open teamwork are coordination and collaboration. Setting out to develop an aspect of open teamwork at any level will have to involve others affected, otherwise collaboration will be worsened rather than improved. Leadership in starting out on development may come from any source in a network. A colleague professional may propose the need to change a way of working, and this may lead other professional groups to reconsider how they operate. Users or carers may raise issues, which lead to a reorganisation of how a team works with them. An individual team member may feel the need to press for development in a particular area or more

68

generally. So may a team leader or more senior manager. Often people with particular responsibilities for leadership and management will set the process off. Just as often, others identify changes they would like to see and need to take responsibility for raising the need for a development process to take place. Leadership never resides always with an appointed manager. However, equally, management responsibility does not confer a right to impose changes on a complex network and team. An essential process, therefore, in team development is to develop discussion and secure agreement about what is needed and how to approach it. Sometimes this might be done through a clear assessment process, following perhaps some of the possibilities offered in Chapter 3. At other times, a less extensive negotiation and agreement process may be adopted.

Ideas about team development

There are two views about how teams develop (see Chapter 1). I call these developmental and situational views. *Developmental* views argue that teams go through a process of building up from being 'not a team' towards a better and perhaps eventually ideal state of 'teamness'. In Chapter 1, we saw that views differ about what this ideal state might be.

Developmental views contain two shades of opinion. One (for example Brill, 1976) holds that if you put people together, the group will naturally develop through a series of stages and end up as a team. The teambuilder's task is to speed it on its way. The second view (for example Woodcock, 1989) thinks that becoming a team is quite difficult and we need teambuilding to help fight our way through the barriers. Shaw's (1994) study of joint teamwork training supports this view in drawing on research evidence suggesting that cooperation is not natural at policymaking and management levels: incentives are needed to make it work. At the practice level, good everyday relationships over cases may be built up but can get bogged down where, at higher levels, managers fight over resources and policy.

Situational or *contingency* views take this position a bit further and argue that different kinds of team and teamwork are appropriate to different situations in which teams are placed. Teambuilding in this view, therefore, would consist of diagnosing what factors affect a work group, designing an appropriate model of teamwork and building towards it. Burell and Lindström's (1987) 'teamview' team development model takes this view, because it sees teambuilding as responding to and improving work environments.

Developmental views

The classic, and most commonplace, view of team development is based on Tuckman's (1965) review of the literature on group development. He says that groups go through processes of *forming* (getting together), *storming* (fighting over territory in the group), *norming* (coming to general agreement about how the group should work) and *performing* (getting on with sharing work without worrying too much about relationships in the group). This analysis is widely used, either explicitly (for example Adair, 1986; Zenger *et al.* 1994) or taken for granted (for example Brill, 1976). However, it is based mainly on laboratory studies of how small groups work. These studies do not deal with situations where teams have tasks and purposes. Neither do they deal with the situation where the team goes on for ever as part of the structure of some organisation, with new members coming and others going. In this situation, structure may be imposed on the team, such as particular tasks or professional roles for specialists or designation of team leaders or management responsibility. So simply using group development as the basis for team development assumes that teams in an organisation behave in the same way as groups in a neutral environment. This is unproven: there may be connections between groups and teams, but they are not the same thing, and probably the environment makes a difference. We came across the same issue when looking at the assumptions behind group dynamics ideas in Chapter 3.

Responding to these problems, some developmental views see teambuilding as a process, cycle or circle of development. Syer and Connolly (1996) focus on changes in team members' teamworking skills. The first stage involves increasing *awareness* of themselves and others, and the sameness and difference between them. The second stage involves increased *contact and communication*. The third stage arrives when trust, respect and *team spirit* grow.

Situational views

If we take a situational view of teamwork, our approach to teamwork would vary according to the factors which affect our work. Lewis (1975) sums these up into three categories:

- members' *preferences*;
- the *type of work* they do;
- the *kind of organisation* they work in.

Taking this view would imply that a variety of types of team might exist in any organisation, depending on the circumstances. We do not have to feel that we must move towards a collaborative form.

Thinking about members' preferences can help to avoid feeling burdened by an apparent failure to achieve some high degree of bonding. For example, I have worked on a highly collaborative team with very good interpersonal relationships on at least two occasions. In one case, this was in a large organisation, where most staff were young, at the start of their career and single or newly married. Although it was large, relationships were close because many of us shared attitudes and social life. There were many inexperienced and unqualified staff so much work was done in a shared way for learning or safety. In the other case, it was a very small group, again containing people with shared attitudes and social life, and a lot of shared work. In both cases, we started very embattled by outside forces. I have later worked in similarly sized groups, but they were more stable. Members were better established and more specialised. Also, we were not so embattled at the outset, and people had many other outside interests and growing families and separate social lives. Therefore, social contacts were not so extensive. Attempts in these groups to organise social events were reasonable, but members did not have so much of their effort committed to their work.

Your team-type also arises from the type of work you do. Webb and Hobdell (1980), a classic piece of work, categorise this by looking at the tasks the team performs and the skills and roles of their members, see Table 4.1. They suggest that teamwork aims to help specialisation, which is about how skills can be integrated into roles to form sensible jobs that an individual can carry (*role integration*). Teamwork also aims to overcome the problems of specialisation, by working out what tasks have to be done and dividing them up (*task differentiation*). You can see how these two things fit together in the table. A useful way of

Table 4.1   Webb and Hobdell's taxonomy of teams

Tasks (i.e. jobs the team must do)	Skills integrated into roles (i.e. abilities of members available to do the jobs)	
	Homogeneous (members have similar abilities)	Heterogeneous (members have different abilities)
Homogeneous (jobs are rather similar)	**Collegial team** e.g. outreach community psychiatric nursing team	**Apprenticeship team** e.g. genetic SSD intake team with different grades of staff
Heterogeneous (many varied jobs to be done)	**Specialised collegial team** e.g. SSD area team with child and adult services specialist groups	**Complex team** e.g. health centre team

Source: updated from Payne (1982), using Webb and Hobdell's (1980) concepts.

developing teams, therefore, is to focus on task differentiation and role integration – see below. It can also be useful to look at how teams put their work into specialisations and priorities – also dealt with below.

The final factor in situational views of teamwork is the type of organisation in which you undertake the work. Three issues, shown in Figure 4.1, interlock:

- *domain* refers to the subject matter of the work, which leads to the definition of tasks and skills;
- *discipline* defines the expertise and professional commitment of the people who do the work and leads to discussion about the professions involved, their relative status and power issues which arise from that;
- *organisation* refers to the boundaries of the team within various networks.

All these different features of a team network might interact, both in an individual case or in a network service. Figure 4.1 shows three scales, running from one to many in each feature. A simple team

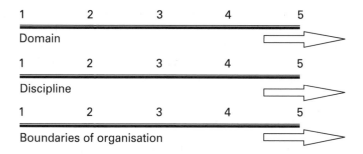

Figure 4.1   Scales of three features of teamworking organisation

might have just one profession, cover one domain and involve one organisation. An example might be a counselling organisation for mentally ill people. Others might have many features. For example, a local council for voluntary service often has several professions (social worker, community worker, youth worker, information worker), coordinates several local government departments with perhaps hundreds of voluntary organisations, and operates in social services, youth, health care, drugs work and a myriad of other domains. Some organisations might be unbalanced. For example, a local community centre might employ no professionals, but deal with every age-group, and involve many different clubs or activities on different days or in different parts of the year.

We can also apply this analysis to the networks in individual cases, and it helps us to be clear whether and how much it is desirable to accept the limitations of an existing network or build additional elements. Chapter 1 proposed that open teamwork implies a concern for both team and network. Therefore, workers and network members may need to shift perceptions between looking at team and network development for the organisation and a daily concern for team and network development in an individual case. Each influences the other. Case team and network building can contribute to wider developments; broader developments will often contribute to better working in the individual case. Some people receive help from only one organisation, one profession within it for only one aspect of their lives. Others pull in more than one professional and agency, and have to deal with more than one aspect of their lives.

Teamwork is not complex where these three features of an organisation or a case involve fewer domains and disciplines with narrowly drawn boundaries of organisation. Teamwork becomes more complex if increasing numbers of domains, disciplines or more complex boundaries are involved. In Chapter 7, for example, I focus on four different contexts for teamwork which have raised multiprofessional teamwork issues:

- *field organisations*, because mutual support for people who go out from their base is important;

- *multiprofessional contexts*, because different disciplines have to be brought together;

- *community networking*, because different organisations have to be brought together;

- *institutional settings*, because all the domains of service users' lives have to be managed within one setting. This may involve several different disciplines or links with a variety of outside organisations in relation to those different domains of living.

Teambuilding approaches

There are four approaches to teambuilding. Three are based in the team, and derive either from the daily effort to improve how things work for individuals, the team, service users or from an explicit decision to work on team issues. Teams can leave it to the necessities of events, assuming that working together on everyday work will stimulate the degree of teamwork needed. An alternative focus may be the second approach of reviewing the way the team is working (see Chapter 3), so that processes are explicit. This would include easing people's feelings within the team relationships. A third approach is self-help as a team or as a team leader, perhaps calling in a consultant or facilitator.

The fourth approach arises when an organisation decides to develop teamwork throughout its work or in a part of its activities. This may be either a coordinated staff development effort to improve collaboration or a reorganisation designed to produce self-managing or self-directed teams. Such an approach implies a strategic decision that the best way of developing an organisation's work would be improving collaboration or coordination. Strategic management sometimes focuses on such things as organisational structure, resource management, broad change management, service development, but it may equally well focus on open teamwork issues such as leadership, culture and values and staff roles in the organisation (Thompson, 1997). The two areas are inseparable: looking at the organisation as a whole is the context for looking at staff teams and changing staff teams will affect how the organisation functions.

Many organisations also seek to develop team functioning around quality assurance processes: we saw in Chapter 2 that quality processes have strongly influenced teamwork thinking from the 1980s onwards. Quality enhancement mechanisms identify teamwork as a failing or an opportunity for development. Alternatively, teamwork may be a central focus on making quality processes work at all. The process is usually to identify standards, appraise the service against those standards and then to try to bring about an improvement. This leads to a further, presumably higher, standard being set and the cycle begins again. Ellis and Whittington (1998) divide the process into making a quality appraisal and taking action for improvement. In both cases, the work is usually based on a group used for consultation, for reference to check standards and to promote action. Developing quality assurance systems is a specialist management area beyond the scope of this book; however there is some discussion of and an activity on benchmarking applied to teamworking below, and it is possible for teams to similarly adapt other aspects of quality assurance to look at their own work. Ellis and Whittington (1993, 1998) offer practical and introductory guides in, respectively, health and social care.

Teambuilding helps you achieve several results. Rushmer's (1997) research suggests gains which may be made through teambuilding processes. Members feel more free to speak to others, sometimes about difficult issues, because they know them better as people. Then, members test out taking on leadership roles, but learn to avoid pulling rank, so that they take on leadership in various tasks and pass it round to appropriate people in the open team. Members try out new behaviours and skills, and see themselves as modifying their approach to work for the team's benefit. Having fun and building enthusiasm were also important. It motivates members if there is a successful outcome and members feel they contributed. Another motivating factor is effective participation and a feeling that this leads to better organisation; part of this is feeling that members helped each other. A positive feature is to end the process seeing that there is more to do: that a team is always travelling, but never arrives. Demotivating factors, on the other hand, arise where the teambuilding is uncomfortable and unpleasant in some way, and where interpersonal contact and shared working are missing from the teambuilding process. Many of these things connect to the characteristics of teams which we reviewed in previous chapters. Probably, teambuilding needs to connect to what people expect.

Practical teambuilding

As with assessment in Chapter 3, teambuilding may focus on a variety of aspects of the team, and may be used to develop not only a group but the open team as well. It is possible to look at general systems of work and coordination among people that work together frequently, or with the network around just one or a few cases.

Individual development

We saw in Chapter 2 that many writers think that promoting individuals' development is important to effective teamwork. One approach to teambuilding is to focus on individual development for team members. This process might concentrate on some like trainees who are thought to need a special focus on their development, but for the widescale development of open teamwork a process of promoting all team members' development might be better.

Individual processes have been very important where particular groups need development or have been excluded from influence in organisations. For example, McDougall (1996) reviews different strategies used in organisations to develop women's progress into more senior roles:

- explicit *career planning* as part of the team's work, and giving advice and support in this area of development;
- *confidence-building*, to help women believe in their capacity and contribution;
- *assertiveness skills* to help women make interventions in circumstances which exclude them;
- skill development in *organisational politics*;
- *stress management*.

Allan *et al.* (1992) studied the experience of women in SSDs of such efforts and support many of these points. Aids and hindrances to

Table 4.2   Aids, hindrances and organisational
strategies for women's personal development

Aids	Hindrances	Organisational strategies
Line management support	Lack of career planning	Supervision and consultation to build confidence
Personal determination	Recognition of skills and expertise	Appraisal systems to recognise aims, skills and expertise
Commitment to the agency and its work	Attitudes to senior management roles	Creating development opportunities, through coaching and mentoring (see Chapter 2), encouraging networks and consultancy, encouraging peer-group problem-solving to build learning
Opportunities for 'acting up' in more senior posts	Family and domestic commitments	Creating flexible career paths by developing transferable skills, giving experience of 'acting up' or 'acting across' in different settings, project work, secondments and job swaps
	Role of equal opportunities policies creates over-formal and restrictive processes	

Source: Allan *et al.* (1992)

effective career development together with actions an organisation might make to improve things were identified (see Table 4.2). While these particularly apply to women, similar strategies might be used with many excluded groups. Training was found to be supportive, but was less helpful when it was too late after considerable experience. Early training in new roles is likely to be important.

Teams could develop plans for professional supervision and staff development. A multiprofessional approach might involve some cross-professional or joint supervision and staff development, perhaps as a demonstration or in a few cases. Open teamwork requires consideration of networks outside the team within professional supervision; perhaps it might be done in the presence of service users, or with their involvement or that of their carers. It also involves those networks in the supervision, review and teambuilding and networking plans and processes. Payne and Scott (1982) suggest five aims of supervision, which we should include in a plan. These form one side of the matrix in Figure 4.2. They also propose a list of skill and knowledge requirements which we should build up in supervision, within each aim. These form the second aspect of Figure 4.2 (*logistics* in the figure means skill in finding and delivering appropriate resources). Finally, they suggest that supervision should take into account the stage which workers have reached. This is the third aspect of Figure 4.2. Each individual worker would have a supervision plan for their stage, taking into account each aim and requirement. The team has an overall plan making sure that within it there are people at appropriate stages in the different professions, that they cover all skills at appropriate stages and that all the aims are met.

Individuals' plans are adapted by open team needs, perhaps expressed through consultation with service users and carers, who will have views about the services that they are offered and the skills represented. They may need to be facilitated in a development conference periodically to contribute.

The process of setting up such plans can use a snowballing exercise building up from individuals' needs. For example, we could use Johari windows and brainstorming and filtering to explore knowledge and skill needs and aims. This whole process, while focusing on individuals' needs, can build team and network involvement and skills.

Another way of looking at individual development which is more directly related to teamwork is improving team members' motivation and satisfaction. Merry and Allerhand (1977: 217–19) suggest that in work situations it is useful to examine five areas of organisation which can make a difference to how people feel:

- *Security*. Do people feel comfortable and safe in the workplace and with colleagues in the team? Are they able to assimilate change that is taking place without getting anxious?
- *Affiliation*. Do they feel part of the team, well-supported by colleagues?
- *Competence*. Do they feel they can handle the work or is it too difficult for them?

Aims: **Skill and knowledge requirements:**	*Maintain team's task*	*Make roles/ responsibilities clear*	*Create good climate for practice*	*Help people cope with stress*	*Aid professional development*
Understand agency function and tasks					
Assessment skills					
Personal interaction skills					
Social interests and activity skills					
Planning skills					
Logistical skills					
Teamwork skills					
Communication skills					

Recruitment ⬆ Selection ⬆ Induction ⬆ Pre-professional experience ⬆ Professional training ⬆ Post-qualifying experience ⬆ Further career development ⬆

Figure 4.2   Aims, requirements and stages in supervision

Source: derived from Payne and Scott (1982: 15–26)

- *Achievement.* Do they feel they are making progress in their careers and in their current work?
- *Power.* Do they feel in control of what happens to them?

These areas draw on Maslow's (1970) hierarchy of needs. We can apply them to everyone in an open team. We should not assume that only workers, but also carers in the community and volunteers can benefit from an explicit emphasis on thinking about people's development needs. We sometimes unthinkingly forget that an elderly person with Alzheimer's or someone close to death has personal development and learning needs as well as team members in the prime of their careers or carers under pressure. It is a human right always to have opportunities for education and personal development. In many situations, we cannot deal with everything which might produce problems in each of these areas. However, making good progress with some or a little bit with all may take away some of the pressure which people face. Especially, note where there are differences between identifiable groups, such as ethnic minorities, gender groups and groups such as disabled people. They may identify greater safety needs, for example, because the way people speak or behave towards others makes them feel more unsafe.

Drawing on a job enrichment perspective, Merry and Allerhand (1977: 230–41) suggest that we should focus on improving particular aspects of team members' jobs:

- *Autonomy and achievement.* Can we give people more control over how they plan and do their work?

- *Interest, challenge and satisfaction.* This would allow people to finish something worthwhile regularly, and may involve designing contracts with service users in stages: this also benefits users, who can see where they are going better too. We can organise work to have more challenging parts to it, using more and different skills. Team members can also explicitly take on a wider range of activities. We should organise days so that people can change location and do different kinds of things within each day.

- *Rotation.* We can rotate routine and regular tasks among team members.

- *Career and personal development planning.* We should openly make and commit ourselves to explicit plans for personal development, participation in courses, and taking up special projects.

We can also apply each of these to the open team's work, perhaps working with another team. Open teamwork means taking the network into your confidence with these things. Training should not take you away from service users. They and team members should be aware in advance about moves made and be able to see the team trying to improve its work. Users and carers can contribute their special perspective to what you are doing. Such approaches can also be used with carers in the network to help them find the work satisfying and worthwhile. Open teamwork means making it clear to everyone that we are trying to make the things we do more satisfying and interesting for everyone.

Strategic teambuilding – mission and vision

Some approaches to teambuilding are concerned with ensuring that overall aspects of the team and its mission are made clear.

Mission and vision are related, but different. Mission is about what the team wants to achieve, vision is about how it understands its working. West (1994: 22–4) usefully identifies different aspects of each:

Mission:

- *Consistent objectives.* What aims can be stated that are relevant for each aspect of their service and each type of service user?

- *Service users' needs.* What activities will meet the needs of different service users? What would be an excellent standard of meeting them?

- *Quality of service.* What would be a good standard of service, overall and for different aspects of the service?

- *Value to wider society.* What is the point of it all? What are the team's shared values about what society gains from what they do? Protection from abuse, security in old age, freedom of action in spite of disabilities, reduction in discrimination might all be usefully defined.

Vision:

- *Team climate and relationships.* What kind of relationships and climate does the team want to have? Constant social interaction, a stronger task focus, more shared working, more clearly defined roles?

- *Growth and well-being of team members.* What could the team do to help people feel good about working in the team?

- *Relationships with other teams or agencies.* What could the team do to ease its work and improve the quality of service for clients by developing its relationships in the network? West separates relationships inside and outside the host organisation: this is not a distinction which should be drawn in open teamwork.

Another way of understanding team climate is the concept of 'culture' (Saul, 1991). This comes from ideas of organisational culture. Kakabadse (1982), for example, found three types of culture in SSDs. The *power culture* was based on a strong central leader: there were low levels of support, mistakes were punished and rewards offered for pleasing the key figures in the organisation. In the *role culture* rules and procedures were the important guiding features. *Task cultures* recognised expertise, mutual respect and control over workers' own activities: there was much mutual support. Handy (1985) also identifies a highly individualised *person* culture, which might exist in smaller organisations such as consultancies or in more separated groups within residential or day care organisations. These respond to personal characteristics and preferences. Kakabadse argues that communication is sometimes difficult because different cultures in different parts of the organisation speak different management 'languages'. These ideas are also relevant to different organisations coordinating or collaborating, since different cultures might speak different 'languages' and find it hard to understand each other.

One area in which this has been important is in gender differences. Case (1994) reviews extensive research which shows that men and women have different patterns of communication. They describe experience and frame problems differently. In speech patterns, women typically cooperate and seek to develop relationships through joint interaction. Their problem-solving is an interactive process in which ideas from all participants are used collectively to build a view of the problem and create a response. Men, on the other hand, use interactions to achieve outcomes, to attract and maintain an audience and maintain the focus on their ideas. Their problem-solving involves taking turns to present ideas which are then compared and contrasted. Both sexes interrupt, but women do it to achieve collaboration, men to attain dominance. Women focus on getting people engaged in the process, men on achieving their desired outcomes. Organisations generally have a culture of interaction which favours men's conversational cultures, and this may exclude women. It may also create a male image of the way leaders and managers behave which excludes women both from participation in the organisation but also from promotion. The differences may also mean that both sexes restrict their conversational styles when in mixed groups, so that the full capacity to communicate is lost. Clearly, all this may lead to failures in collaboration and communication which open teamwork tries to overcome. However, because teamwork and networking involve interactions in groups failures in communication may prevent an organisation with a restricted culture from tackling these problems effectively. A focus on how people talk in teams may therefore be useful, and Donnellon's (1996) work is discussed below and adapted to an activity.

Many of these aspects of communication and interaction are reflected in the experience of an agency for women. Allan *et al.*'s (1992) study of women managers in SSDs found that they felt that they had a more participative style of management than men, who sometimes went into 'instruction mode', they felt excluded from male groupings and codes of behaviour, and by being less interested in organisational politics. Their view was that women had to be better than men to get on, and women were frequently ignored in meetings.

There are problems with a strong focus on cultures. As with ideas of ethnic culture, talking about management, organisational or team cultures often implies too much uniformity. It may create a simplified idea of what a complex group is like, based on a few factors. Such usage fails to recognise the range of behaviour, views and attitudes in a team. Thompson *et al.* (1996) suggest a team culture might contain national and ethnic factors, sector and organisational values, professional values and individuals' beliefs. Some views imply that a culture is very stable, almost unchangeable. People stereotype artists or youth and community workers as chaotic, for example, social workers as woolly-minded idealists, doctors as never seeing the whole person and worrying about drugs, while police are sometimes seen as authoritarian and aggressive. A climate or culture approach also focuses on intangible things about personality and style, and can lead to criticisms of individuals, or even bullying, based on unclear criteria. Clear definitions of failings in skill, specific behaviours and roles and tasks make it much easier for people to understand their job and change their behaviour if that is needed. Since the work of Peters and Waterman (1982), it has become widely accepted that managements should intervene in the organisation to create a culture that is effective in achieving their purposes. While this may allow teams and networks to focus on culture to try to achieve desired changes, cultural factors such as gender differences may make it difficult to tackle such uncertain issues. It is important, therefore, to try to be explicit about behaviours and activities which need intervention or change and define clearly what changes will be required.

Holder and Wardle (1981: 124–31) usefully analyse the features of 'atmosphere' which contributed to successful teamworking in an informal, small voluntary agency:

- willingness to share information from the member's own specialist background, and learn from others' specialist skills;

- preparedness to share, and take on, responsibility for managing particular aspects of work;

- preparedness to accept flows of information in different directions, not just in hierarchies;

- preparedness to give time to working on team relationships, but in a structured and planned way;

- an assumption of confidence and trust in people, which came from members' preparedness to identify the reasons for a mistake, and explicitly plan to learn from it;

- preparedness to allow authority and power to move around members of the team, where they were motivated and skilled enough to take the lead.

Task differentiation – competencies

This approach to open teambuilding and the next derive from a central feature of teamwork designed to overcome specialisation in all organisations, discussed above. That is, once you get beyond one person doing everything, you must have a division of labour, dividing the tasks that an organisation aims to achieve among the 'more-than-one-person'. So you have to specify the tasks to be done and divide them among the people available to do them. This is *task differentiation*. Unless you differentiate the tasks sensibly, you probably could not get people to do their tasks in a useful pattern with others in the organisation. It gets worse when you have to get organisations to work together. One way of improving teamwork, therefore, is to sort out the way tasks or divided and be clear about how they fit together. When I used to argue this (in Payne, 1982, for instance) it all seemed impossibly theoretical. However, nowadays, this is a central feature of the planning for training and development across all occupational groups in Britain. Most occupational and increasingly professional training is now organised on the basis of defined competencies. These state precisely what you ought to be able to do, and backs it up with the knowledge and skills that you need to do it. Most care professions, then, now have a clear system of definitions of the tasks they need to carry out. We may not agree with every word, but at least it gives us something clear to test ourselves against. If we add various professional statements about tasks and responsibilities, and government and other guidance that comes from policy and legislation, there is a wide range of task statements that we can take into account in thinking about our own teamwork.

Rather than specify one particular set of tasks, a useful approach would be for teams to collect formal statements of competencies, tasks and skills from their constituent professions. They might devise rating scales, as in several activities in this book. Factors which we might rate are: how much I possess this skill or competence and how much my work needs it; alternatively seen on a team basis, what skills or competences do the team have, and what does it need. We can combine the team assessment with the individual assessment to plan enhancements or training for specific skills and competences.

Another modern management approach, relating quality management to these issues, is *benchmarking*; where the quality of activities in the organisation are compared with agreed standards. Oakland (1999) summarises four different approaches to benchmarking:

- *internal*, where actions are compared with other practices in the organisation;

- *competitive*, where actions are compared to the standards of alternative services to the agency's own;

- *functional*, where actions are compared to similar functions in health, social or related agencies;

- *generic*, where actions are compared with standards in many different kinds of organisation.

For example, where a team wants to think about how well it receives users at the office or visitors to a care establishment it could look at teams in other parts of the agency (internal), at similar agencies in another sector. For example, local authority teams might look at local voluntary or private sector teams (competitive), at housing department teams (functional) or what banks and building societies do (generic). One of the activities in this chapter provides a model of benchmarking.

Role integration – occupational standards

In the previous section, we looked at task differentiation. But obviously when we have divided up tasks, we then have to collect them up again into sensible jobs for people to do. This is not a random process. We try to do it on the basis of tasks that reasonably go together to form a *work role* for a person. We try to make the work role one which is consistent within itself. Also, we try to fit the roles together in a sensible pattern for the whole agency and for work groups within it. This is *role integration*. This meaning of role is different from the meaning discussed in Chapter 5. There, role is about the part people play in interpersonal relationships within a team or group.

Before looking at roles more closely, just a word of caution about being concerned with roles at all. Handy (1985) associates the idea of roles with a particular style of organisation, which he calls a 'role culture'; we met this idea above. Another word for a role culture is a bureaucracy, where job descriptions and functions are clearly defined according to a hierarchy of authority. Taken to the extreme this can be very inflexible. For example, some workers want every task defined and allocated to someone and their own job, responsibilities and powers clearly defined. Trade unions strongly support this kind of approach, because it allows them influence on negotiating jobs in the organisation, whereas flexibility in teams can exclude them. Cynics might suggest that this is a reason for the popularity of self-directed teamwork in management writing in the 1990s. Lack of clarity in job descriptions or constant change in roles might make an organisation more flexible. It is an assumption, perhaps an unjustified convention, that role clarity is worth attaining. Certainly, in any organisation we need a balance between flexible uncertainty and constraining definition. Getting the right balance is one of the problems of teamwork, and the controversy and conflict which swirl around role problems is one sign of how difficult this can be.

I only have to mention the three most important practical issues which arise when dealing with roles, to indicate how controversial this area is: deciding *priorities, specialisation* and *workload allocation*. All of these areas raise both problems for managers and for teams because they go to the heart of the teamwork paradox of trying to meet the organisation's task objectives while also trying to achieve a supportive participation for team members. The open team goes further: it tries to involve the wider network of professionals and service users.

Systems for deciding these issues often start from one of the following categories of activity:

- legal requirements;
- types of work (for example groupwork, cognitive–behavioural therapy);
- service user categories (for example client problems);
- levels of risk, difficulty or complexity;
- organisational or political policies (for example performance indicators).

Sometimes these combine to form a more complex system of priorities or specialisations. In teams organised on a geographical basis, people may simply do all the work for their 'patch'. However, this has usually been modified either by workers' practice interests or by the organisation's exigencies, such as the need for liaison with other organisations, or the need to meet particular legal or policy requirements.

Priority and specialisation systems are also affected by the development of teams with a wide range of expertise and levels of education and practice. This leads to what has been called 'skill-mix' in, for example, community nursing, where work of different levels of risk, difficulty or complexity are allocated to staff with different skills. Research investigates the make-up of the patient population in an area to set the mix of specialist expertise or levels of ancillary or professionally trained staff required.

In many organisations, teams have a standard make-up, and they have to work within this to decide the arrangement of work within their existing personnel. While there are formal systems for doing this (see Parsloe, 1981, for a review of systems available in SSDs), teams may find it useful to build up their own, which reflects their particular organisation (see activities). This would start from legal and organisational requirements and possibly a comprehensive list of problems presented by service users. A profile of team expertise and potential contributions can be mapped out and compared with the requirements. An open team would want to involve service users and wider networks in devising their system of priorities. One important factor may be the nature of work that the team undertakes. For example, Fuller and Tulle-Winton (1996) studied specialisation in community care teams for elderly people. In a complex pattern of results, they found that specialisation made no difference to collaboration with other services in short-term work, which non-specialists could handle routinely. However, in long-term care cases and in assessment and planning, specialisation mattered and produced better collaboration and better results for service users.

Examples of teams doing this in SSDs (for example Burke, 1987, 1990; Day *et al.*, 1978) often rely on Hall's (1975) operational priority system, Goldberg and Warburton's (1979) case review system and Vickery's (1977) caseload management system.

Role clarity or role blurring?

Many discussions of teamwork promote the idea that team members should be clear about their roles. Parker (1990: 47–50) presents the mainstream arguments for doing so. He argues that since team members depend on each other, avoiding conflict and confusion means that they must be clear about expectations of each other. Seeing actions as attached to roles can lessen the tendency to blame, in an emotional way, conflicts on personality or criticise behaviour as negative or irrational. Since most work takes place away from colleagues, clarity about roles can lead to consistency in expectations. For example, service users can be told that someone will do something because this is their accepted role. Definitions of role also help to make clear where a team member is overburdened or underworked. In addition to these points, Harrington-Mackin (1996: 35) suggests that role clarity can help rotation of roles for training purposes or to avoid one person getting left with unpleasant jobs for too long. Quick (1992: 47) argues that identifying roles can help to see where behaviour is inappropriate. Kane (1975b) quotes research findings that suggest that while flexibility is necessary at the early stages, role clarity is more important as the team progresses. Garner (1994: 8) argues that role ambiguity is common in helping professions, because skills and knowledge in the different disciplines overlap, while training is largely isolated, being based within professions.

Most of the general management literature discussed above refers to role clarity within groups of managers or workers with similar responsibilities. The issue is even stronger in multiprofessional care because it brings together teams of people with clearly defined professional boundaries with long traditions and authoritative and powerful professional interests. Sometimes legal requirements support them; doctors' medical responsibility, for example. They are trained separately, and operate from different departments in sometimes different organisations, such as health trusts, social services departments, police services, housing and education departments. This may define roles clearly, but in conventional terms, rather than offering the possibility of flexibility. Authoritative professions, such as law and medicine, sometimes assume the definitions they have been taught are correct, whereas the observer might note variations. Recently, for example, I took part in a discussion in a multiprofessional organisation about advocacy for young people. Social workers, lawyers and service users discussed the approaches of different organisations in the field, and suggested that there were different forms of advocacy. The definition of advocacy was contested and unclear. A lawyer present, however, stated very firmly and finally, that lawyers had a clear professional definition of what advocacy was, and made everyone else feel woolly and disorganised for being open to uncertainty and alternatives.

Whatever the formal definitions, roles overlap. In any team, different professionals often perform similar tasks: mental health social workers and community psychiatric nurses, for example (see Chapter 7).

Moreover, there is ambiguity in the approach to role clarity. Professional assumptions and government policy statements sometimes promote role blurring for flexibility, and at the same time promote role clarity for accountability and efficiency. Calling out a social worker to do what a nurse could easily do and vice versa seems unnecessary. However, apparently similar work can conceal real differences. For example, in one psychiatric hospital, nurses often supervised visits where patients were likely to become distressed or difficult. They followed the principle that they should take a back seat, because the purpose of the visit was interaction between patient and family; nurses were just there for safety reasons. On occasion, though, social workers supervised the visits. They saw doing so as an opportunity to observe and assist interaction between family members and patients – often the patients' illness had made them inarticulate. Feedback suggested that at least some families found this made their visits more satisfying. Also, the multiprofessional team found the information gleaned from the social workers' observation helpful in assessing the patients. However, as the nurses might have surmised, some families found the social workers' approach intrusive. So an apparently similar task was interpreted in different ways. The difference in approach identified for the team that they had not given enough thought to the purpose of supervising visits. Those purposes might vary in different circumstances and justify different team members doing the task on particular occasions. It was something that needed to be planned for professional reasons, not just left to chance.

Corney (1982), Dingwall (1980), Dingwall *et al.* (1983) and Fox and Dingwall (1985) all argue that some redundancy and tension in different professional perceptions benefit service users. This is because it may avoid problems being missed and may protect civil liberties by ensuring that over-zealous or oppressive professional behaviour is curbed. It also allows service users to extract resources by playing different professional perceptions against each other. Clarity may usefully promote service users' certainty about who does what, too.

Simon (1991) describes 'caseswop', an informal development among members of teams to share work in cases. While one worker retained keyworker responsibility for the case, another, often from another agency, contracted to provide a specific input to the case. Sometimes this was simultaneous with the keyworker's activity, sometimes interventions followed on from one another. The advantages are that they put a new and additional resource into play, without disrupting agency accountability or demanding new resources. It proved stimulating to workers, and built links within the network of professionals working with similar cases in the area. Such approaches to training and development through building on experience as we practise can develop role clarity and flexibility, provided it is well-supervised and supported.

In summary, the picture of commentary and research on role clarity is mixed. Service users have complex and unified life experiences: it seems wrong to divide them following professional distinctions. Therefore, there may be real conflicts and ambiguity in roles within a team. Yet we need clarity to provide some certainty for workers and service users, so that they can understand their aims as they approach open teamworking in their teams and networks, which might otherwise be confusing and complex. How might we deal with this? A number of points come out of this discussion:

- In the early stages of multiprofessional teamwork, be prepared for some role blurring. Use the experience of this to review roles regularly and tighten up conventions, by devising agreed protocols for who does what. Over time, this will cut down uncertainty.

- Use role clarification within the team as a training device and to review management of areas of work. This will build up a pattern of shared assumptions.

- Expect to review and adapt roles in each individual case, rather than assuming that some unstated conventional view will always apply.

- Involve service users and all network members in devising roles in a particular case, so that they understand and can work with the decisions you have made. Do not take for granted that they will understand and accept your decisions.

Problem-solving

Does your team have problems in working together over something? Sometimes, members find it hard to say, and speaking too generally or behaving as though everything is a problem is unhelpful. Therefore, being specific about something which has gone wrong may help members to see it as a problem of teamwork. There are processes for problem-solving in teamwork. They involve the following sequence:

- does a problem *exist*?
- *define* the problem;
- get members' *commitment* to doing something about the problem;
- *plan* actions to solve the problem;
- *carry out* the plan;
- *review* what happened and learn lessons for future teamwork.

This approach may be effective with general team processes, in a particular case or with open teamwork issues. One of the most important issues is specifying who does what precisely. The 5WH system (defining who does what, when, where, why and how – see activities) can be a good test of whether a plan has been set out with enough clarity. Another crucial aspect is effective feedback between the people involved, looking explicitly at differences in point of view. Answering 5WH will also help define the plan of action.

This process of identifying the problem and planning aims to give problem-solving more focus. Next, we need to gain commitment to a solution. 5WH will help here too, by suggesting who should be involved and what should be done. Three important aspects of gaining commitment are that the people involved should agree what they want to do about the problems. These should be stated as an outcome: precisely what change in the situation would be satisfactory and how will you know when you see it? You can then specify exactly how you intend to get from here to there.

In problem-solving, people often think about outcomes before or at the same time as problems. When you say to them: 'what is the problem here?', they will say: 'we need a...' or 'we should...'. This relies on their experience of answers that have worked previously, or brings out their assumptions about who is responsible and how things should be done. Experience and assumptions, by their nature, will often suggest ready-made answers, rather than outcomes negotiated through the team. The problem-solving process is being used here to put pressure on others to achieve your own solution. It contravenes the power principle (see Chapter 6) that you should only use pressure (a form of power) in open team situations to achieve things for service users and the community through teamwork. If it benefits one agency above others and does not involve team members working together, it will not work in a teamwork situation.

Often, in problem-solving, people agree to exchange information. They assume that more and better information will lead others to change their reaction in whatever direction they are trying to achieve (and avoid their having to do anything). The open team needs to agree what they want the recipient of the information to do about it. It is better if they set out to agree that all or several will make a contribution, rather than all focusing on one agency to do something.

When evaluating problems and proposed solutions, analysing the factors that will affect each possibility often helps. One approach to this is forcefield analysis, based on Lewin's field theory – see the activities.

Problem-solving often leads to disagreements and conflict. Sometimes these arise because of misinformation, and sometimes because of differences in values and approach. It is important to have a process of discussion which enables conflicts to be dealt with (see Chapter 6 for some ideas on doing this).

Consultation

Process consultation is a mode of intervention in teams devised by Schein (1988 – see Chapter 2). It has many similarities to consultation in multiprofessional work in mental health and psychiatry (see Chapter 1).

Process consultation proposes that a good way of teambuilding is to examine the way in which interactions take place in teams or networks and try to improve them. It is largely about improving communication and decision-making. Process is the interactions, both spoken and unspoken, which take place between people, together with the reflexive cycle by which an interaction affects how we perceive the situation, and then changes our thinking and behaviour as a consequence. We then display our behaviour in the next interaction, which affects others' perceptions, thoughts and behaviour, and so on. Process consultation, therefore, does not just look at interactions. It also examines how interactions affect subsequent interactions and create consistent modes of thinking and behaviour. It requires external consultation because this can be difficult to do while the interactions are progressing. As we saw in relation to assessment in Chapter 3, team development often needs a process for looking at and standing outside the interactions, as well as being a participant. However, this may be difficult when interactions affect the review. So, the argument goes, outside consultants help with reviewing and evaluating the process of teamwork. Six headings may be relevant:

- communication;
- member roles and functions;
- problem-solving and decision-making;
- group norms and group growth;
- leadership and authority;
- intergroup cooperation and competition.

One of the weaknesses of this approach, which focuses strongly on processes of communication, is that, again as with many other conventional approaches to teamwork, it assumes that the most progress can be made with improving interpersonal and group working skills. I think it is often better to focus on the actual tasks that need to be carried out.

Consultation in mental health and psychiatry offers an alternative approach focused on the content of work, rather than its process, and comes from the work of Caplan (1974 – see Chapter 1). It is related to supervision, but the distinction is that the supervisor has part of the responsibility on behalf of the agency for working with the service user, which is shared with the worker. The consultant works indirectly, trying to help the worker develop his or her own perceptions, analyses and skills in working with the user, within the worker's own frame of reference. Consultation may be used with a primarily educative purpose, to enhance the worker's analysis and skill. Alternatively, it may be used with a service user or agency focus, to help the worker solve problems in the user's life or the agency's functions. The problem-solving may lead to the worker's personal development and education, and improving the worker's capacity might lead to improved problem-solving. Steinberg (1989: 27) envisages four focuses of consultation:

- the service user;
- the worker;
- the agency or team;
- the consultation, to help the worker use the consultation.

Steinberg's analysis suggests starting with clarifying the aims of the consultation and who is to be involved. Then there should be a process of reflection on the nature of the problem or area for educational development, how it is done now, what has helped and hindered progress and possible options for change. The continuing work involves:

- clear definition of an issue on which to work;
- clarifying resources available to deal with it;
- considering and building up resources to act;
- considering and planning strategies for using the resources;
- evaluating attempts to act;
- using the evaluations to redefine the problem, resources and strategies.

There should be a clear end to the process.

Many of these consultative processes are used interprofessionally. Thus, a colleague from another profession can consult with you while you deal with something which they might otherwise have to deal with. This can enhance multiprofessional training, communication and collaborative working.

A useful process can involve looking at the way people in the team and network talk. I mentioned earlier in this chapter how different management languages could get in the way of effective collaboration. Schein (1969) makes the distinction between behaviour aimed at dealing with the task the team has to perform, and behaviour which maintains the capacity of the group to work together.

Donnellon (1996) studied a variety of teams and divided the way they talk into six categories. She argues that the team's typical way of talking reveals something of its team dynamics. We should look at:

- *Identification.* What groups in the team or network do members feel attached to: informal groups, functional or professional groups, service groups? Or do they call the team 'we?'

- *Interdependence.* People are independent if they talk about doing things on their own, or say: 'I'll do that', and if they miss answering questions or comments put to them. They are interdependent if they talk about mutual interest, expressing their need for others' responses, ask for others' views, propose joint action and refer to doing things together.

- *Power differentiation.* They feel relatively powerful if they express things certainly, interrupt, speak confidently, challenge others to get things right, give direct orders or instructions, ask leading questions (that is, questions which include or suggest the expected answer), repeat questions or comments they make, speak aggressively and are excessively polite as an aggressive tactic. They feel powerless if they apologise a lot, dissociate themselves from comments or questions (for example, 'the team will need to take this on...' instead of: 'I think we should work on this...'), make disclaimers ('I don't know a lot about it, but...'), hedge ('I'll play devil's advocate...'), are polite and always state how much they owe others. You can often see this among particular groups in the team, having found out who identifies with whom. Examples might be particular professional groups, gender groups and ethnic groups.

- *Social distance.* Members feel distant socially if they use formal language and forms of address, full sentences, excessive politeness, impersonal requests ('Would it be possible for you to evaluate this?' instead of: 'Could you have a look at this, please...?'), impersonal responses to questions about relationships ('Managers always have to take up a lonely position'). They feel close socially if they use casual speech, slur pronunciation, use nicknames, claim common interests with the team, express knowledge and concern for others' wishes, empathy, feelings of reciprocity and cooperation and similar language.

- *Conflict management.* Members use forcing, avoiding and accommodating forms if they give directions, make threats, acquiesce in something they disagree with, use power differences or want to vote. The use collaborative styles if they treat disagreements as issues, problems or needs, ask questions about others' interests or needs, talk about balancing needs, make suggestions in a non-threatening way, restate views which disagree with theirs and analyse implications or consequences.

- *Negotiation process.* People negotiate about problems in a way in which they seek to win or lose ('win–lose' negotiating): for example, they express 'positions' in a debate, talk about making concessions or losing out, and they use power differences to win or always accept a losing position. People negotiate about problems with the aim of helping everyone get something out of it when they reinterpret or reframe what they are saying in the light of others' ideas, explore implications or possibilities, ask 'what if?' questions and try to find objective criteria for sorting out the problem.

Practical networking

So far, this chapter has focused on the work of teams as groups within agencies or in established team relationships, because this book draws on this tradition of studying team development. I suggested that many of these techniques may be used within networks of service users and carers. However, open teams involve wider networks of professionals and service users in development, and require us to look specifically at networking techniques as well. This may involve daily action to improve situations that arise, or it may involve a more explicit decision in the team to develop in a particular direction. In either case, team and network members cannot precipitate changes entirely on their own. Changes and developments will always involve others, who need then to participate in the process of decision-making about the development.

The main elements of networks are points (in social networks, people and their organisational and sometimes family and community structures) and links between them. I said in Chapter 1 that networking in care services means seeing 'points' in personal, not mechanistic, ways. So practical networking means not only identifying who is or might be in the network, but also the personal characteristics that they bring. This means seeing individuals very much as individuals, but also looking at their professional, family and community background which contributes to the network. We must distinguish between different characteristics and see people as more than 'doctors', 'police officers', 'mothers' or 'carers'. What particular approaches to this role do they bring? The next chapter, particularly where it looks at what individuals bring to a team, provides a good basis for exploring the individual contribution of 'points' to the network. *Developing* a network means changing the attitudes, strengthening the skills and building the contribution of the people in it (perhaps only potentially).

The essence of networking, however, is connecting the points through links. This section focuses on that issue. The first stage is to assess the network. Then action to follow up on the assessment can be taken, which will then need to be evaluated. Finally, clear decisions will need to be taken about when interventions to improve the network have finished, and what action will be taken to maintain it in a good state afterwards.

Assessment

Developing links in networks means considering three factors:

● the link's nature and direction;
● its strength;
● its quality.

Table 4.3 presents an assessment format which allows these factors to be evaluated, as the basis for a discussion.

Table 4.3   Network assessment

Focal person:

Linked person:

Link assessment:
(circle the relevant option)

Type of contact:	family	leisure/ community	work	professional
Interpersonal contact:	individual	casual	in a group	professional service
Direction:	user-initiated	link-initiated	regular	mutual
Transport:	at home	at work/ leisure	professional service	special transport: *specify:*
Ease of travel to link:	at home/ practical to walk	easy public transport	car/other available personal transport	special arrangements
Frequency:	daily	weekly or more frequent	monthly or more frequent	less frequent than monthly
How long is a typical contact?	a few minutes	an hour	a few hours	more than a day
User assessment of link:	very important	important	not very important	not important at all
Link's assessment of contact:	very important	important	not very important	not important at all

How could it be
improved?

If it could be
improved, what would
be the benefits

- to the user
- to the link
- to the service

We saw in Chapter 1 that links might be of many different types. In Wenger's (1994) analysis, for example, it might be focused on the family, on the wider community or mainly on professionals. Seed's work concentrated on the mode of connection. Was it interpersonal, or a transport link, for example? Direction was also relevant. Another example from Seed is whether the link was part of work, leisure or service support networks. Was it outwards from the service user, or inwards towards them from someone else, or reciprocal?

Strength might come from the quality of a relationship, whether the participants experience it as close. Alternatively, it may be measured by proxies for quality, such as frequency, physical distance or how much time is spent together. We have to be careful not to place our own assumptions on judgements about strength. For example, a husband might spend all his time caring for a disabled spouse, but their personal relationship might be poor or unsatisfying. On the other hand, his daughter may live in another town, and only telephone, but the mother may see this as close and supportive.

This point leads us to quality. For example, does the link meet the needs of the people involved, or only some of them or none of them? And how does it meet their needs? For example, a social worker who informs a GP about the progress on a case when the GP's involvement is needed meets the social worker's needs. However, GPs like to feel involved with their patients' progress all the time, and would not have this need met by the social worker's priorities.

Assessment of individual links may need to be followed by assessment of other links in a network and of the interconnection as a whole.

Action

Action as a result of network assessment may be considered in three ways:

- Whom do we work with? We might work with the focal person, or people that they already link with. Alternatively, we might identify other potential links or identify people to become links who are not in the person's network at all. For example, if a mental health service user has good links at the day centre, it may be possible to demonstrate to family members that the user has developed skills in relationships that make it worthwhile building up family contacts. At an earlier point in this process, we might focus on the user to build up those skills, with the aim of persuading family members to build up lost contacts.

- What aspects of the link do we work on? We can decide to develop links by altering any of the factors in the assessment from Table 4.3. For example, we can improve a network by increasing the number of types of contact, creating opportunities for developing the interpersonal nature of the contact, making links more mutual or regular, developing the direction, so that other people make the effort as well as the focal person, or the focal person makes approaches and does not rely on others. We might strengthen the arrangements for transport, so that we may rebuild a lost link.

- What do we want to achieve? As always, we need to agree with service users and other potential and actual parts of the user's network the purpose of building links and building them in this particular way. Part of this is to provide contacts into the team. For example, if we agree that a health visitor will build up and maintain contact with an elderly person, this network-building will be strengthened by participation in other work and planning for the whole situation.

This last element, that is, what we want to achieve, forms our performance indicator.

Evaluation and ending

The assessment provides a clear basis for deciding what is to be achieved and the actions can be clearly specified from this. A further assessment of the network may help to see what improvements or changes have taken place. Alternatively we can make a more limited evaluation of the success of particular actions to achieve limited objectives. Crucial to this is the participation of the people who form the network, and in particular the quality and feelings arising from changing the links in the networks.

If we have achieved our aims, or at least enough of them as seem practical, we should be clear that we are not trying to develop the links any further, or we are changing the focus of our activities. Otherwise, people can be troubled by not progressing further. For example, a hospital social worker set out to encourage family members to maintain contact with a bereaved man, who had just suffered a major heart operation. Two family members did invite him for meals with their family and took him for visits. However, because they were not clear that this was enough for the man although the social worker thought they had improved the network sufficiently, his sister worried that she had not managed to involve more members of the family, and that she did not do more herself, when in fact this would have been too much for her and for her brother.

Conclusion

In this chapter, I have focused on development, that is working in a planned way to improve how the open team works for the benefit of the users of its services, and for the satisfaction and support of the workers involved. Much of the chapter looks at different ways of improving the team. These methods apply both to the group within an agency, or an attempt to weld a wider network of professionals into better cooperative relationships. I pointed out frequently that an attempt to develop open teamwork requires not just a focus on the group you are trying to weld together, but also with their wider links and networks. The latter part of the chapter has concentrated on this networking beyond any clear group. I have tried to show how both are related: we must be aware of and develop the wider network, but as we develop networks, we must integrate those developments with the team which sees itself more as a group with shared aims. I want to re-emphasise the starting point, however. That is, there is no one way of defining a team. You may have an ideal to aim at; that ideal may be shared. More likely, you will only be able to go so far and circumstances will stop you. They may not stop you for ever or in every way. This chapter contains a myriad of factors you can look at. There must be some you could make a start on – in a particular case, or something that fits with what your team wants to do. Start there, and you might find that progress in one way will lead to a cycle of steps which will move you closer to better teamwork. There may not be an ideal answer: nobody else may agree with you about the ideal. Even so, improved working is available through team development. Remember the ideas of writers who suggest that, outside the group relations laboratory, work groups go on for long periods of time, have constantly changing personnel, and move in cycles of development, rather than ever reaching an ideal state of teamwork. There is always something you can do.

Activities

The activities in every chapter of this book offer ways of working on team- and network-building, because each chapter looks at a different aspect of teams and networks. I have selected here, therefore, activities which work on particular ideas presented in this chapter, or which do not achieve a strong focus elsewhere in the book. See the Appendix for basic team development activities.

Before and after teambuilding

This activity is based on Rushmer's research, discussed above.

Stage 1:	Distribute the questionnaire in Table 4.4 and invite team or network members to complete it. They keep their own copy. Collect anonymous copies.
Additional option:	Average the points chosen by team members to see where there is agreement, or where there are differences in view. Discuss the results.
Stage 2:	Carry out your teambuilding work.
Stage 3:	After several activities and at least a week's time, administer the questionnaire again. Invite team members to see how their attitudes have changed.
Additional option:	Average the points and see whether general change has occurred. Discuss the results.

Our teamworking situation

Stage 1:	Each team member takes Figure 4.1 and circles the number of domains they work with, the number of disciplines and the number of organisational boundaries (within your own organisation plus with outside organisations) they have to cross.
Alternative:	Do this in a case, with team and network members, including service users and carers.

Stage 2: In pairs, list and check the veracity of the domains, disciplines and boundaries identified. If there are differences, explain why they occurred.

Stage 3: In the group, list on a blackboard or flipchart the domains, disciplines and organisational boundaries. Then identify the differences between individuals and groups and why they occur. Are there any groups in the team or network whose domains, disciplines and boundaries are markedly different?

Stage 4: Discuss how you could plan to develop understanding and shared work in each domain, discipline and across each boundary.

Motivation and satisfaction

(based on Merry and Allerhand, 1977: 217–19)

Stage 1: Using the rating form (Table 4.5) ask people to rate how they feel about the team under each aspect of your work situation.

Stage 2: Collate the ratings to get an average of the team's ratings.

Optional: Discuss how you understand the different aspects, and agree if any is more important than others: perhaps agree a list of priorities. This optional stage could also be done before Stage 1.

Stage 3: In pairs, discuss the factors (positive and negative) which affected your ratings and identify actions which would improve your ratings.

Stage 4: Report back (with an intermediate small group stage if this is a large group) and list positive and negative factors for each rating and actions which could lead to improvement.

Stage 5: Filter the suggested actions and propose a plan – look at possible actions within the job enrichment perspective in the chapter, for example.

Table 4.4   Scale: helpful and unhelpful aspects of team relationships

Please circle the point on the scale which is closest to how you feel about your team or network: if you agree very strongly with the statement on the left, circle '1', if you agree very strongly with the statement on the right, circle '7'. Circle the intermediate figures where they reflect your view: for example, '4' would be a neutral view.

#	Left statement	Scale							Right statement
1	If I have a difficult issue, I feel very free to talk with other team or network members	1	2	3	4	5	6	7	If I have a difficult issue, I do not very free to talk with other team or network members
2	I know other team and network members very well	1	2	3	4	5	6	7	I do not know other team and network members very well
3	I feel OK about taking on leadership roles in my team and network	1	2	3	4	5	6	7	I feel uncertain about taking on leadership roles in my team and network
4	I feel OK about encouraging others to take on leadership roles in my team and network	1	2	3	4	5	6	7	I feel uncertain about encouraging others to take on leadership roles in my team and network
5	Responsibility in our team and network passes easily round different members	1	2	3	4	5	6	7	Getting different members to accept responsibility in our team and network is hard
6	I keep changing my approach to work in ways which benefit my team and network	1	2	3	4	5	6	7	I maintain my approach to work consistently in my team and network
7	We enjoy working together in our team or network	1	2	3	4	5	6	7	Working together in our team or network is sometimes a struggle
8	It is easy to build enthusiasm in our team or network	1	2	3	4	5	6	7	It is hard to build enthusiasm in our team or network

Table 4.4 (cont'd)

9	We often achieve successful outcomes in our team or network	1	2	3	4	5	6	7	We often feel we get nowhere in our team or network
10	I feel I make a good contribution to our team or network	1	2	3	4	5	6	7	I find it hard to make a good contribution to our team or network
11	I feel I participate in improving how our team works	1	2	3	4	5	6	7	I find it hard to participate in improving how our team works
12	We help each other in our team or network	1	2	3	4	5	6	7	We tend to follow our own interests in our team or network
13	We always look forward to future opportunities to improve our work in our team or network	1	2	3	4	5	6	7	It is hard to see things we could improve in our team or network
14	I find working on improving teamwork or networking is often enjoyable	1	2	3	4	5	6	7	I find working on improving teamwork or networking is often unpleasant
15	When we try to improve teamwork, we seem to have a lot of contact with each other	1	2	3	4	5	6	7	When we try to improve teamwork, we seem to have little contact with each other
16	When we try to improve teamwork, we seem to have a lot of shared activity to work on	1	2	3	4	5	6	7	When we try to improve teamwork, we seem to have very little shared activity to work on

Source: based on Rushmer (1997)

Table 4.5   Rating scale: motivation and satisfaction in the team

Please circle the point on the scale which is closest to how you feel about your team or network: if you agree very strongly with the statement on the left, circle '1, if you agree very strongly with the statement on the right, circle '7'. Circle the intermediate figures where they reflect your view: for example, '4' would be a neutral view.

1	I feel comfortable with other members of the team	1 2 3 4 5 6 7	I feel most comfortable away from the team
2	I can live with the amount of change and stress in the team	1 2 3 4 5 6 7	I find the amount of change in the team stressful
3	I usually feel part of the team	1 2 3 4 5 6 7	I sometimes feel loyalties elsewhere than the team
4	I usually feel well-supported by team colleagues	1 2 3 4 5 6 7	I sometimes have to look elsewhere for my support
5	I feel I can usually handle the work l have to do	1 2 3 4 5 6 7	I sometimes cannot see how to handle my work
6	I generally feel I am making progress in my career	1 2 3 4 5 6 7	I often feel I am going nowhere in my career
7	I usually feel I am making progress with most of my work	1 2 3 4 5 6 7	I sometimes feel I am not getting anywhere with my work
8	I usually feel in control of what happens in my work	1 2 3 4 5 6 7	I sometimes feel that everything at work is out of control

Source: derived from Merry and Allerhand (1977: 217–19)

Developing mission and vision

(developed from Gawlinski and Graessle, 1988: 35–43)

Stage 1: Snowball or brainstorm to get a series of one-sentence statements about team purposes.

Alternative: Team members draw a badge representing their service.

Alternative: Team members create a press release describing their service in one double-spaced page of text in the form the local newspaper would publish.

Alternative: Team members (without conferring in advance) give a short talk of 2 minutes on their view of the single most important aspect of the team's work.

Stage 2: Divide the statements into 5WH aims (*why* you want to do it or the change in society you expect to see as a result); objectives (precisely *what* you want to achieve for the people you work with); services (*how* you will work with them). Gawlinski and Graessle (1988: 36) add *who* you are, that is the combination of skills in the team and how it will work together; and *when* for example office hours, out-of-hours availability. We might also add *where*, for example office-based, home visiting, day centre, residential care, in community settings or the local team area, impact on local agencies, wider professional impact, change in the public perception of the professions involved.

Stage 3: From the statements under each heading, create formal statements of purpose.

Alternative: Form groups or pairs to make part of the statement: why, what, where, who, when and how groups.

Benchmarking

(based on Oakland, 1999)

Stage 1: Plan the approach by:
Selecting comparison group
Identifying the issues to focus on
Defining the main performance indicators

> Creating a working group to compare the team with the comparator
>
> Deciding how to collect information
>
> Organising and prepare visits or interaction with the comparator

Stage 2:   Compare the organisations and identify:

> The main differences: in what ways is the team or the comparator better?
>
> The main competencies which make the difference
>
> What helped the other agency achieve their better standard, or helped the team be better than the comparator? How can these be developed?

Stage 3:   Set new performance levels and competencies and identify how they are different. Develop action plans and integrate them into the organisations present way of doing things.

Stage 4:   Try it out.

Stage 5:   Monitor the problems and gains of the new processes, and if necessary adapt the new standards, comparing them with the benchmark organisation.

Deciding priorities and team profiling

This activity moves towards agreements about priorities and who does what from two different directions at once, neither giving priority to the agency's requirements, nor the individual preferences. The activity can be carried out through a series of team meetings, or within a three-day event, provided suitable documentation about legal requirements and agency and political policies is available. Alternatively, only parts of the activity, relevant to particular team needs, can be tried.

Stage 1:   Snowball, brainstorm or carry out a team information project to identify specific *legal requirements* which make demands on the team's work. Report these to a team meeting.

Stage 2:   Snowball from individual lists the *types of work* (not user groups) in which team members each regard themselves as trained, competent, untrained but experienced and competent and interested but needing development to perform. Report these to a team meeting, making a 'table of expertise and potential', and offering a profile of each team member's expertise and potential.

Option: Develop plans to meet the potential. Identify gaps (snowball, brainstorm or project) and see whether there are wider members of the network or potential network who could be organised to fill them.

Stage 3: Snowball or brainstorm *service user categories*, either problems or categories of user or both. Report these to a team meeting.

Stage 4: Snowball to identify a list of legal requirements for each service user group and which types of work are relevant to each user group.

Stage 5: Snowball or brainstorm ways of defining *levels of risk, difficulty or complexity* (RDC). Filter to identify no more than three ways of defining service users in this way.

Stage 6: Set up a debate over each (speakers for and against) and vote for the best. After the vote (do not let the vote finally determine decisions; this may not be inclusive enough), discuss ways in which you could combine the preferred methods of defining risk, difficulty or complexity. As a project, create a complete list of user categories and divide types of user or requirements for service into levels of risk, difficult or complexity for each group.

Stage 7: Snowball, brainstorm or set a team project to identify *organisational or political policies* which affect the team's work. Report this to a team meeting.

Stage 8: In an open team meeting, or as a team project, work through the list of user categories and RDC identifying where legal requirements and policies apply, and allocate a grade of priority (no more than five grades, fewer is possible) to each RDC level within each group. Then in an open meeting, decide whether at each grade level, the order of priority between user categories.

Stage 9: Divide the team into pairs or threes. Each pair/three takes one or more prioritised user categories and identifies which worker profiles could meet the top priority in each category. Report back and gain agreement for the decisions. Look for clashes where different user groups require the same people. Repeat for the next priority, until all priorities are covered.

Stage 10: Test out in practice whether allocation according to these priorities and profiles works, noting for an agreed period what works and what produces difficulties. At the end of the agreed period, decide on adjustments.

5WH × 2

5WH means: Who? What? When? Where? Why? How? You ask these questions about any teamwork situation to analyse what should happen, and if you cannot answer all these questions, you have not fully analysed the situation. It is '×2' because you do it from two points of view: workers and service users. Sometimes, it is '×3', because you also look at another team's point of view.

Stage 1:   Snowball or brainstorm to define the issue.

Stage 2:   Each member answers the questions 5WH from their understanding of the situation; then from the point of view of service users and in the view of any other teams involved.

Stage 3:   Answers are collated on a chalkboard or flipchart, so that self-views are first, followed by others' views. So, the social workers', nurses' and service users' understandings are listed first, then the nurses' and service users' views about the social worker's tasks, then the others' views of the nurses' tasks and so on.

Stage 4:   Discuss any identified inconsistency and the uncertainty revealed and define the answer to the issue.

Stage 5:   Discuss the reasons for the inconsistencies in view; then make plans to overcome (or make explicit and review regularly) the inconsistencies.

Forcefield analysis

Stage 1:   Brainstorm or snowball to define a problem or possible solutions.

Stage 2:   For each problem or solution, identify factors which press for a solution in one direction, and all the factors which press against it.

Alternative: Allocate each problem or solution to a separate group or pair

Stage 3:   Weight the factors for their power (1 = minor; 5 = major).

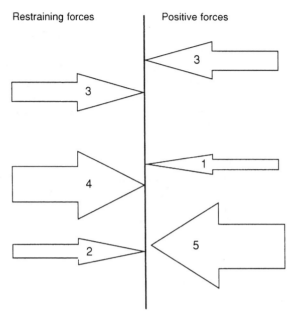

Numbers = weights (also reflected in the width of the arrow)

Figure 4.3   Forcefield analysis

Stage 4:   Plot the factors for and against on a forcefield diagram, like Figure 4.3.

Stage 5:   Decide which problems have immovable forces enforcing or constraining particular actions; pick off forces that you can do something about, and plan what to do.

Team talk styles

(derived from Donnellon, 1996)

Stage 1:   Videotape a typical team meeting or discussion.

Alternative: Role play; if you have no video recorder, use audio or have one group observe others.

Stage 2:   Divide into six pairs or threes, giving each pair the responsibility to identify the alternative styles of talk in each of Donnellon's six categories. If you cannot create six, do the exercise twice, changing the categories so that all are covered.

Stage 3:   View the videotape. Each pair notes different talk styles among team members and *examples* giving evidence of each. Work out an agreed report form.

Stage 4:   Each pair reports back on team talk: they do *not* discuss individuals or attribute examples to individuals, but discuss the evidence of different styles in the team.

Stage 5:   The team discusses what the styles reveal about how the team works and changes in style that they want to pursue.

5

Individuals and the Open Team

Introduction

Individuals bring themselves to the open team: they bring their own personality, values, knowledge and skills; they also bring their own networks. They need to keep their individuality, but also to become part of wider structures. This places the issue of our personal identity and its place in a group identity at the centre of multiprofessional teamwork (Hornby, 1993: 95–157). It is also central to *open* teamwork that we understand and work with the boundaries of the team as a group and groups within the wider network. We have to retain a picture of the identity of the team and of the network as wholes, at the same time as understanding the identity and importance of their parts.

This chapter, therefore, looks at identity. Members of open teams need to identify for themselves and be able to express to others their own identity as they understand it. This means being clear about what their role is in the network. It may be a professional role in a multiprofessional team, it may be a specific agreed role in a network. However, team members must also collectively create a team and network identity, to some extent subverting or perhaps enhancing their own identity. Team members need to be clear about how they see their individual identity within the team as a group, the group's identity within the wider network and the part they play as individuals in creating the group's connections with the wider network. Of course, in all matters of identity a team member's own understanding may differ from the understanding of others. Also, various factors may have different meanings for different people. For example, an ethnic or gender identity may be an important aspect of a person's identity from their own perception, but it may lead them to be excluded from participation in some groups or lead to prejudice from some others.

The individual

We start from the individual. How can we understand what an individual brings to an open team? Brill (1976) suggests that members bring four aspects of themselves to a team: the *tasks* that they undertake, their specialist *role* (considered in the previous chapter), their *position* in the interpersonal relationships of the team and their *person*, which refers to their personal characteristics and history. The last two are the focus of this chapter, and affect how the tasks are differentiated and roles integrated. Building up our understanding our position and person and that of others helps team functioning.

Brill suggests seven personal characteristics which team members might find it useful to think about. They are given in ascending order of privacy in Table 5.1, although all of them are more or less visible to others. All these factors affect each other and may be more or less important in particular circumstances. For example, my generalist skill in playing the piano was worthless in my social work career until I happened to get involved with a residential care home for older people needing an accompanist for singing evenings. The existence of some characteristics often blinds us to others. For example, I once worked with a social worker who specialised mainly with elderly and disabled people. He also had experience as a foster carer for children. However, nobody recognised that this might be valuable in child care work, until new groups for foster carers were set up and he offered to take part. Often we ignore latent characteristics and behaviour patterns in this way. The way someone feels about their age and sex or about conventions of dress and politeness is relevant to how others see them and how they behave towards others.

Of course, team members do not only bring things to an open team, they also take things from it. We saw in Chapter 3 that meeting individual needs and respecting individuals' contributions are usually regarded as an important aspect of effective teamwork. However, in the concern to build teamwork, we often neglect individuals' personal needs and their development. Schein (cited by Clark, 1994: 37) identifies four crucial personal needs that people bring to teams:

- *Identity* – their interpersonal role and their tasks in the open team must connect to their self-image and identity.
- *Control and influence.*
- *Needs and goals* – open team goals must include those of members.
- *Acceptance and intimacy* – members want to be liked and are worried about being too close or too distant.

Table 5.1   Personal factors in team membership

	Factor	*Comment*	*Example*
Least private	Specialist knowledge and skill	Related to work	Professional training, experience as foster carer
	Generalist knowledge and skill	Not related to work	Piano-playing, woodwork
	Reference groups	Groups aspired to or valued	Professional groups, political party
	Latent characteristics	Natural characteristics of member	Age, sex, ethnic origin, religion, class
	Behaviour patterns and norms	Typical behaviour and socialised expectations	Dress, courtesy, loyalty, use of authority
	Values and attitudes	Attitudes to how humans are and should be	Worth of human life, 'everyone can grow'
	Self-image	How members see themselves	'Do-gooders', caring, competent, worthless
Most private			

Source: Brill (1976)

Similarly, Adair (1986) argues that individuals have needs which their work must meet, in addition to the team satisfaction and motivation factors examined in Chapter 4:

- *Trust* – they must trust themselves and their capacity and others in the team.

- *Autonomy* – members need to be part of the team, and also to have distinctiveness from it.

- *Initiative* – members need to feel that in at least some areas of work they can act on their own decisions, and their freedom to do so needs defining.

- *Industry* – people want to work, and have activities which are valid and worthwhile.

- *Integrity* – people want to be able to act consistently according to beliefs and value that they espouse.

- *Security* – members like to understand how others regard them in their work role, and that they are making a valid contribution which the organisation values. This is related to whether they feel that their job will continue to exist and that they will continue to be employed.

If the open team does not meet these needs, people will become frustrated, tense, anxious and insecure. Note 'open team': both service users and professionals get these satisfactions from each other when they are working together to provide a service or on an individual's case. The 'together' aspect of collaboration means that satisfactions come from the joint working, rather than from what some people see as 'normal' sources, that is, professionals from colleagues, users from family and community. Not getting satisfactions from team or network relationships can lead people to demand them from elsewhere. For example, if professionals or users are not clear about their role, they will seek reassurance from other people. There are three types of responses if members are feeling bad about not having their personal needs met. *'Tough'* responses tend to lead to fighting, controlling and resisting authority. *'Tender'* responses lead to supporting, helping alliance and dependency behaviour. *Withdrawal* responses lead to passivity, indifference and too much use of logic or reason in debates.

So far I have been looking at the 'person' factor in open teamwork. Turning now to 'position', this relates not only to professional and work roles, discussed in Chapter 4, but also to informal roles which people play in interpersonal relations. A lot of work has been done on this during the last 20 years, and I consider it next.

Interpersonal factors and roles

In Chapter 4 we looked at integrating roles to form viable jobs: that definition of 'role' was concerned with the work tasks performed, and I called it 'work role'. Another strand of teamwork writing is concerned with members' roles in interpersonal relations. The assumption lying behind this work is that people have typical ways of behaving towards others, which then condition how people in groups relate to one another. Teamwork writing from the 1950s to the 1970s reflected the early concern with teams as groups. One of the earliest accounts of team roles (Benne and Skeats, 1948, used in Adair, 1986) derives from the study of group dynamics. They divide roles into three types: those which help the group fulfil its task, those which help to build or maintain group cohesion and those which are concerned to pursue personal needs. The lists of roles are set out in Table 5.2.

In a simplified version of personality role types, Quick (1992) proposes roles which support and develop the team ('team-building roles') and those which disadvantage the team ('team-subverting roles').

One strand of analysis of team roles, building on this sort of work, describes the effect of different types of personality or styles of behaviour on the group process within a team. Many accounts of roles like this depend on the experiences of the writer, rather than presenting a comprehensive, researched analysis. Often categories mimic those created half a century ago by Benne and Skeats (1948). Whatever the origin of this agreement, it suggests that this way of looking at roles relies on seeing a team primarily as a group, and team roles as primarily contributions to group relations, rather than the functions the team has to perform. Adair (1986: 40) makes this point when he criticises the way we personalise functions within an organisation as roles. Similarly, Spencer and Pruss (1992: 39) suggest that this approach relies on defining psychological personality traits, and that different kinds of interpersonal skills used in organisations are a

Table 5.2 Benne and Skeats' group roles

Group task roles	Group cohesion roles	'Individual', personal roles
Initiator-contributor – suggests innovations	**Encourager** – praises, agrees, warm understanding	**Aggressor** – deflates others' status, attacks or criticises
Information-seeker – asks for information or clarification	**Gatekeeper, expediter** – encourages others to participate; limits lengthy contributions	**Recognition-seeker** – seeks attention; reports personal achievements; seeks important roles
Opinion-seeker – asks for information and values	**Compromiser** – yields status, admits error, 'comes halfway'	**Blocker** – negative; disagrees without reason; goes back on agreements
Information-giver – offers facts or experience	**Harmoniser** – mediates disagreements	**Playboy** – cynical, displays lack of involvement
Opinion-giver – states beliefs or opinions	**Standard-setter** – expresses or applies group standards	**Dominator** – exerts authority; manipulates by flattery; interrupts
Elaborator – spells out reasons, examples or consequences	**Group observer-commentator** – feeds back interpretations of group process	**Self-confessor** – expresses irrelevant personal feelings to receive attention
Coordinator – connects ideas; coordinates activities	**Follower** – acts as audience; accepts direction of group progress	**Help-seeker** – seeks sympathy through expressing insecurity or confusion
Orienter – summarises or defines positions		**Special interest pleader** – cloaks own biases through pleading for important interests (e.g. on behalf of users)
Recorder – acts as memory for the group		
Evaluator-critic – compares achievements with standards		
Energiser – simulates more or better-quality action		
Procedural technician – does routine, supportive tasks		

Note: The roles are not given in any particular order, and items in columns do not relate horizontally to items in other columns.
Source: adapted from Adair's (1986) summary

more appropriate basis for defining roles: their argument reflects a 1990s focus on skills and competences, rather than personality.

One example of personality type role definitions (Brill, 1976), discusses multiprofessional teams in health and social care. She refers to:

- leaders;
- fighters, on behalf of service users against organisational authority;
- catalysts, who disarm conflict among team members;
- 'know-it-alls', who promote research, but whose absolutist approach to knowledge irritates others;
- manipulators, who seek their own rather than group interests;
- peace-makers, who seek consensus at all costs.

Many such analyses are negative about team members' personalities, without any research base to justify the labels. However, Lundy (1994) usefully makes the point that team members may take on helpful and unhelpful roles simultaneously: we never only have a single role. Also, he shows others may push team members into unhelpful roles.

A significant advance on this view of roles as a contribution of personality to the group process was made in the early 1980s. New research examined roles taken within the work tasks that the team undertook. The most important and influential researcher was Belbin (1981). However, although this is a completely new approach, based on research among management teams, many of the roles reflect the personality-type analysis discussed above.

Belbin's (1981) work originated from a management training exercise. Simulated teams were set up to carry out tasks in groups, and teams were selected in various ways, partly using psychological tests. This led to ideas for the sort of people who would be useful in making a team work well. Eventually eight roles were identified which were found necessary for a successful team. These are set out in Table 5.3. A self-test questionnaire was devised to elicit which of these roles was most typical of particular individuals. This work has been followed up in practice by Belbin (1993) and others and has been widely applied. In particular, Platt *et al.* (1988) devised a card-game exercise for people in the voluntary housing movement. This adapted the terminology to be more familiar and appropriate to public and socially oriented services. Platt *et al.*'s additions to Belbin's (1981) roles also provide more information about how they fit together and may be managed, and these have been included in Table 5.3. I have kept Belbin's original terms, since they are more widely used elsewhere.

The argument is that a successful team will have all or most of these roles contained within it. If significant roles are missing, the team will be unbalanced and will function less well. Most people have main and secondary roles and therefore can contribute skills arising from one or

Table 5.3 Belbin's team role

Role	Personality features	Strengths	Possible weaknesses	Relates well to	Powerful role combinations	Potential conflict with
Company worker (Platt *et al.*: organiser)	Methodical, practical, reliable, conscientious	Turns plans and ideas into practical projects; sets about tasks that need doing, even if it's boring; pursues the organisation's interests	Inflexible, lacks imagination, does not inspire or motivate others	Chair, completer-finisher	Completer-finisher, shaper, monitor-evaluator	Plant, resource investigator, teamworker
Chairman (Platt *et al.*: chair)	Calm, enthusiastic, self-confident, self-disciplined, good listener, positive, talent-spotter	Guides group and uses each member's talents to achieve aims, accepting, intervenes decisively to pull team together, sums up well	Bossy, intimidates group and limits their self-confidence and communication	All members; needs to work with plant and monitor-evaluator	Completer-finisher, teamworker	Shaper (over leadership)
Shaper	Dynamic, out-going, challenging, opportunistic, emotional	Driving force, good project leader, galvanises group, makes things happen, challenges inertia	Overreacts to disappointment, impatient, abrasive, argumentative	Teamworker, resource investigator	Resource investigator, completer-finisher	Plant, chair, monitor-evaluator
Plant (Platt *et al.*: innovator)	Individualistic, serious, clever, loner, unorthodox, original, radical, forthright	Produces imaginative ideas, complex and strategic planning, wide knowledge	Over-sensitive, unrealistic, disregards protocol and can be isolated or scapegoated	Chair, teamworker, monitor-evaluator	Shaper, completer-finisher	All other roles except teamworker

more roles. Which roles we take on depends on other skills in the team. In one team we might be more of an 'evaluator', say, while in another we might be a 'chair'. Relationships between some roles are easier than between others (Platt *et al.*, 1988: 16–19): shapers, resource investigators, teamworkers and completer-finishers often work well together. So do plants, company workers, chairs and evaluators. If we have a choice for a working group, it may be worth trying to put people occupying these roles together. More dynamic, but perhaps more conflictual, working groups come from putting contrasting roles together. Shapers are good special project leaders, with a chair to smooth the way. On the other hand, resource investigators need the analytic skills of an evaluator, but react badly to the rejection of the evaluation of their ideas, so a teamworker may help to leaven the relationships. Conflicting roles carried out by a single personality can be powerful. One advantage of this formulation of team roles is that both pluses and minuses in each role are acknowledged, so that the definition of some roles is not tainted, as in some of the examples given above, by a negative slant. This also points out the positive side of some traits which can seem negative.

Although Belbin's work has been influential, there are several cautions in using it. First, people are not always consistent and the roles they take up may change (Syer and Connolly, 1996: 84). As a result, we may label people or groups with their roles, and this does not reflect the full complexity of their approach to their work. We may collude with them in a fantasy about how they are, thus preventing them from changing (Syer and Connolly, 1996: 96). Most people have a range of possible ways of acting, and can decide to take on several different roles. Second, more important, Clark (1994) argues that Belbin's model only proposes changing team membership, or influencing recruitment, rather than offering some intervention which can help an existing team make progress. However, we have seen that some later additions can provide guidance for this purpose. He suggests that Belbin's work, treated light-heartedly, is a useful introduction to the idea of team roles, rather than being of practical use in teambuilding. My own experience confirms this view. Third, Belbin's work is based on research on teams of managers of other people. It is not clear how useful it might be for professionals who work individually and come together to coordinate their work, or teams with a designated leader and group of variously skilled subordinates.

From the point of view of open teamwork, the problem with these approaches is that the early focus on group relations limits applicability to network relationships. Even Belbin's work focuses on relatively small groups. It can be hard to apply beyond the focal team and outwards into the network. Some modern work shifts the emphasis.

For example, Parker's (1990) helpful analysis of team roles simplifies the sort of analysis found in Belbin (1981), by identifying four team-player styles:

- *Contributors* focus on the task, contribute good information and hard work and are dependable. They combine Belbin's company workers and completer-finishers.

- *Collaborators* focus on goals and the 'big picture', are flexible and open to new ideas. They combine Belbin's shapers and resource investigators.

- *Communicators* focus on team process, are good listeners and resolve conflicts. They combine Belbin's chairs and teamworkers.

- *Challengers* focus on questions and issues, both evaluate standards and push the team forward. They combine Belbin's monitor-evaluators and plants.

The analogies with Belbin's analysis are not exact. For example, contributors also contain elements of Belbin's teamworkers. Parker's work is useful first because he shows how different aspects of these elements can combine to benefit particular functions in the team. For example, a team leader in a new project might usefully have substantial elements of collaborator and challenger styles in their make-up. On the other hand, leaders of an ongoing long-term care team might lean towards being contributors and communicators. Second, Parker's work shows how different styles and roles of working focus on different issues for the team: task, goals, process and issues. Third, and most usefully for open teamwork, this analysis helps to identify contributions and limitations of even marginal or distant members of a network.

Margerison and McCann's (1990) 'role preferences' are similarly an example of a more modern approach, mentioned above, which focuses on skills rather than personality types or interpersonal roles. These were identified in discussions with successful teams:

- *creator-innovators*, independent people who come up with ideas;
- *explorer-promoters*, sociable people who bring back ideas, contacts and resources;

- *assessor-developers*, practical people who get ideas to work and test them against practical requirements;
- *thruster-organisers*, motivators who organise people and systems;
- *concluder-producers*, consistent people who maintain quality standards;
- *controller-inspectors*, careful people who check and evaluate work;
- *upholder-maintainers*, stable people who support others;
- *reporter-advisers*, patient people who are good at collecting and presenting information.

The modern analyses claim, then, to include both positives and negatives, to focus on skills rather than personalities and to develop their ideas from a research base of group exercises or discussions with managers. However, many of the descriptive statements still carry elements of personality styles within them and often carry negative emphases, even where they include a positive element. Many also bear remarkable similarities to each other, reflecting, probably, well-established categorisations of personalities from work over the last half-century as well as a consistent pattern of role division in workplaces around the world.

Identifying interpersonal roles helpfully identifies continuities in behaviour, but may cause us to believe that people are fixed, rather than being able to change. All these analyses make clear that this is not so. Teambuilding activity designed to look at interpersonal roles should, therefore, always do so with a focus on possibilities for change and development, such as every team member learning new and additional roles. However, such analyses can help to get away from simply defining team members by their profession or job role, as we did in Chapter 4, and help to see the broader contributions that they make as people to the team or wider network.

The individual and the open team identity

Personal characteristics, then, create a 'person' and interpersonal roles a 'position' and these form an individual identity within an open team. To understand how these are incorporated into and form *team* identity, we need to feed back work or professional role integration and task differentiation into the equation. People's person and position are clearly different and come from different sources than their work role and the collection of tasks undertaken by the organisation. It is sometimes taken for granted in over-simplified management thinking that what you do in a profession or for an organisation is untainted by your person and position; the latter are private and outside the organisation. But this is clearly not so; as Brill (1976) said in the discussion with which I started this chapter, all four factors must influence one another.

How do person, position, role and tasks influence one another? Open multiprofessional teamwork does not require conformity, to a standard work or professional role or solely to tasks defined by an organisation, because it requires team members who will be flexible in their capacity to build new links and look for unobvious network strengths, and it requires incorporation of professional and community networks from outside the organisations represented by employees.

To make progress with individual development, as part of team-building (one of the approaches in Chapter 4) we need to find ways of seeing how individuals can relate to an open team, and the organisations surrounding it. Margerison and McCann (1990: 26–9) raise four issues:

- *Relationship preferences.* Members find a balance between being extroverted and introverted.
- *Information use.* Members find a balance between pragmatism and creativity in finding and applying information.
- *Decision-making.* Members have different balances between being analytical and critical and basing their decisions on conventions and values.
- *Organisational approaches.* Members vary in their tendency to prefer structured, planned ways and flexible, open ways of organising.

One activity proposes looking at these four dimensions of members' relationships with an open team that they work in. These dimensions form preferences for a style of operating which personalises the tasks and work roles in the organisation, but this still comes from the individuals' identities. Another part of the interaction between person, position and organisation comes from the organisation's impact on defining the identity of a team.

Based on consultancy in health care organisations, Øvretveit (1997) suggests that the shift from being the personal identity of an individual or their identity as a representative of another team arises when *membership* of the team is defined. It can be specified in various ways. For example, people who are full-time, or who are governed by team policy, managed by a specified person or who have formal rights to be consulted or participate in decisions may be full members. Others who do not meet all or some of these criteria may be associate members or peripheral in some way. Where the boundary is drawn defines membership of a team as against a network and starts to create identity as a team or network member. That identity then needs satisfaction as part of the joint working, not only from the individual sources that we considered at the beginning of this chapter. Other aspects of team membership may arise around which *professions* should be represented. Sometimes this is a political matter, and each relevant group must be included; alternatively, some groups may be contracted for some work. Differences in type of work, status, payment and autonomy may be crucial elements in how decisions are made. Sometimes differences in seniority or even uncertainty about membership are denied. Øvretveit (1997: 18) suggests this may be because the team is committed to participation and stress democracy and equality to promote it, avoiding questions which may upset a balance of participation. I look at this issue in Chapter 6 on power in teams.

Being people, what team members contribute comes from their personality. However, in any work situation, as Hornby (1993:107) points out, our contribution is bounded by that work situation and the role we play within it. She also notes (pp. 98–101) that service users and their carers make their contribution deriving from their role in the network. So, as in Figure 5.1, we can identify the work group part of the network, as it is clustered around the workplace of the team member we are looking at. The user and carer networks are clustered around the people whose roles are 'user' and 'carer'. Third, the multiprofessional team network connects the various professionals with links to the team member, user and carer we are concerned with. These people are all individuals, but their points in the network are their roles, whether these are professional roles or roles such as carer, user or family or community member.

How can we understand these separate roles as part of an open team? Some descriptions of the formation of team and network are concentric: that is, an aspect of the network is taken as a centre point and others spread out from it, as in Figure 5.2a. Hornby (1993: 9), for example, argues that the most appropriate focus for teamwork should be service users, who are their own self-helpers. In contact with them

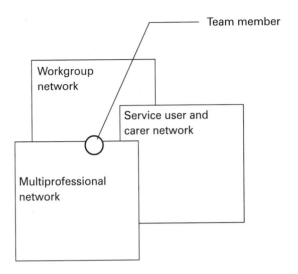

Figure 5.1 Three interlocking networks
in multiprofessional teamwork

are face-workers, including informal carers from the community and members of the family. All these people are often encouraged or required to collaborate in teamwork, as we have seen in Chapter 2. They in turn are part of agencies and community and family networks which form a wider context. Policy seeks to involve these in a wider coordinated network of provision. Ethically, this stance places an emphasis where it perhaps should be, on the service user. However, it does not permit a complex understanding of the interaction of different blocks because it is difficult to consider the detail of links between different interests in the network. It may also exclude some members of the team who are not part of the obvious user–professional relationships. For example, in residential care and other institutions, different shifts (day and night) and the impact of domestic and maintenance staff must be considered (CPA, 1996). In all settings, we must include the role of managerial and administrative staff. Also, as we saw in Chapter 3, we need to start team development by looking at whom members think is in the team, and whom they have left out. A network analysis of the open team is therefore often a better representation of the range of relationships between the team's elements, as in Figure 5.2b. As you see, it is still possible to put the service user at the centre.

Figure 5.2a   Concentric open team analysis

A network view deals with this problem by seeing roles as points in a field (in this case 'the community', with connections to other points. Seed's approach (see Chapter 1), for example, identifies different forms of transport and distances between the settings where the roles are taken up. Network views tend to focus on the amount, direction and quality of connections. This has an advantage when you are looking at improving linkages, whereas it is neutral about the main focus of work. It helps to identify the complexity of and potential for alternative approaches to a network.

Another view, taken by Rawson (1994) for example, is to see work and interpersonal roles as sets within a field (see Chapter 1 for the terminology). In Figure 5.3, we can see professionals within their agencies, or isolated, we can see where overlaps occur or where connections are precise. Some boundaries are firm and clear, but we

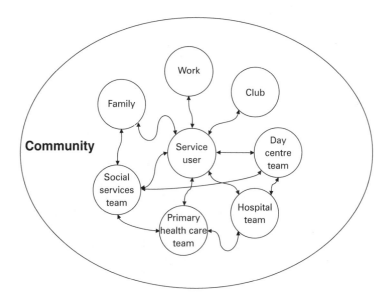

Figure 5.2b   Network open team analysis

can also consider where boundaries are blurred or permeable. This approach, then, helps us to think about identity and boundary. What exactly is the connection between one role and another? Is the consultant psychiatrist part of the hospital or the community team, or partly within both and partly outside both? What aspects of her hospital role hinder her community role and vice versa? Thinking in this way helps to understand how the network interacts in practice and includes within discussion of a network how people perceive roles and boundaries.

Each of these ways of understanding how people as people and people's roles can fit within a team or network has something to offer, then. The different views suggest that we need to think about different issues in considering teams and networks:

● Where is our focus and how does the existence of the team and network affect that focus?

- The extent and quality of the links within the network: how do these form different focuses?
- What is the identity and boundary of different people's and agencies' roles as they form points within a network?

Focus

As we have seen, anyone in a network may become a focus of the way we think about it. There may be several focuses or just one. Thinking about the focus gives us a point of view. Very often, we see things from our own point of view and we concentrate on people who have relationships directly with us – our 'client' or 'patient' or our 'opposite number' in another department. Network analyses, whether using a diagram or not, help us to see things from someone else's point of view: we can ask about what links are important to a service user, and the quality of them. This takes us on to links.

Links

What does a link consist of? Network ideas suggest to us that if we can draw a line between two points, that is, make a connection between two people, we have made a link. A link only really exists when everyone involved is aware of it and the connection has an impact on them. Just seeing someone, or just meeting them may be a link, but in social networks, we should identify the nature of communication. For example a letter seems to be just one-way, but it communicates to and affects the person who receives it. They might feel more warmly towards us, or angry about what we have said. This then affects how they deal with us in the future.

Whittington (1983) shows how social workers use three methods to work on links: rhetoric, that is language and argument; relationships which engage the service user and promote mutual interests and influence; and resources which are used to negotiate or influence the direction of the work. One of the activities helps to assess links in this way.

In another book about making links (Payne, 1993), I also suggested that we can identify four kinds of professional linkages:

- *Liaison* is about making and maintaining contact with other organisations and people.

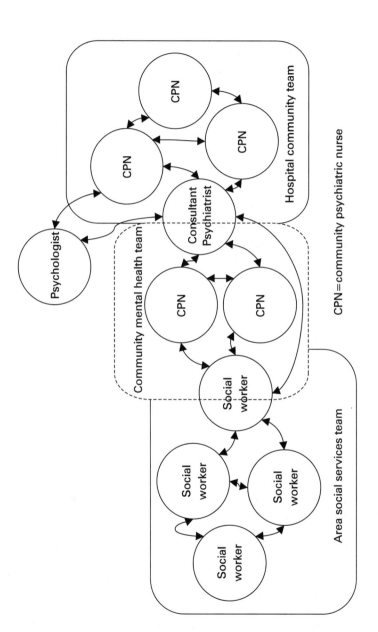

Figure 5.3 Interpersonal professional roles as sets in fields

- *Coordination* means ensuring that organisations and people work in ways which support and complement each other's work.
- *Representation* is acting on behalf of one agency or person in their relationships with another.
- *Presentation* means promoting and demonstrating understanding about your work with another person or organisation.

These kinds of linkages need to be planned, take account of interpersonal relationships which affect the link and relate to formal structures and financial relationships between people or agencies.

Identity and boundary

Identity and boundary are concerned with how people see their position in the network and where they see its boundary as being. They might see themselves as individuals, or as part of a group, with a wider boundary. Other groups or individuals will exist in their perception of the network. This may be more complex than a single identity and boundary, because, as we saw above, we participate in different aspects of the network. Each aspect might have different boundaries. To some extent, different boundaries create different groups, within which we have different identities. However, one of the points about open teamwork (as opposed to seeing the team as a separate group) is that these different groups interlock. Therefore, different identities have their effects, perhaps indirectly, on the whole network. For example, at one time I specialised in mental health work in a social services area team, but also liaised with a community project in the area. I had a reasonable multiprofessional team with the social worker, community psychiatric nurse and psychiatrist based at the local hospital psychiatric ward. They, of course, had links with many other mental health workers. A health visitor from a large health centre in the area was also involved in the community project and we had good links. However, a new GP in her centre was suspicious of social workers and proved difficult to work with over two complex compulsory admissions to hospital. He was then dubious about my involvement in the discharge arrangements for these patients. My links with the health visitor, and evident successful participation with the psychiatrist's team, convinced him to give it another go, and we developed quite a useful liaison, which helped in future cases. My identity as a person involved with the community, as a participant in the hospital, benefited, through indirect influence, my involvement in the area team's links with the health centre. My alternative identities, as committed to community development and as more expert in and committed to mental health than many of my colleagues, benefited my identity as a part of the health centre team.

Potential professions in a team and network

It may seem surprising to leave the formal professional identities of potential open team members until the last section of this chapter. By doing so, I have been keen to emphasise that many other aspects of individuality are important to successful multiprofessional working. Much of the teamwork literature and experience *outside* the health and social services world does not consider professional background at all or only as a minor factor among many others. From this point of view it is just as surprising that, in health and social care, professional background looms so large. The evidence I discuss in Chapter 7 shows how important this can be in obstructing effective teamwork and inter-agency cooperation. It is so much of a problem in health and social care because of the different areas of legal, independent personal and professional responsibility within the roles of health and social care professionals. The management teamwork literature deals more with superior–subordinate relationships and groups of similar staff. Therefore, although it offers useful ideas about teamworking, it sometimes does not deal with particular factors which affect care services.

In another way, while profession seems important, where multiprofessional teamwork operates successfully, its importance may decline, as different areas of skill and contribution are made clear and acknowledged. Also open teamwork implies a wide range of professional, non-professional and user and carer involvements. Dealing with risk and complexity requires listening to many different people, valuing their contribution and taking it into one's professional thinking, rather than working in different professional ghettos.

However, clearly different professional expertise and contributions must be recognised, to ensure that the full range of expertise is called on when necessary. Also, divisions, difficulties and conflicts arising from professional roles and responsibilities need to be dealt with. However, alliances and strengths from cross-professional links may be built on – the picture of relationships among the professions is not all negative.

A crucial element in developing open teamwork is to avoid assumptions about appropriate professions to be involved in any particular team. We must also leave open the possibility of involving unexpected professions or roles in particular cases. User and carer involvement will also need to be provided for. Labelling people 'core' members of a team either in general or for a particular case, can sometimes seem to exclude others from equal consideration.

A useful analysis of the possible agencies involved appears in Figure 5.4. It takes into account several different factors. First the network is divided into broad areas of social provision which might yield relevant team members. One area is the family and community of the service user. Second, there are three different sectors of provision: state, private and voluntary (or third) sectors. Third, the areas are divided into 'authorities' (the planners and organisers of an area), the agencies within it and individual professionals. So, for example, in dealing with the education area, we may need contact with the organising agency in the area. Here, this is still the education department of the local authority, insofar as any agency has overall responsibilities. This comment draws attention, though, to the fact that as the organisational system of public services has become more complex with elements of privatisation everywhere, we have to take into account a more complex set of relationships. Then we may need to deal with schools, or with specialist agencies, such as psychological services. Professionals are attached to these institutions, but may also operate independently. There are complexities in these divisions. For example, employment services have traditionally been associated with social security. However, the national government Department of State is now the Department for Education and Employment (DfEE), and careers guidance has always been part of education, although since the mid-1990s, it is often privatised and no longer part of the local authority education department.

This diagrammatic analysis may be used as an analysis of a team's information resources or contacts. You can test out how far your networks extend. Teams may also use it to help analyse the network in a particular case, overlaying the relationships in a different colour.

Looking at potential professional connections in your network in this way raises the possibility of seeing them in an institutional and service context, but also seeing the whole pattern of community and professional networks which might be involved or which are uninvolved in a particular case or in a particular agency's work. Open teamwork implies, not a set 'team', but openness to a range of professional relationships tied to other aspects of the network. It also suggests that, rather than assuming conventional professional involvements, a range of possibilities needs to be provided for, and constant variation assumed.

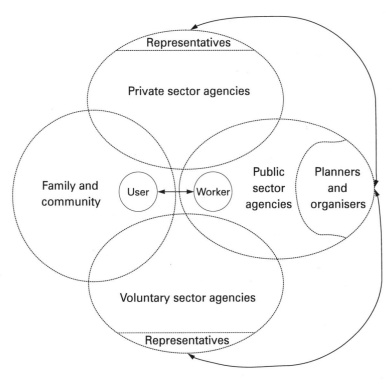

Figure 5.4 Network analysis of some agency relations

Conclusion

In this chapter, we have focused on the different identities of the individuals which they contribute in various patterns to the open team. Open teamwork requires us to look not just for established roles, or accepted personal contributions, but to think anew and frequently about the open team's personal and interpersonal membership. We must be flexible to include the necessary aspects of the network, rather than closed to the possibilities of surprising involvements.

Activities

See the Appendix for basic team development activities.

What can I offer?

(derived from Brill, 1976)

This is a good starter for any team development activities which aim to bring together disparate individuals, or people who do not know each other well. It can also produce surprises in teams who think they know each other well.

Stage 1:	Individuals think about their work and personal life over the past three months and list different characteristics of themselves under each heading in Table 5.1.
Stage 2:	In pairs or threes, discuss which characteristics and skills are new to others.
Stage 3:	Report back the 'new to the team' characteristics (anonymously if you want). Brainstorm ways in which they might be used in the team.
Optional stage:	Snowball or brainstorm issues which have arisen with service users over the past three months, and match these with possible characteristics identified in the team which would help respond to those issues.

Team member maps

This exercise works well as an enjoyable and not-too-demanding starter with residential care or hospital ward teams, but can work with any team where they share a physical base.

Stage 1:	Each team member is asked to draw a map of the team's territory (the office or residential care establishment for example).
Stage 2:	Discuss the different maps. How do different positions in the area lead to different perceptions of it? For example, does the clerical worker draw the office as bigger than the nurse on the ward? Do some people forget parts of the territory? Do people agree what the territory is?
Stage 3:	Returning to their maps, team members place others and themselves on their map where they are usually to be found.
Stage 4:	Discuss the outcomes. Do perceptions differ? Why? Does the placement of people reveal their roles in relationships in the team?
Optional stage:	Snowball or use a Johari window around what individuals learned about themselves and others' perceptions of them from the exercise.

How do I work in my team?

(derived from Margerison and McCann, 1990)

Stage 1:	Individuals rate how they see their own preferences, how they think their colleagues see them and the style of what their organisation prefers in the rating scale in Table 5.4.
Stage 2:	Report back scales first on organisation preferences, and discuss. Are there different views about what the organisation likes? Do the differences in view create different groups in the team?
Stage 3:	Snowball individuals' preferences and differences between how they see themselves and how they think others see them.
Stage 4:	Discuss, without necessarily reporting actual members' differences, how the team should handle differences in perception.
Additional stage:	Individuals rate each other team member, and the different views of each team member are

reported and discussed (with the raters remaining anonymous). This can be more demanding emotionally, and should be handled with care.

Table 5.4   How I work in my team rating scale

Work style	*Please circle the rating which reflects your preference*	Work style
Relationship preferences I like to develop new contacts	3 2 1 0 1 2 3	*Relationship preferences* I like to focus on strengthening existing ties
Information use The agency should develop effective information resources for us to use	3 2 1 0 1 2 3	*Information use* I like to search out new resources and ways of doing things
Decision-making It is important to make decisions by following professional values, law, policy and procedures	3 2 1 0 1 2 3	*Decision-making* It is important to think carefully about each new situation when making decisions
Organisational approaches I prefer to structure my work within a carefully planned organisation	3 2 1 0 1 2 3	*Organisational approaches* I prefer a flexible agency structure which gives wide discretion in planning my work

(0 = neutral, 3 = strong preference for this statement)
Source: derived from Margerison and McCann (1990)

FLIBbers – Focus, Links, Identity and Boundaries

This activity uses network analysis to examine how individuals fit with the team and use their identity in wider network links.

Stage 1:   Agree with participants *either* to focus on a particular case *or* to focus on team relationships. Snowball from individual network diagrams of the case or team relationships.

Stage 2:   Report back the agreed diagrams, and arrive at an agreed diagram of the network relationships. Organise copies of the agreed diagram for everyone to use.

Stage 3:   Review in the group the areas of disagreement, and note them. What difference of *Focus* did they imply? Remember, there may be several different focuses in a team or individual case, according to your role or interests. Agree in the group which individual or group within the network is the focus.

Stage 4:   In at least two subgroups, work on *Links* from the focus to other aspects of the network (you may want to agree diagrammatic conventions for showing links, but it may also be interesting to compare in the next stage the different approaches the subgroups take to describing the links). Think about the type and quality of links.

Stage 5:   In the full group, compare how the subgroups have identified and described the links diagrammatically. Arrive at an agreed diagram of the links. Looking at team relationships, stage 4 should require seeing how different members of the team give access to different groups in the community or different agencies. It should also be necessary to look at relationships in the team to see how ones links within the team make it easier or harder to use links that particular individuals have.

Stage 6:   In the subgroups, try to draw *Boundaries* round identifiable groups in the network diagram. As the subgroups do this, they must write a definition of the *Identity* of the group(s) whose boundaries they are drawing. Sometimes those group(s) will be individuals whose identity is not shared with any of those they link with.

Stage 7:   Review the outcomes in the full group. What different groups have the subgroups identified? If they are the same groups, do the boundaries and definitions differ? How and why?

Example: In an individual case, you may get different definitions of the working team, or members of the family or carers, or interested members of the community. Looking at team relationships, you may get different definitions of the role of particular links. The court may be central to social services child care team members, the psychiatric unit to mental health team members, the social security office to them all.

6

Power Issues in Open Teamwork

The power principle in open teamwork

This chapter and the next are about overcoming the things that sometimes cause difficulties in open teamwork. Many issues come from problems about power, dealt with in this chapter, and organisational structure, dealt with in the next. Issues about power arise because we assume that teamwork is about openness, democratic processes and equality between people, when our society sometimes works in the opposite way. So our open team seems to be working well, until the leader weighs in with his management responsibility to follow some organisational policy. Or, we all think we are involving our mentally ill patient and his family, when the psychiatrist does a home visit at the behest of the GP and says he has medical responsibility and admission is the only answer. Apparently the niece has pressurised the GP because she thinks her uncle should not be left on his own.

The reason for being concerned about power in teamwork is not only that unequal power may be oppressive against some members of a team or some service users. A concern for power may also be positive in ensuring that open teamwork overcomes inequalities and imbalances in power and stimulates power sharing, to the benefit of the people we serve. We can understand power as people's capacity to achieve a desired outcome, that is, to get what they want. Power comes from a variety of sources. Three sources which are important for teamwork are: power in interpersonal relationships, political power and social power.

Interpersonal power

French and Raven (1959) distinguish six different kinds of interpersonal power. They propose that an individual can get someone else to do what they want by bringing one or, more often, a mixture of these into play:

- *reward power*, where person A thinks powerful person B can offer rewards;
- *coercive power*, where A thinks B can damage or punish;
- *referent power*, where A identifies with B;
- *expert power*, where A thinks B is skilful or knows more;
- *legitimate power*, or authority where A accepts a general view in society that B should be able to influence things is correct.

Understanding sources of interpersonal power is only the beginning of a basis for understanding more complex power relationships. However, since the open team is concerned to draw people in the network into participation and reach out to people, an understanding of a range of power relationships allows us to see how our actual or potential power relations will affect how people see us and respond to participation and reaching out. While participation is supposed to give people more power in the network, some members of the network may not see that they have much power in the situation. We can see from these sources, for example, that a service user or carer may not feel that they have any of these forms of personal power. To facilitate their participation, it may be necessary to be explicit about the influence that they may have: legitimate power, for example, because practice and procedures give them rights, or expert power in their own problems and the contributions they make to caring are two examples. Equally, it may be necessary to prevent team members' power from damaging relationships. For example, in multiprofessional teams, doctors are often seen as having overriding expert power. This may impose an unnecessary burden on them, because things will be referred to them which are not required. Equally, it may stimulate resistance and avoidance. A mentally ill user may avoid seeing the doctor for fear of being readmitted to hospital, for example. Another user might take no notice of a nurse's advice because it does not come from a doctor's position of expertise.

This discussion emphasises that power is not a matter of actuality but of perception. How people see the power possessed and how they attribute power to particular pieces of behaviour is an important aspect of relationships in teams and networks. In an open team, members need to be aware of power relationships and how behaviour might be perceived as reflecting or expressing power in all relationships. Then it should be possible to help people deal with these issues in the network.

For example, the parents of an adult man with learning disabilities had found a care assistant from the SSD offered valuable advice and support and responded well to her guidance. This is an example of the assistant's referent power. For a long time, as they aged they tried to get independent housing for their son, and the social worker assisted in this. They perceived the social worker as having a great deal of reward power, when this was successful. However, when their son was allocated special housing near them, he had difficulties in managing independently, and the housing assistant was particularly critical and demanding, in response to pressure from neighbours. The parents and the care assistant who supported them saw this as demanding unreasonable achievements from their son and as an example of coercive power. Their response rather set the care assistant against the housing assistant. The parents' response to this was to approach their doctor to get an opinion which would influence the housing department to be more reasonable. This is an example of expectations of the doctor being too high, because of his general referent power. He referred the matter back to social services, and the social worker's past help enabled her to engage in a negotiation with the housing department. The care assistant felt this was 'siding with the enemy' and some careful work on repairing relationships was needed.

As power is a matter of perception and relationship, this inevitably means that it is expressed and diffused in political relationships and structures.

Political power

Political power is about how the capacity to achieve desired outcomes becomes associated with organisational and social structures. Organisations and social structures diffuse and concentrate power. All the forms of interpersonal power may be relevant, but most political power is concerned with coercion and legitimacy. In conventional democratic structures, election confers legitimacy.

Forming a government then confers coercive power, through the legitimated right to pass legislation and enforce it, ultimately through using physical force.

One characteristic of political power is that, although it might ultimately be sanctioned by legitimated physical force, the power persists by custom and expectation, even without physical force. Thus, capacity to achieve a desired outcome continues to be associated with social institutions and ways of behaving long after the physical force that sanctions it ceases to be used. This leads us to the importance of social power.

Social power

Social power derives from conventions and expectations about social institutions, social status and organisations. Power does not only come from the ability to use force, for example to discipline staff or remove a benefit or service from a client. It comes from the knowledge or fear among staff or service users that you have this capacity. Such knowledge or fear of power becomes associated with organisations or social institutions. Black service users, for example, might expect all organisations dominated by white people to ignore or minimise their interests. So, social divisions may cause excluded people in or outside organisations to assume that we can impose our will on them, or that we will try to do so, even if we do not see it like this. Therefore, others often mistrust our potential use of power. We have to find ways to deal with these problems of social power. In teamwork, we have to respond to a fundamental mistrust that arises between employees and employers, and between different groups, such as professional groups. In networking, we have to overcome the social expectations of many people in the network. We have to do this by being aware of and dealing explicitly with issues of power in our relationships.

The power principle

The starting point for dealing with these issues is the *power principle*. It says that power in open teamwork should be used for the benefit of service users and their community through the open team. This makes three points: our concern is for power used within the team, for user and community benefit and for action within the open team. The benefit of the service user and their community seems obvious, but we tend also to take for granted arguments about benefit to the agency.

However, people, perhaps without realising it, sometimes produce 'service user-benefit' explanations of power which conceal their own advantage. For example, managers often produce 'efficiency' arguments and professionals produce 'expert knowledge' arguments which may have some justification in them, but also, and perhaps mainly, reinforce their personal power. We have seen why: power subsists in factors which are independent of individuals, such as information, social divisions and structures, or expectations. For example, medical knowledge is more powerful than social knowledge because it has had longer to establish itself as a widely accepted system of knowledge. Also, it is backed by widely accepted social assumptions valuing scientifically created knowledge whereas social knowledge is claimed to be less 'scientific'. There is also a pattern of social assumptions related to the acceptability of scientific knowledge; it is associated with middle-class education which confers social authority. Another example: women professionals in a team may be expected to take on caring roles which confer less social authority. This might allow male doctors or lawyers to be more distant and less involved in personal tasks, which makes them less aware of the reality of the problems which the necessity for care imposes on their colleague professionals and carers in the family and community network. Different kinds of power may be mistaken or misunderstood. For example, someone with expert power may assume that this also gives them high legitimate power. Others may think this too; where people take power, others often allow them to.

Any division in or between groups is ripe for power conflicts. Power crucially operates around divisions. Where divisions between groups of people exist, inequalities in the capacity to obtain and use resources often arise. The reason for teamwork and networking is at least partly to facilitate connections and relationships which will spread power across, and reduce the ill-effects of, the divisions. This is the reason for the third aspect of the power principle focusing on working through the open team. By extending collaboration beyond a group of workers into interagency collaboration and user participation, we make teamwork development available to combat power imbalances and conflicts. This takes up the other aspect of power, that it may be positive. It is possible to build on divisions to create alliances between people who have shared interests. However, another positive approach can be to build bridges across divisions to create stronger alliances, for example between users and carers, and between users and professionals. Such alliances may be stronger because they draw on different social sources of power and support.

Power issues and social divisions in teams

Power issues sometimes arise around conventional divisions, such as gender and ethnic origins. In open teamwork there are complications. Discrimination arises because of gender and ethnic differences between individuals. This happens both within the team and within the network. Some people may assume that women should be in an assistant, domestic or caring role, while men make the plans and 'professional decisions'. You can see these patterns of power relations in talk and language use in teams and networks. I have seen some managers, for example, who seem to miss what women – even senior women – say in a meeting. They only 'hear' and respond to it when a man says it. When I see a woman's comment passed over, I say things like: 'I think we should go back to Jane's idea...', rather than just making the point again, because it is important to acknowledge both how we do this and the contribution made. People from minority ethnic groups may be regarded as less competent, say, because their use of language may reflect the style of their ethnic origins. So they write reports or speak in ways which are experienced as unusual forms. These personal prejudices are not only backed up by conventional attitudes in society, but also by conventional professional divisions. So, in teams, men may have gained high status because they are likely to be promoted to management positions or work in high-status professions, such as medicine or law. They often have a more extended, more conventional education, and this strengthens their command of conventional behaviour and English. Women are more likely to be in ancillary roles or work in lower-status professions such as nursing, social work or occupational therapy. These patterns are changing as both high- and low-status professions gain a more balanced entry and equal opportunities policies affect behaviour and practice in organisations. Attitudes, equality and personal power follow some way behind this. Among people in the network, attitudes may vary widely. It is easy to offend people of different views. So people from conventional masculine backgrounds find insistence on not using gender-specific language amusing or irritating.

Similarly in dealing with people from minority ethnic groups, the health service was an early focus of new Commonwealth immigration in the 1950s. People have become accustomed to working alongside professionals from minority ethnic groups. However, we cannot take this for granted. Discrimination and prejudice also arise in other services where workers from ethnic minorities are less commonplace.

In teams, gender and other power differences sometimes come out in sexual relations. Many people form close personal relationships with work colleagues: a lot of people marry people they met at work. It is pleasing to like people that you work with, and it eases teamwork if team members like one another. However, other team members may find close personal relationships excluding, and the special features of such relationships can worry or confuse people in other agencies and service users. A couple, married or not, may be seen as favouring one another even if they are careful not to.

Another problem with forming close personal relationships is the risk of harassment, where one person presses a relationship or behaves intimately in ways that another does not want. Harassment may be even more of a problem if someone appears to offer career advancement for sexual favours or personal attention or appears to threaten detrimental consequences if they do not get the kind of relationship they want. Such behaviour needs to be recorded and confronted. A team would ideally all take responsibility for this, or at least offer support to people worried by harassment. However, the person who is offended often needs to do it, making it clear precisely what is unacceptable. At its extreme, dealing with harassment may be a matter of taking a formal grievance or disciplinary action.

Sometimes differences in power such as formal organisational status or around professional divisions becomes important. Kane (1975b), in an important American study, identified a crucial difficulty in multiprofessional health and social care. 'Aspiring professions' gain greater influence in multiprofessional work for their personnel and world view and sanction for their yet-to-be established work from trusted older professions. Established professions, on the other hand, pay for this by more cumbersome methods of working and decision-making, higher costs and overheads and the loss of part of their functions. Also, unless work is reassigned from established professions, new professions appear to offer completely new services and there may be dispute about whether this is needed. The gain for older professions is that the newer professions may improve the quality of the overall service and take on what is lower-status work to the senior profession. For a nurse or social worker, however, accepting the lower-status work without also fighting for a renewed view of the value of their particular skill and expertise fails to gain the advantage for service users of what they can offer to the overall service.

Conflict

How conflict arises

One important aspect of teams is how they manage conflict. Much of the commentary I reviewed in Chapters 2 to 4 says that we should always be able to see conflict in a team. 'Bad' teams hide it; 'good' teams succeed in handling it constructively. Conflict often builds up around the inappropriate use of power to resolve issues in relationships and action within the open team. It may be inappropriate in two ways. Sometimes people do not take the power that they should have within the open team to resolve issues among themselves. Alternatively, power is used against the power principle to resolve an issue, and team members feel oppressed. This should not arise in open teams, since participation is a priority and the purpose is to allow the group to achieve more than individuals might achieve on their own. It follows then that unresolved conflict is likely to make achieving both these objectives problematic. Following the power principle, we should focus on constructive techniques to manage conflict and resolve the issues which underlie it. Eisenhardt *et al.* (1997) suggest three important strategies, and ways of moving towards them, set out in Table 6.1.

How does conflict occur? Walton (1987) suggests that it is cyclical. Several issues exist in the team which might provoke conflict. Few problems arise unless a triggering event brings the issues into play. Conflict behaviour then appears as the team tries to deal with the trigger. With more experience of conflict, more issues arise which cause it. Then, triggering events lead to conflict which, previously, would have been neutral. *Substantive* issues, that is, where there are real differences of view, often arise about philosophical or principled differences or invasion of roles which are important to us. Other important issues arise around task or opportunity deprivation where people are unable to follow deeply held views, or cannot pursue aspects of their work. This happens when others cut across them or the team or managers do not allow them to make progress, perhaps because they do not have the right level of training. *Emotional* issues, that is, where the problem arises from feelings about others, can arise from people not having satisfying roles or having incompatible styles of dealing with issues. Sometimes conflicts arise from unfulfilled expectations and we should look at assumptions and expectations to see if they are reasonable. There may be barriers to dealing with conflicts, where one member thinks that another is too vulnerable or risky to criticise, so an issue does not get raised, or they prefer to maintain an image of equanimity.

Table 6.1   Strategies for dealing with conflict

Strategy for dealing with conflict	Do this by...
Focus on issues, not personalities	Find and discuss current, factual information
Frame proposed outcomes as collaborations to achieve the best results for team, agency and service users	Identify several alternatives, not one
	Identify and rally round goals
	Make the process humorous and cheerful
Make the process of decision-making seem fair	Balance the power structure (e.g. in who does what)
	Do not force consensus

Source: Eisenhardt *et al.* (1977)

Filley (1975: 9–12) suggests that the following kinds of social relationships lead to conflict:

- ambiguous domains, where people are uncertain about who is responsible for what;
- conflicts of interest;
- communication barriers caused by distance in time (for example, part-timers) or space (for example, out-posted workers);
- one person depends on another, who does not behave as expected;
- roles are strongly differentiated by status or convention;

- where people have very frequent dealings with each other. This increases opportunities for things to go wrong and may accentuate personal differences;
- where consensus is needed, raising the risk of something going wrong if agreement is impossible;
- where there is a history of past conflict.

One helpful preventive strategy is to look out for these situations and try to prevent them arising.

Another useful preventive is to make sure that everyone actively participates in team and network decisions. This, however, although the next few paragraphs offer some suggestions, is a counsel of perfection. Most people find interpersonal conflict where they work wearing, unpleasant and difficult to change. They therefore try to reduce the consequences of it, rather than deal with the conflict itself. While this seems workable with minor issues, it very often leads to a problem which expands to take over other areas of activity. Generally, then, tackling every disagreement in the early stages is best, before it escalates. But this can be stressful, and needs energy: I often find myself gearing up with a heavy heart to deal with some conflict – 'Oh, not again'. This often causes us to put off dealing with it in the hope that it will go away. However, we should plan this, waiting for the right moment, rather than putting action off without knowing when we will deal with it.

It is also useful to arrange things to reduce the possibilities for conflict. Chang (1995a: 59) suggests some helpful ground rules for team behaviour (see Table 6.2). I have adapted these to a health and social care content and restructured them.

How can you tell when conflict is becoming difficult? Feelings of conflict include anger, attack and rejection. Also, conflict behaviour often leads to competitive strategies such as blocking others' attempts to take action, interruptions, ignoring others, making alliances with one group against another and manoeuvring for advantage. Very often feelings of regret, sympathy, guilt and cooperative strategies balance these, because few people can sustain all-out war. Chang (1995a: 40) offers some helpful guidance. He suggests keeping a lookout for the beginnings of conflict situations. For example, team members say things with emotion, attack ideas before someone has finished talking about them, accuse others of not understanding the point, refuse to compromise and make subtle personal attacks. Behaviour like this then escalates into members wanting to win an argument, rather than reach the best outcome. Their position becomes firmer and they are emotionally committed to it. They limit involvement with people who disagree, and do not see the need to come to agreement. Different people react in different ways. Some are aggressive, some go in for politicking, others put any discussion off and yet others simply avoid communication and discussion about anything – 'I'm just doing my job and not getting involved'.

Table 6.2   Ground rules for team behaviour

Area	Ground rule
Listen	Hear others out completely before responding
Opinion	Opinions differ about most things
Disagreement	If you disagree with someone, tell them, not others
Acknowledge	When you see a difference of opinion, say so: do not ignore it or exaggerate it
Referring	Do not refer work on in a form in which you would not wish to receive it
Intake	Do not accept work in a form in which they should not have passed it on
Doubt	When in doubt, find out
Assumptions	Do not assume anything: it is risky
Responsibility	Find out your responsibility and how others fit with it
Update	Keep others informed of what you know, keep yourself informed of what they know

Source: adapted from Chang (1995a: 59)

Dealing with conflict

All of these responses are usually unhelpful. It is usually better to engage directly with the conflict in a 'problem-solving' way. Members should avoid reacting emotionally and should try explicitly to react rationally – 'let's just stop and think this out'. First, try to avoid the conflict escalating while you find a way of dealing with the issues rationally. Then, try to manage interpersonal conflicts helpfully. Third, help the team find ways of dealing with the issues which underlie the conflict.

First, avoiding the conflict. Table 6.3 suggests some ways in which you might control conflict until you can deal with the personality problems and the basic issues.

Table 6.3   Limiting conflict behaviour

Strategy	Possible actions	Examples
Avoidance	Avoid situations where disputes arose; reduce triggering events; cooling-off periods	Reduce contact between the parties; set up system for dealing with conflict subjects; adjourn meetings
Alteration	Change the form or place of the conflict	Agree not to argue in front of others; or to criticise each other without making a positive suggestion; meet before conflict situations to resolve problems
Feedback	Help parties to understand how others are affected	Other people are upset; team is losing resources or cooperation from others; loss of dignity
Help with consequences	Provide support, more rest, more thinking time	Neutral person to listen to stressed people; time off; more social events; encourage getting away from the office at lunchtime; discourage overwork

Source: Payne (1982: 79), slightly adapted

Managing interpersonal conflict management is the next thing to tackle. Harrington-Mackin (1996: 121–36) suggests managing information according to the RISC strategy:

● you **R**eport the behaviour which is a problem in specific terms ('You said yesterday at the team meeting that I made a bad decision in the Ali case and you have made several similar criticisms about other cases in front of other team members in that last two weeks...');

- you state the Impact that the behaviour had on you ('Saying that while I was describing the case in that way interrupted my explanation of a complicated case before I had explained the details, distracted me and others from the plans we need to make and undermined other staff's confidence in my work, especially my student...');

- you Specify what behaviour you would prefer ('If you do have criticisms about my work, please talk to me about them in private, and listen carefully to the full circumstances before jumping in with a comment...');

- and you state the Consequences, both good and bad, if the other person does not respond ('We'll be able to use your ideas in making our plans if you make criticisms positively like that. If you keep interrupting with negative points in meetings, I'll have to ask the team leader to set up a case referral meeting in a way which will restrict all of us from such active involvement...').

If you are being criticised in this way, Harrington-Mackin recommends the PAUSE strategy:

- you Paraphrase the objection, showing that you have heard and understood it ('Are you saying I should have contacted the doctor first?...');

- you Ask questions to clarify and specify it: do not ask why questions which might lead to self-justification ('What information do you think the doctor could help us with?...');

- you Use time to cool down and think over what was said. Ask to discuss it later ('Perhaps we could think about ways of doing that. Could I talk over the possibilities with you after our lunch meeting?...');

- you Summarise what you decide to do ('We'll talk this over in our supervision meeting this afternoon...');

- you Evaluate how you responded – a bit over-anxious, angry? – because you may have to deal with that later and work out how you will move on.

Moving on to team management of disagreements, Chang (1995a: 45–55) also makes helpful suggestions about a process for sorting out conflict:

- *Acknowledge the conflict.* If someone reacts unusually strongly to something you said, ask to get involved in a resolution: 'I thought that would be ok, but you seem to think there's a better way. Perhaps we should talk over the possibilities.'

- *Identify underlying conflicts.* Most conflicts have underlying issues that have led to them. Others are about emotional issues. Examples of common underlying issues are uncertainty about who does what, disagreement about how something should be done, what the purpose is, the procedures that they should follow, who is responsible for what, and about values and facts. Examples of emotional issues are incompatible personal styles (for example, easy-going against driving; free-and-easy against careful), struggles for control over other people or over resources, threats to self-esteem, jealousy and resentment about past decisions or actions. You have to resolve both underlying and emotional issues to overcome a conflict.

- *Hear all points of view.* Because this may mean getting views from timid or non-communicative people, this may have to be done privately at a suitable time in a suitable place. This does not mean putting off working on the conflict. Team members can do this among themselves, but sometimes a peer, the team leader or even an outside consultant may have to act as mediator. In discussion, focus on facts and behaviour, not feelings and personalities. Avoid blaming and focus on similarities or agreements. Also, look at different levels of the conflict: people may differ on what the problem is, or agree about that but view it differently, or they may view it in the same way, but differ on the solution. The mediator might produce evidence about how the conflict hurts the team.

- *Work together to find ways of resolving the conflict.* Do not put it all on one person. Both sides should make a contribution. Try to remain open and keep channels of communication going. Involve others in building up a response to the problem.

- *Agree and allocate responsibility for action to resolve the conflict.* This may involve finding out information, seeking changes in policy or getting agreement to change the way things are done.

- *Arrange (and keep to) a session to review how things are going.* This holds people accountable for working on the solution. It also provides the opportunity to find out if any other problems are hovering around, and for self-congratulation all round if things are working well.

Some people are not amenable to all these rational measures because they have built up an image of themselves as right and others as wrong or incompetent. They do not hear or understand others' comments and always find something wrong. Their behaviour is often rude or inconsiderate. They often see themselves as defending the underdog and fighting against injustice. Dealing with such people requires careful planning in almost every encounter in order to manage your relationship with them. Meet with them at a specified time for a specified period. Report your views clearly, if necessary reading a prepared script. Refuse to be interrupted: comment on or question every interruption and every hostile or negative comment. You may be attacked personally and professionally. Do not allow yourself to respond to any attacking comments. Do not apologise, do not retreat, do not get angry. Paraphrase what they say in temperate language. Specifically and openly note down what they agree to or disagree with. Set deadlines for any action you are going to take and stick with them. There is very little possibility of changing people with extreme behaviour problems; they just have to be managed with as little damage as possible to everyone else. Public organisations, particularly, have employment procedures which are inadequate to remove people who fail to perform because of personal relationship difficulties and there is often very little to be done except hope that they do not cause a major disaster, such as a user's death. If this does occur, it is useful to maintain a detailed record of attempts to get such people to function. This needs to include evidence that matters have been passed with adequate evidence to managerial or professional disciplinary procedures to deal with so that responsibility for the failure to take action can reside with the upper reaches of the organisation where it belongs.

Among the problems which many teams face is conflict over insufficient or unequal commitment to work or to achievement. Fatout and Rose (1995: 84–6) call this 'social loafing'. It arises where team members take more part in meeting their own goals or in social activities, rather than in task-related activities. Social loafing, they claim, occurs just about everywhere, but needs to be controlled, as well as leading to an assessment of underlying reasons why people feel the need to behave like this. Possible ways of controlling it are to select team members who are committed to its particular purpose and setting up processes for defining work publicly and openly so that everybody can see that work is comparable. With a longer focus, team members may need to attack issues which are leading to disaffection. For example, team members can raise problems which are obstructing the team's work and 'turning people off'. Managerial action might include enriching individuals' work (see Chapter 5). Social loafing may be a symptom of problems in the organisation which need managerial action to set and reinforce specific targets.

Teams may also get into conflicts with managers or other parts of the organisation. We may see these as opportunities to develop participation in the wider organisation thus developing the network. Many of these techniques for dealing with conflict are useful here too.

Promoting participation

In Chapter 2, one of the most commonly identified characteristics of teams was a participative style. It is, however, uncommonly difficult to achieve. People often resist participation if it means taking on responsibility, particularly where they see participation as a way of others avoiding responsibility. An example is where, intentionally or otherwise, managers or well-paid people with high professional status use others' participation to avoid responsibility for which they are paid, or to impose their own views by dominating agenda-setting and decision-making. Sometimes, status and power differentials make participation difficult for either those with responsibility, power and status, or those without. For example, doctors who worry about their clinical responsibility for medical decisions sometimes behave as though this means that no other colleagues or patients have the right to pursue their own responsibilities or interests. On the other hand, nurses, social workers or patients often accept imposition of opinion by doctors, without standing up for their own responsibilities, knowledge and skill contribution. Similarly, legal knowledge or powers which police officers or social workers sometimes have seem to make it impossible for someone to participate. However, choices always exist. West (1994: 25–9), quoting Wall, identifies three aspects of team participation:

- *Interaction.* Team and network members need to meet, talk and work with each other. You need to build in opportunities for this to happen. These may be informal or formal meetings or 'handovers' from one shift or group to another.

- *Information-sharing.* Team and network members need to identify information that each needs to know and find out where that information will come from. Then you need to make sure there are ways of passing that information on to whoever needs to know it. Also you should avoid passing information on to people who do not want it, so that information does not build up unnecessarily.

- *Influence over decision-making.* Teams and networks need to know what decisions are needed. When are you making a decision? Often we just fall into deciding something. When a decision comes up, who needs to take part in it? Decisions which arise regularly need a programme of meetings to take them; decisions which are more occasional or one-off need careful consideration to make sure people can participate.

All these relate closely to communication. In Chapter 4, we met Donnellon's (1996: 25–39) analysis of how language in team communication helps understanding of relationships. Words and word-formations used can help to show how members understand and interpret their team and its environment. They also indicate relationships such as who identifies with whom, who is interdependent with others, power relations, social distance, how members manage conflict and how they negotiate. Pietroni (1992) shows how different disciplinary languages are used in different aspects of health and social care. He identifies languages drawn from linguistic traditions in:

- medicine/molecular/material;
- psychology/psychosomatic/psychoanalytic;
- epidemiological/social/cultural;
- anthropology/ethnology/ethology;
- symbolic/metaphorical/archetypal;
- natural/energetic/spiritual;
- prevention/promotion/education;
- environmental/ecological/planetary;
- legal/moral/ethical;
- research/evaluation/audit;
- economic/administrative/political.

However, his medical background means that his 'social' excludes virtually all sociological and social work languages. He also excludes languages of 'caring' and nursing, and his 'legal' includes only ethics-related issues, such as confidentiality and consent. What this illustrates is how easily even the most open-minded and committed multiprofessional operator is conditioned by the languages of their training and daily involvements. We must be aware, then, that there are different languages and different interpretations and emphases in similar languages.

Networks can also be difficult to participate in. Burton and Kagan (1995: 52–7) discuss 'penetration' of social situations. They suggest that we can assess the extent to which we can take part in a social situation in four ways:

- *Physical access.* This may be about wheelchair access or lifts. Equally, it may be about being allowed to go to particular meetings or to particular places. For example, social workers usually participate better in a hospital team if they are allowed to go to ward meetings and have access to ward records.

- *Who may participate.* This may be stated formally, as in club membership, or informally, for example, where people from minority ethnic groups or with learning disabilities feel unwelcome.

- *What kind of activities people can do.* There is little point in being able to go to a pub, for example, if you dislike drinking and loud music.

- *What kind of roles people can play.* For example, sometimes leadership or caring roles are limited.

Looking at these issues of access to social contact may help us identify actions which will help people participate more fully.

Communication

We have seen that promoting participation and dealing with power issues involve skilled communication, another important aspect of successful team- and networking. Failures in communication become power issues because the essence of cooperation and participation is effective communication. People who do not or cannot communicate make it impossible for others to participate; if they do so intentionally or carelessly, it is an abuse of their power over communication. We will see in Chapter 7 that much of the policy development which has sought improved collaboration and cooperation among agencies and professionals has arisen from concerns that failures in communication have led to serious service failures. Often they have arisen from misuse of professional and group power, to the disadvantage of service users. Again, the power principle comes into play. Another point is that communication is a widely recognised good, accepted in a range of professions (Abramson and Mizrahi, 1996), and so improving it may gain support from different stakeholders. On the other hand, communication does not mean that you can avoid acting: you must *do*, as well as communicate.

Lindström (1987) emphasises more prosaic but nonetheless important aspects of communication skill:

- *Encouragement and criticism.* Both should be appropriate, be aimed at positive improvement and be specific. Team members should not say to others: 'You're always arguing', because it is non-encouraging, non-critical and non-specific. Being encouraging means finding and saying what is useful and helpful about a piece of behaviour; a comment is only worthwhile if change is possible. Being critical means identifying exactly was wrong about a piece of behaviour and how it could have been helpful. Being specific means defining exactly what the other person said or did, speaking near to the time of the event, but preferably when the other can be receptive, that is, not in the heat of the moment. It also helps to get feedback about why someone did something that others criticise. 'It would have helped me to deal with John's behaviour, if you had been on my side during the meeting and mentioned your doubts afterwards in private.' Mentioning good consequences of your proposed solution and bad consequences of what went wrong also helps.

- *Active listening.* Team members should try not to let their attention wander when others are speaking or doing, should be responsive and encourage them to express themselves. Table 6.4 sets out a variety of useful techniques for improving listening skills.

- *Being open.* Team members should express their feelings, good and bad, at appropriate moments. They should be prepared to share information and be available to help or respond to others in the team. Table 6.5 sets out techniques for facilitating openness. Some of these draw on active listening skills, given in Table 6.4.

Table 6.4   Active listening

Technique	Why	How
Focus on speaker	Reduces their focus on your personal characteristics, emphasises the importance of their communication	Look at them, frequent eye contact, reduce your contribution, do not take over discussion
Encourage speaker	Stimulates better communication	Ask questions to gain elaboration, indicate you have heard and want to hear more
Reduce communication problems	Provides the best conditions for communication	Ask if there are problems in their communication, offer to change setting, ask what you can do to help communication, say if things are difficult for you to hear and suggest alternative arrangements
Paraphrase	Calms and clarifies, helps the speaker gauge your understanding, summarises repetition	Say: 'Let me see if I understand you…', use your own words to say what you think the speaker said; if they spoke for a long time, summarise; then ask: 'Is that right?'
Draw people out	Helps speaker clarify and refine ideas and reduce listener's uncertainty	Paraphrase, then ask open-ended, non-directive questions
Mirror	Builds trust, emphasises listener's neutrality, speeds discussion	Repeat short communications, use speaker's keywords in summarising
Gathering ideas	Builds ideas quickly	Specify task, suspend judgement (like brainstorming)
Stacking	Makes order of speaking in a meeting clear, frees people to listen	Ask or say who wants to speak, put them in order, call on them in turn
Tracking	Makes clear that several ideas are being followed and that speakers' lines of thought are not being neglected	Summarise discussion, point out different areas, ask 'Is that right?'

Table 6.4 (cont'd)

Technique	Why	How
Encouraging	Especially early in a discussion, creates openings for participation	Who else has ideas? Is there a nurse's perspective? Is there an example of that principle in action? Has anyone not spoken for a while?
Balancing	Completes range of alternative views, undercuts manipulation by 'silence means consent', supports people who find it difficult to speak	Is there a different position? Are there other ways of looking at this? What do others think?
Making space	Helps non-communicators contribute	Do you have a point of view? Hold others off, use a round
Intentional silence	Helps someone who is struggling to clarify what they are saying	Count to five, focusing on the speaker with no reactions – as though you expect more. Stop others speaking. Suggest everyone thinks over what has been said for a moment
Seek common ground	Identifies agreements in a conflict	Say you will summarise group's differences and similarities; summarise differences, then common ground, say 'Is that right?' Highlight areas of potential agreement

Source: Summarised from Lindström (1987: 43–5) and Kaner *et al.* (1996: 41–54)

- *Argue to convince, not to win.* We should be well-prepared for meetings, think out the various different positions and try to understand them. It also helps to think up practical illustrations of what we want to say, so that people can understand their relevance to the matter under discussion. In particular, we should look at the skills and experience of the other team members to see where their contribution is likely to be particularly strong.

West (1994: 40–1) calls this way of behaving 'constructive controversy', where people explore opposing opinions, are open-minded, considerate and understanding of others' positions. They want to inte-

Table 6.5   Being open in meetings

Ways of working	*Examples*
Make the discussion flow	Ask who wants to speak and put them in order... but allow interruptions to the order when there is a controversial comment
Broaden participation	Encourage... 'who wants to say something?' Balance... 'Does anyone have a different view on that?' Make space... 'Do you have something you want to add?' Use the clock... 'Perhaps we should move on in five minutes – are there any more contributions to this?'
Help people make points	Paraphrase and mirror (see Table 6.3) Draw people out... 'could you say a bit more about that?'
Manage different points of view	Call for alternative responses... 'Does anyone have an alternative view?'
	Refocus... 'We've been talking about *x* for a while, perhaps we should look at the other aspects.' or 'Jill made a point a few minutes ago, shall we pick that up before we lose it?'
	Tracking... 'We're discussing several points here. Let's split them up.' and afterwards: 'Have we picked up all the points?'

Source: adapted from Kaner *et al.* (1996: 55–67)

grate not separate ideas, always look for high-quality solutions and can tolerate diversity of opinion, personality, background and profession in the team.

One important area of communication is regular briefing. In management conventions, this is part of a process of passing down *and up* information through the organisation through a planned series of regular meetings. We can learn from this idea for making sure feedback works between team members and leaders, between team members and each other and among networks concerned with particular cases or communities. You can cover liaison responsibilities, as well as management instructions or staff or network feedback.

McGeough, (1995: 79–86) suggests the following process: good news, then not so good news including progress, policy, people, points for action, plans, praise, priorities and procedures.

Movement and change

Does the team move forward, progress? Should it? These questions are always a worry for team leaders and for many team members. Somehow, their work seems unchanging, stultified. This is a power issue, because they do not seem to have control over their own development and progress: either nothing seems to change, or change is imposed from outside. If open teamwork is about engaging the team and wider networks in resolving their own issues, they must also take power over change. Some teams are worried by constant change but it leads to the same thing: they cannot make positive progress, as opposed to running to keep up.

Smale (1996), basing his work on extensive consultancy activity in the social services, suggests that rather than looking at change as an event, we should see it as a process of managing progression through a series of innovations. The feeling of powerlessness to create change comes from a number of fallacies (see Table 6.6), which may be summarised by saying that we often think that change can happen without our doing too much about it. Virtually all his fallacies may be overcome by careful planning and working on innovations. Instead, his model of *managing change through innovation* proposes identifying specific changes that can be achieved and actively pursuing them. This involves identifying the major people involved, being clear about the innovation to be introduced and understanding the social and organisational context in which it is to be introduced. The innovations then need to be carefully negotiated and planned within the teams that will use them, with training in what do to. What happens as a result of introducing the innovation needs to be carefully reviewed and adaptations made as problems arise.

Jerome (1995) usefully examines team change processes. He suggests that we need to prepare for a change, map out what will change, navigate through the change and then evaluate our successes and failures, so that we can manage change better next time. *Preparation* involves being aware of events which might lead to changes: law, policy, education and training, personnel, resources all vary, and changes in them are often signalled in advance, but we

Table 6.6   Fallacies which lead to
powerlessness over making changes

Type of fallacy	Fallacy	Explanation
'Tell and do nothing'	cascade	senior managers announce changes in procedure and expect the organisation to work them out
	anthropomorphic	people assume that good innovations will naturally arise and diffuse within the organisation
	natural selection	people will adopt examples of good practice that they see in other teams and reject practices known to be ineffective
	Trojan horse	people assume that a successful pilot project will be adopted by others
People	heroines and villains	people assume that all innovation comes from individual 'champions' and obstruction of changes is due to 'difficult people'
	not reinventing the wheel	people do not accept innovations 'not invented here' or at least specifically adapted to their needs
	to know is to act	even though people know something is wrong or possible, they do not necessarily act on that knowledge
Innovation	innovation is always progress	there are often disadvantages to many proposed changes
	all innovations are additions	some innovations do not require new resources, and can be introduced by working better
	more of the same	not all innovations can be introduced by the same methods as previous innovations; people may have too much faith in present methods
	new ways of working require restructuring	it is not inevitable that innovations require a restructured organisation

Source: Smale (1996)

just carry on rather than planning to cope. *Mapping* involves deciding who and what will be affected, how, why and where: a 5WH exercise (see Chapter 4) may be relevant. Jerome (1995: 41–76) suggests that we have to look at all aspects of team responsibilities and resources. Think of this even if only one team member is coming or leaving, because this will have implications for everyone. If Mrs Jones can no longer shop for her neighbour, an extra burden might fall on the home help or relatives. If the social services specialist in work with Deaf people leaves, occupational therapists, day centre staff, district nurses and all sorts of others will be affected within the adult services team of the SSD and outside. All involved should look at consequent changes in the pattern of how resources are used. Money, equipment, materials, time, policies and procedures and skills, knowledge and training may all have to change. We cannot assume that we understand how the responsibility was carried out, or that a new worker or family member will do it in the same way. Therefore, we may have to look at tasks and roles again. There may have to be changes in the accuracy, frequency or thoroughness with which we do things, our availability, costs and timing and the quantity of work we take on. Each may improve or worsen. Responsibilities may have to be reshaped, eliminated or reassigned as they stand. Resource check circles (see activities) may help you to think about the issues.

Navigating changes involves looking at each item of our plan of change and seeing how it might best be carried out. It is also important to look for things or people that might get in the way of achieving results. Finally, *evaluating* what has been achieved and how enables you to prepare for and manage change more effectively in the future.

Conclusion

In this chapter, we have examined power issues. I identified a 'power principle' that power in open teamwork should be used for the benefit of service users and their community through the open team. We looked at some aspects of power, and the activities contain a process for examining power in teams. More important, I have tried to show how conflict, participation, communication, movement and change all involve power issues, which may be resolved through applying the power principle in team development.

Activities

See the Appendix for basic team development activities.

Power and divisions

Stage 1: Role play a recent team or network event (for example, case conference, care planning meeting) *or* have two or more independent observers watch and record the event *or* video or audio record the event.

Stage 2: Snowball examples of the use of each type of personal power.

Stage 3: Report the examples agreed in pairs to the large group. For each team member, list the times they used power, what kinds of power they used, the times others used power with them, and the types of power used. Agree if there are patterns.

Stage 4: Snowball network diagrams of the team or network, dividing it into groups or sets according to the use of power, to gender divisions, to professional divisions, to educational background and to ethnic divisions.

Stage 5: Review the network diagrams in the group: can it be agreed? What are the differences in pairs'/small groups' diagrams? What are the issues of agreement or disagreement? Which groups are more/less powerful? What is the basis of those power differences? Are they aligned with social divisions? Which? Are there clear divisions which are not accounted for by social divisions?

Developing team participation

Stage 1: Snowball or brainstorm a list of all the occasions that team or network members met (as a whole group or in smaller groups) within the last month, the aims of the meeting and the extent to which they were achieved.

Stage 2: Record and review the accumulated lists in the large group. Is there agreement about what was achieved?

Stage 3: Snowball (brainstorming is not personal enough to pick up everyone's information needs) examples of information individuals received from others which was useful to their work within the last month, and why it was useful. Then snowball examples where they would have liked to receive information, but did not do so.

Stage 4: Record and review the accumulated lists in the large group. From these lists, work out a set of policies about information communication.

Stage 5: Snowball (do not brainstorm) examples for each individual where they could participate in a decision which was important to them, and an example where something was decided where they did not participate when they wanted.

Stage 6: Record and review the accumulated lists (perhaps anonymised in the pairs/smaller groups) in the large group. From these lists, work out a set of rules about decisions which require participation.

What are our languages?

Stage 1: Using Pietroni's list, above, each team member rates the extent to which they think they use each area of language (1 = very high use, 5 = very low use). Then, each rates all the others on their language usage.

Stage 2: Report and record each individual's rating against the average of others' ratings of them. Review and discuss if the team, network or individuals within them need to change language usage.

7

Open Teamwork: Structure and Context

The power issues we looked at in Chapter 6 are worked out in organisations. An organisation is a collectivity designed to achieve aims. This definition implies that it brings together people ('collectivity') in some thought-out, rational structure ('designed'). So the people have to work jointly to achieve the purposes and the structure implies that they take responsibility through the structure for meeting the aims. In turn, they have to take, or be given, power and resources to do so. Even though open teamwork may be used as part of any kind of organisational structure, it implies an organisation ('the team') within the wider organisation (sometimes called the 'host' organisation). *Open* teamwork implies working across the team's boundaries within the wider organisation and across the host's boundaries with other organisations. Also, we have seen that most people understand teamwork as being about the sense of commitment to the team and participation. There is a risk that the team will sometimes compete for commitment and participation with the host. Also, commitment to cooperation may compete with commitment to the team and the host organisation.

To carry out open teamwork, therefore, we need to understand how teams fit into organisations. The central issue is accountability. How do open team aims connect with the host organisation's aims? If teamwork involves collaboration between different professional groups, in different agencies, how do we manage the conflicts between those organisations' aims and practices? If open teamwork aims to include user and community networks, how can their diffuse and individualistic aims be aligned with organisational purposes? Should they be? We are addressing here the paradoxes described at the outset of Chapter 1.

So far in this book, I have treated teamwork as something which happens between *people*. Even so, I described (Chapter 1) modern approaches to self-directed, high-achieving teamwork which require the host organisation to support team independence. Also, developing open teamwork has so far seemed generic: you can do it anywhere. How can it work in different settings? This chapter, therefore, starts from various options for connecting open teamwork to a host structure and context. We then move on to how care services have used these structures to cope with the problems of collaboration and teamwork. I have identified four types of context which each create different demands for teamwork. In each case I discuss some of the experience of trying to make teamwork work in that context. These are:

- *Field organisations.* Here team members work mainly as individuals, going out from an office, or seeing people who come into an office. They deal with people already in the community, who therefore have existing networks of both professionals and family and community around them. Multiprofessional work is by different professionals involved with the same service users, going out from different organisations with responsibilities to the users. The teamwork problem is organising collaboration between these different professions and their organisations.

- *Multiprofessional contexts.* Here team members work in organisations which are multiprofessional in their staff, so that the multiprofessional network *is* the team. Connections with community and service users networks need to be built up. The teamwork problem is managing the strains of different professions working together daily with their different roles, and coordinating contacts with community and service user networks in spite of those strains.

- *Community networking contexts.* Here the essence of the team's work is creating, developing and involving community and service user networks as a prerequisite to delivering professional services. The teamwork problem is how to interweave professional roles with a service which should focus on the community.

- *Institutional organisations.* Here the team works with service users inside an institution, with all its requirements for close, continuing interpersonal relationships. The teamwork problem is being creative in everyday living and working together, and bridging the boundary of the institution with community and service user networks beyond.

Who does the work of developing teams in these contexts? Everyone contributes, but mostly team leaders or managers carry this role, and the next chapter takes up managing structure and context.

Teamwork structures in organisations

Four approaches to thinking about the structure of teamwork in and between organisations are shown in Figure 7.1.

Link pin structure (Likert, 1961). Here teams are encapsulated in a conventional organisational structure with its hierarchy. In Figure 7.1a, after the director at the top, people at each level are both members of the team of the person above in the hierarchy and managers of the team below. They are the 'link pin' between these teams. Each person is responsible to a person in the level above. This forms a line of accountability, which they can follow up and down the hierarchy, with people being 'line managers' of those below them and responsible to those above them. The people at the lowest level of the hierarchy are members of a team, but have nobody to manage.

The advantage of this approach is that it fits teamwork into a clear structure of accountability within an organisation where authority comes from the top downwards. However, it does not reflect the complexities of relationships between groups in most organisations, and it assumes that leadership in teams must always reside with an appointed manager. As we have seen, power relationships are more complex than this. Also, in effective teams, leadership sometimes moves among members according to who is most appropriate for a particular task. Conventional hierarchical link pin structures make such flexibility insecure. They also exclude the influence of other organisations and of service users. The assumption is that workers at the bottom of one organisation will communicate up the hierarchy to their director who will communicate across the organisations. The other director will communicate downwards. It used to be common in local government for all letters to be signed in the name of the director for example, although this is now old-fashioned. In reality, workers communicate where they need to. If there is a problem, however, people sometimes stand on ceremony and insist on communication up and down and this inhibits relationships and does not reflect the

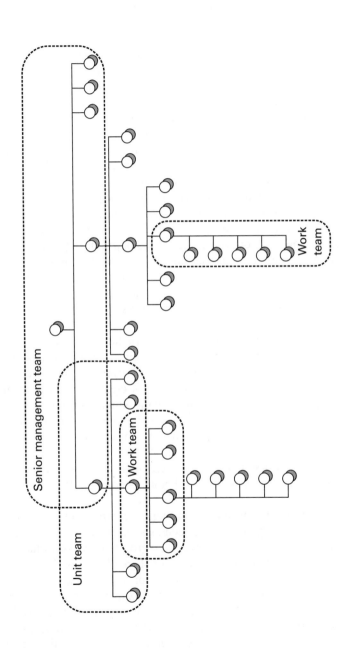

Figure 7.1a Link pin structure: teams in a hierarchy

reality of responsibilities and contacts. However, the hierarchy is preserved in job descriptions, because your level is often partly defined by the sort of people you have regular contacts with.

For open teamwork, the problem with this approach is that it assumes that the crucial network is within the organisation. Influences from community and service users networks come from the top through people gaining authority to set the policy of the organisation through election or formal appointment. Community and service user influence also comes from the bottom, as people present their needs to the organisation's workers. However, this hierarchical structure puts service users and external communities at the bottom as supplicants to the organisation, rather than participants in it. Of course, systems for their participation can be set up, but this structure gives the organisation power to offer and to take away participation.

Matrix structures try to deal with some of these problems. Figure 7.1b shows how workers can be taken from within their hierarchy and work in a group from another hierarchy. The other hierarchy can be either from their own organisation, but a different line of managers, or can be from another organisation altogether. Within the same organisation, matrix teams are often used for projects where expertise is called on from a variety of teams. Between organisations, matrix teams can be used to set up a new structure for a multiagency service. Community mental health and learning disability teams and child guidance clinics are sometimes created using this structure. An additional sophistication is the possibility of creating a matrix team of managers of the workers' matrix team which can manage the project. This structure allows flexibility within hierarchical organisations, without losing the accountability of people within their management lines.

For open teamwork, matrix structures again focus too much on the professional organisations, and not on community, user and carer networks.

Systems approaches to understanding team structures recognise even more complexity. Teams are seen as spheres of influence, with boundaries. Where boundaries overlap, there are flows of influence through communication, joint working or shared interests. The influence may be overlapping membership, or represent groupings of interests. Where teams share many cases, for example, you might see overlapping interests. People in a community may have an interest in the community in general and contacts and group memberships in different areas of interest to them. In Figure 7.1c, we can still see two

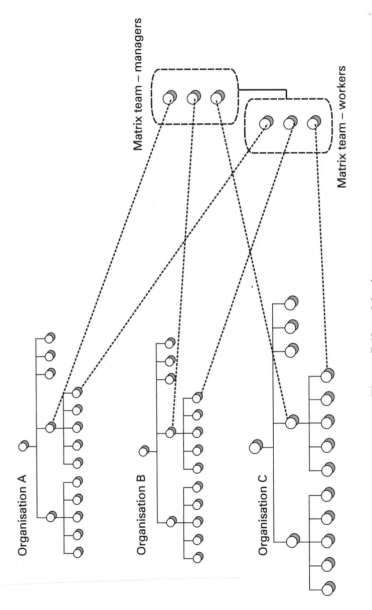

Figure 7.1b Matrix structure

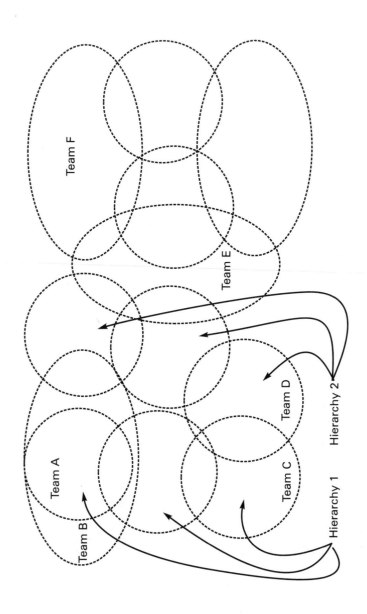

Figure 7.1c Systems analysis of an organisation

conventional hierarchies, with their overlapping link pin, but this analysis acknowledges much greater complexity in the connections within and between organisations. Team A, for example, is wholly within a larger Team B. Teams C and D overlap a lot, but note that their managers in the hierarchies do not overlap at all. Within an organisation, this might be typical of children and adults' services teams within an SSD area. Sometimes, children and adults' work is nowadays separated in different corporate structures in local authorities. Between organisations, this might be typical of SSD and community health teams covering the same area. Team E works in different hierarchies and also interacts at different levels in the hierarchies. This is typical of specialist teams. It might also represent the interests and contacts of a family or self-help group in contact with different levels of different hierarchies for different reasons. Team F incorporates upper levels of two hierarchies. The lack of boundary between them suggests a complete merger, and might be typical of an area where there is joint SSD and health commissioning of community services.

Network approaches go further than systems approaches by trying to specify the amount and nature of the relationships within and between different groups. There are several network diagrams (see Figure 1.1 for example) throughout the book: I do not repeat information about this approach here. Networking is a good way of understanding structures very flexibly, but it does not represent the formal structure of organisations very well.

Each of these approaches to understanding teamwork in organisational structures can tell us something. However, open teamwork requires us to acknowledge the complexity of relationships beyond and across boundaries. Teamworking tries overcome limitations of perception and relationship in more conventional understandings of organisations and their boundaries.

Teamwork and field organisations

Many agencies involved in aspects of social care, are field organisations, that is, their workers operate mainly individualistically from an office with 'cases' of people who remain in the community. Many local government agencies such as SSDs or the police, are like this and have formal hierarchical structures. Teamwork is included in them through link pin structures (often taken for granted) and through special structures for collaboration across the hierarchies or with other

organisations. Good examples of these structures arise within area
social services teams and in child protection.

Area social services teams

Area teams were established for the first time in the 1970s after the
Seebohm reorganisation of the personal social services. The aim was
to promote accessibility for service users, and staff feeling accountability to and involvement with identifiable communities. Some
views promoted the idea of community development as part of the
role of SSDs. The aim was to build community links. Teamwork
developed mainly around bringing together groups of staff from
previously separate agencies. Therefore, open teamwork was not a
major feature of most teams.

The development of area SSD teamwork over three decades is in
part a continuing struggle between promoting mutual support and joint
service objectives against the constantly recurring ideal of connection
with and participation in the community and its networks and with
other professions (Hadley and McGrath, 1980; DHSS, 1978; Cockburn, 1990). Early teams were social work professionals grouped for
convenience around a manager, who provided individual supervision.
Teamwork became more important as group supervision and allocation of work were carried out in this group. Some non-professional
staff, such as social work assistants, were attached to the team (Austin,
1978; Schindler and Brawley, 1987). Different specialisms became
allocated to teams, for example intake teams received referrals and did
short-term work to reduce work pressure (Buckle, 1981; Hillman and
McKenzie, 1993: 31–6). An important trend of the 1970s and 80s,
community social work, allocated smaller work groups to geographical
'patches' in pursuit of better links with the community, better preventive work and better integration of domiciliary and home care staff
(Hadley and McGrath, 1980; Hadley and Hatch, 1981; Bayley *et al.*,
1987; Hadley and McGrath, 1984; Barclay Report, 1982; Smale *et al.*,
1988). In the 1990s, teams became specialised around adult and child
protection services, responding to the Children Act 1989 and the NHS
and Community Care Act 1990.

Three major lessons arise from these developments. First, the
agency has an important role in setting the environment in which
teams can work effectively, even where it is an authoritative, hierarchical agency. Bamford (1982: 50) argues, for example, that agencies

have a responsibility to provide for adequate professional supervision and team development with the time, privacy and recording systems to make that work. On the other hand, it is difficult to change and develop a team in a particular direction such as community social work unless the agency is organised so that the ideology of the development suits its environment. Management ideologies for teamwork and the wishes of particular teams or their leaders have to be suitable for the agency. Acquiescence is probably not enough, otherwise the team will be fighting its corner all the time. Much team development carried to its conclusions implies widespread agency change, and managers agreeing to a team development process need to consider what they are setting off. Otherwise, it is better to improve interpersonal support and collaboration, rather than try to promote a widespread participative team ethos, which will not work with strenuously enforced hierarchical responsibilities.

Second, teamwork showed the policy tensions which affect all SSDs, and by extension, evident policy tensions in any setting will affect teams and teamwork. Challis (1990) identifies four policy tensions affecting SSDs, and these are relevant to all care services:

- *specialisation versus genericism*, for example the area team as against children and adult services debate;

- *residential care versus field services*, for example the debate about deinstitutionalisation as against secure care which protects the public and service user;

- *localisation versus centralisation*, for example the community social work debate; district vs cottage hospitals;

- *direct provision versus being a regulator or purchaser.*

Each team has to deal with such tensions continuously, and they form a useful basis for exploring teamwork (see activities – the tension grid).

Third, the experience of working with paraprofessionals and volunteers has extended concepts of teamwork beyond the purely professional team. Including indigenous workers has, with community social work, formed the basis of including the team in a wider community network which is the basis of open teamwork. Darvill and Munday (1984: 155–81) identify the requirements for effective work with volunteers, in a way which also points up the following lessons from including paraprofessionals in the team and network:

- The policy and its implementation need evaluation, to see how networking and participation are working.

- A clear structure of responsibilities, roles and communication is needed so that decision-making is clear, especially in risky cases involving child protection and public safety. This is also needed when, as for example because of a purchaser–provider split, volunteer or paraprofessional are in a separate agency.

- Staff will not work effectively with volunteers and paraprofessionals unless they are secure and valued in their own roles. Rewards for them in their work and the agency's commitment to paraprofessionals and volunteers including respect for the professionals' work is an important basis for helping collaboration work. The director should not go about saying: 'anyone could do this job – we don't need social workers really' (or nurses), because this values the special contributions of neither the professionals nor the volunteers.

- There needs to be effective in-service training about defining roles and managing work within a team of paraprofessionals and volunteers, backed by inclusion of this in qualifying training. Some staff need more extended post-qualifying training in this field.

- Having a coordinator who develops and supports the involvement of volunteers may help, if they can facilitate others' participation in relationships, rather than taking everything over.

We can take the lessons from these three areas of progress forward into other multiprofessional open teamwork and applied in other multiprofessional settings. Indeed we shall see below that they have their echoes in other contexts which also contribute their experience to different aspects of multiprofessional open teamwork.

Child protection

Child protection has been controversial since soon after SSDs were established in the 1970s. Specialist child care officers were merged into departments with wider generic responsibilities and poor resources. Size made them more politically important and visible than the previously existing children's departments. Since the early 1970s, a number of cases shifted the focus of concern from child deprivation and neglect and general family problems affecting children towards child protection from abuse. Later child sexual abuse became the focus as awareness of its extent grew. The reaction to this illustrates the inadequacies of the formal management hierarchies of government agencies in securing consistent cooperation across organisations. The initial concern with poor communication was dealt with by multiagency coordinating machinery, based around area child protection committees focused mainly on investigation and registration of children at risk. Gibbons *et al.* (1995: 117–18) show, however, that much of this has focused on investigation and that, since education and health authorities control specialist treatment and care resources, they need to be involved in later stages as well. Later developments focused on coordinating investigation of suspected cases of child abuse, particularly where the police were involved (Pence and Wilson, 1994; Lloyd and Burman, 1996; Waterhouse and Carnie, 1990; Metropolitan Police and Bexley London Borough, 1987; Home Office, 1988; SWSG, 1988).

Furniss (1991: 59–110) sees the intervention stage in child protection work as concerning the involvement of a professional network with a family. Thus, he sees the team's work as open to the family network. This presents problems, since the family may transfer some of its relationship problems to the professional team. For example, different members of the team often relate to different parts of the family: residential workers with children, field social workers with the mother, criminal justice workers with the father. The interests and problems of each family member then have a representative in the professional team. For example, in one case, child protection workers dealt with the family, and a violent mother was the responsibility of a forensic mental health team. It was easy for each to see the priority of the other as negating the interests of their client or patient, whereas the children's needs were probably better served by taking forward the interests of both children and mother in step.

The child protection process potentially makes it possible to work within networks of services and family and community. However, the need to make risky official decisions has tied the collaborative process closely to accountable hierarchical structures. It makes more sense, therefore, to see child abuse team structures as matrix structures. Individuals working together must constantly refer back to the management structures which sanction their authority. However, looking at network links can help to identify problems within the matrix structure where relationships are ineffective.

Although the child protection system has achieved the highest profile on the need for collaboration, other children's services need this just as much. Three areas have particular importance: very young children – the 'early years' group (David, 1994), children needing care and treatment because of disability (AMA, 1994; Middleton, 1992; SSI, 1996) and preventive work, particularly in family centres and using community work techniques (Cannan and Warren, 1997; DoH, 1991; Henderson, 1995; Stones, 1994). Effective teamwork, through for example multiagency forums, is also required in cases of domestic violence which are so often a hidden factor with child abuse and other family problems (Mullender, 1996).

Multiprofessional contexts

Considering multiprofessional contexts for teamwork offers the opportunity to learn from situations where different professions work together regularly in the same organisation on the same cases. Two good examples of such contexts, which have developed significantly in recent years, are primary health care and community mental health teams.

Primary health care

Primary health care, that is general health services which are the first point of call for people in the community, is a classic setting for the development of multiprofessional practice. It is also important because the GP's surgery or local health centre is a non-stigmatised port of call for people with all sorts of problems, which then get referred on. Attaching more stigmatised services such as social services to it, and focusing on early identification of problems, have the potential to prevent problems arriving at other agencies when they are too well-developed to be sorted out easily. Twinn and Cowley (1992) quote the World Health Organisation on the reason for the importance of primary care: 'The focus of the health care system should be on meeting the basic needs of each community. Services should be readily accessible and acceptable to all and involve full community participation. This is the basis for primary health care. A full, equal partnership between health care professionals and the people they serve is essential to translate this belief into action.'

Teamwork began to develop with financial incentives offered to GPs for group practice and employing staff in 1965 and delegating GPs' work was permitted in 1969 (Bowling, 1981: 29). Government priorities announced in the 1970s (DHSS, 1976: 16–19) emphasised developing primary health care teams, mainly for preventive reasons and to respond to the increasing number of older people. Team-working also improved after the 1974 NHS reorganisation connected GP services better to wider health provision. A working party of the Royal College of General Practitioners (RCGP, 1985) recommended that good communication with ancillary and primary health care team (PHCT) staff, through informal and regular planned meetings, with a knowledge of respective roles, should be among the criteria of good general practice standards. There have been various development projects, but Bowling (1981: 31) argues that the small size of many GP practices prevents a substantial range of attachments from other professionals. Bryar and Bytheway's (1996) recent study in South Wales emphasised the role of effective practice management, audit of professional standards, supportive education and training and careful assessment of community needs. In these ways, clear work practices were identified and checked. McIntosh and Dingwall (1978; see also Kane, 1975b), identified a crucial and continuing issue. They suggest that doctors may see teamwork as a way of reinforcing their position in health services and maintaining their control of decisions as the work and involvement of others become more complex. Other professions, who enjoy less status, see teamwork as a way of sharing decisions with powerful professionals. In many PHCTs there is a clash between a medical model of thinking in which people present deviations from assumed 'good health' are 'cured' by the intervention of expert professionals. This may, more often in a community setting than in a hospital, bring tensions with a social model, associated particularly with social workers, which locates the origins of some health problems and certainly many practical consequences of ill health with social assumptions and social reactions.

The team usually includes secretaries and receptionists and often provides for nurses, health visitors, midwives and occasionally social workers or counsellors. Dunnell and Dobbs (1982) studied community nurses in the early 1980s and found that most, except community psychiatric nurses and 25 per cent of health visitors, regarded themselves as part of a PHCT. Auxiliaries had little contact with GPs, but most nurse professionals had daily contact. Most regarded their contact with most other staff as good. Staff attached to GP practices had better relationships with GPs. Jeffreys (1986) suggests that in the 1980s social workers, health visitors and home or district nurses were re-evaluating their roles and this made tidily interlocking roles impossible to achieve. In the 1980s, GPs have begun to employ counsellors in their practices. Corney (1993) reviews the research, which shows that GPs, counsellors and patients were satisfied. Return to the GP, use of psychotropic drugs and reduction in referrals to psychiatrists were among the results. However, health visitors with minimal training, social workers, psychologists and GPs themselves could carry out effective counselling.

Employed by SSDs and with a non-health care background, social workers have been marginal members of PHCTs. Bruce's (1980) and Huntingdon's (1981) important studies of GPs and social workers identified extensive differences in many aspects of professional structure and culture. However, there were similarities in the experience of work, both groups experiencing identity crises within their occupation and fatigue and despair at the limitless nature of their role. Differences in culture, technology, training, identity and attitude to service users, underpinned by differences in the structure of the professions, made for difficult relations. Research covering a range of primary care professions identified many similar issues. Dalley (1989) describes this as a form of tribalism, but the issues are increasingly recognised and training efforts made to overcome them (for example Pritchard and Pritchard, 1994). Sheppard's (1996) review of research on social work–GP relations in mental health suggests that where GPs have regular contacts, in compulsory admissions to mental hospital, they are satisfied with social work services. However, they have little contact with the full range of SSD provision and little conception of the wider social and environmental roles of social work. Sheppard (1992) suggests that, generally, GPs are a homogeneous group which resists changes in opinion, and in spite of good consumer feedback, they do not seem to appreciate the kind of work done by social workers. GPs mainly used it, successfully, for practical services as an extension of health care provision. All this suggests that given time and appropriate relationships, social work can offer worthwhile and unique services in primary care. Either side could help improve the position by feeding back to the other positively. There is also evidence of improvement where social workers are attached to PHCTs but not with formal liaison systems; in particular, service users' views are positive.

What can we learn from all this research which might have wider applicability? The important aspects of good provision are as follows:

- Facilities, especially a room at a health centre, should be adequate.

- Primary health care staff and especially GPs need education in the roles and skills of social workers.

- Personal relationships of trust and confidence with GPs are needed. The whole approach to collaboration in the medical profession, for example between GPs and specialists, is based on personal relationships of trust, rather than formal systematised contacts with an organisation.

- All sides need to be committed to the attachment.

- Social workers should be used who can work independently, are confident in their professional role and relate well to other professions.

- Informal and formal meetings involving the social worker are needed.

The complexity of relationships between both organisations involved and professionals suggests that PHCT teamwork is better seen from a perspective of interlocking systems or a network of semi-independent professionals, crossing the boundaries of their organisations and groups.

Mental health care

Mental health care has become an important site of multiprofessional working. This is partly because multiprofessional work arose from the greater complexity of health care services but also because of the development of community mental health provision from the 1950s onwards. The Seebohm reorganisation which set up SSDs removed social work from the ambit of other mental health provision (Fisher *et al.*, 1984). The running down of large psychiatric hospitals led to a need for more community practice and wider collaboration for hospital-based professionals. The loss of social work to SSDs and the loss of nursing work in the hospitals stimulated the development of a new profession, community psychiatric nursing (CPN) (Sheppard, 1992; Morrall; 1997; Corre, 1993; Savio, 1996). More recently, networking in small community residential settings, such as group homes or supported housing schemes, has become more important as research (for example Hatfield *et al.*, 1993) has shown that a substantial minority of mentally ill people in the community have limited support networks. More collaboration and teamwork were needed because long-stay patients were leaving hospitals for the first time. Hospital-based professions had to involve a wider range of community agencies which included other professions. First joint care planning and then, with NHS and community care reforms of the 1990s, joint commissioning between health and social services organisations developed (King, 1991: 64–72).

McGrath's (1991) important study of community learning disability teams contains useful experience. The two main constraints were differences in professional perspective and insufficient delegation of responsibility to the team. There was high commitment, mutual trust and support in the teams. Having a shared base, commitment to clear policy, a single coordinator and management support helped to develop them. Conflicts at more senior management levels adversely affected good teamwork. Individual planning for service users was limited by insufficient flexibility in job descriptions, poor autonomy and lack of resources to implement complex assessments. Networking was helped by formal links backed up by frequent informal contact. Community mental health teams (CMHTs), bringing together psychiatric nurses, social workers, psychologists and community psychiatrists (usually part-time on a sessional basis) have been an important development in the 1990s (Paxton, 1995; Mistral and Velleman, 1997; Onyett and Ford, 1996).

Practical ways of better management have emerged from all this experience. The fundamental requirements are as follows:

- *Well-structured formal links.* Ways of achieving this are: clarity about referral procedures and about the organisational structure and accountability, including regular review processes (Fagin, 1996), training in and recognising and including a wide range of skills and services, a clear focus on the priority client group (Patmore and Weaver, 1991) and effective relationships with voluntary sector organisations, day care, employment facilities, housing providers and joint planning processes (Culhane, 1996). Team development needs specific attention, and budgetary responsibility and coordination may be managed separately from medical case responsibility. One study (Ryrie *et al.*, 1997) shows that 'zoning' the work of small groups of workers, rather as in community social work, can achieve these management objectives well.

- *With extensive informal contacts*. These reinforce the formal systems regularly and allow alert workers to pick up problems early.

- *Balancing tensions*. All such teams must deal with daily conflicts and inconsistencies in the systems they work within. Wells (1997) suggests that such teams need to balance tensions between:
  - political and policy pressures
  - local management's agendas
  - professional and peer cultures
  - perceived personal advantages to different team members.

Other aspects of mental health services which particularly require multiprofessional attention are where people with mental illnesses do not use mainstream services. The Health Advisory Service (1995: 48) argues, for example, that homeless people need special drop-in facilities and a variety of informal groups. Sometimes, these allow people to be fed into more formal mental health provision. A series of public enquiries as extensive and controversial as those in child protection cases have raised concerns about mentally disordered offenders (Reith, 1998). There is extensive guidance in interagency and multiprofessional work with severely mentally ill people (DoH, 1996a). Where patients are 'detained' by court order, Section 117, Mental Health Act 1983 requires health and social services authorities, working with voluntary organisations, to provide after-care. This is done by designating 'social supervisors' in social services or probation services. Guidance is issued for their work (Vaughan and Badger, 1995: 207–34 but updated in 1999). Hospitals must make appropriate arrangements for discharge and provide written information. There must be regular contact with the patient's supervising psychiatrist and with other appropriate professionals. Experimental projects were established in 1990 to encourage cooperation between the mental health and criminal justice systems (Home Office/DoH, 1995). The care programme approach (CPA) was introduced in 1991 (DoH, 1990) to provide a consistent form of case management for mentally ill people to avoid their losing contact with services. They are rather similar to the care management approach adopted as a result of the NHS and Community Care Act 1990. The CPA requires systematic assessment, a care plan, a key worker and a regular review in each case, for a wider group of patients than those affected by Section 117. Multiprofessional teams need only be involved for complex assessments (DoH, 1996a: 47). A tiered CPA is proposed in which a minimal plan would apply to those with minor needs. More complex plans are developed for 'medium level needs' and a full, multiprofessional plan where patients have severe mental illness, represent a significant risk, suffer from severe social dysfunction or have highly volatile needs (DoH, 1996a: 55).

Drawing all this material together, we can see that multiprofessional work is not an easy answer to the problems of coordination and collaboration which assail health and social care services. The lessons which have been learned suggest three important points for planning multiprofessional contexts:

- The physical environment and facilities need planning to facilitate joint working and information sharing.

- Effective systems, time and space for communication need to be established.

- The different professional groups need to invest time in becoming clear about their own professional role and its contribution to the multiprofessional team. They also need to understand, accept and be prepared to work with the different approaches to understanding and responding to problems within different professional perspectives.

It is here that joint training is often thought to play an important part.

Multiprofessional education and training

Joint education and training for better multiprofessional working began to develop in the health care field in the early 1970s in several countries, although there were experiments and pioneering efforts before then (Leathard, 1994; Goble, 1994; Casto, 1994). Early training cooperation in Britain developed between community health nursing staff and social workers. An influential development in multiprofessional education was developed around PHCTs in Exeter (Jones, 1986). A joint committee covering educators in the primary health professions was established. Training days were organised for staff new to multiprofessional collaboration. Out of this training for practice teachers and educators developed. Many such short-course initiatives exist in primary health care and advanced courses in community health and community care (CAIPE, 1992; Storrie, 1992). Shaw (1994) studied local joint training initiatives in community care.

He found that participants in joint training became more aware of other organisations in their locality, and valued the work of other professions more. The role of first-line managers was important: they could help or resist better multiprofessional working by supporting cooperation and helping their staff make good use of training. However, to do so, they needed a good appreciation of the needs of service users and the professional skills needed to practise professionally in their field. Simply concerning themselves with organisational systems was ineffective in producing more multiprofessional competence in their teams.

Public, official and professional concern about poor coordination in child protection led to regular recommendations for joint training in this field from reports on child abuse scandals. The official guidance on working together under the Children Act 1989 formalised this with the recommendation (Home Office *et al.*, 1991: 53) 'that agencies establish joint annual training programmes on child abuse issues with access for all professional groups in direct contact with children and families'. Joint investigation, training for all professional staff and for receptionists and telephonists was recommended. This is usually coordinated in each area by the area children protection committee, although a variety of formal courses are used. Myers and Cooper (1996) report a scheme to draw trainers from a variety of agencies in one area. In some cases, an interagency child protection training role is being established and there is a National Inter-Agency Child Protection Trainers' Symposium (Hendry, 1995).

Community networking contexts

With community networking contexts, the services are set up within a policy which assumes the active participation, and possibly primary role, of community and service user networks in providing social and health care. Such policies are based on the idea that most social care for adults and education and support for families with problems come from families and community networks around service users. Professional services have to interweave their provision, support and enable such community provision. Some ideas for practice within community networking contexts come from community work and community development practice.

Community networking practice can come from an official base, as in community care or family support services, or from a community setting, which may call on some interventions from official agencies as in services for domestic violence.

Community care

Community care policy has a long history in post-war British health and social care. They cover three distinct aspects of policy (Payne, 1995). The first is removing long-stay patients with mental illnesses and learning disabilities from hospital and preventing their long-stay admission. Related to this, but distinct, is providing long-term care services for people with disabilities and elderly people preferably in their own homes, or at least in non-institutional environments. Finally, a more diffuse objective is providing care which responds to the needs and wishes of people in the community, and involves them and their carers more in planning a pattern of more individualised provision for them.

The most recent reincarnation of community care derives from the implementation of the NHS and Community Care Act 1990 (Payne, 1995). This provides for service coordination, by making local authority SSDs responsible for coordinating the production of community care plans, specifying the range of provision by statutory, voluntary and private providers in each locality. Gaps are plugged by new services commissioned by the SSD or other providers. Increasingly, this is done jointly by health authorities and SSDs. Community organisations, and organisations of carers and users should participate in the planning and commissioning.

In addition to service coordination, provision for individuals is coordinated by *care management*. In 'social care entrepreneurship', the most common and government-endorsed model of care management, someone with complex care needs is assessed by a care manager, often a social worker, from the SSD. The assessment leads to a care plan which puts together a package of services individually tailored, from the range available in the local community care plan, for the individual service user. This is then organised, monitored and evaluated periodically by the care manager. Care management replaces the assumption that individual professionals and separate services would assess service users for their services, which they would coordinate among them by cross-referral and joint working. The problem is that this emphasises a managerial process of delivering a package of services, rather than focusing on the service user's continuing relationships with care providers. The quality of what is done as services are provided, then, is hidden from this way of looking at organising collaboration.

There are alternative models of care management. In *'brokerage'* service users take the lead role in care planning, sometimes using direct payments to buy services, helped by a care manager as a consultant. Brokerage is mainly used with adult disabled people, especially where they are given a budget to meet their own needs. Some care management is *multiprofessional*, and a team, with service users participating, creates and implements care plans. This model is often used where patients are being discharged after long stays in hospital, as with mentally disordered offenders, or in community mental health and learning disabilities teams, all of which were discussed above. Some PHCTs have also used multiprofessional care management (Harrison and Thistlethwaite, 1993).

The wide range of people potentially involved in community care services are in many different hierarchies of the two main sets of agencies involved. Many are also in autonomous service-providing units, such as day and community centres, residential care homes and group homes with visiting staff. Therefore, it is easier to see the pattern of services in this case as systems, and relationships among them as networks.

Institutional contexts

In spite of the increased range of community services, much social provision still takes place in institutions such as hospitals, nursing homes and residential homes. Everyone works in the same place, so there is continuity of contact. They also often work in public, so that others can see what they do. Institutional contexts, therefore, have a rich history of learning to convey to other contexts.

Hospital care

Much important provision is offered in hospitals, and we saw in Chapter 2 that they were the origins of multiprofessional work in health care. They are very much institutions, however, and it is easy for that multiprofessional teamwork to be well developed without involving the wider network.

Øvretveit (1992) shows that during the 1980s the NHS developed a variety of models for organising professions within hospitals. These range from the model of an individual private practitioner, through directorates for each profession, providing services to divisions and institutions, systems where each profession has separate management within each unit, or where various professions are combined. He argues (1992: 148) that multiprofessional teams place limitations on good-quality professional practice and that these have not been considered against a general management preference for demonstrating coordination by setting up multiprofessional teams.

Much literature on social work in hospitals assumes a casework model, reflecting the doctor–patient relationship. However, Robertson (1989) usefully points to the value of groupwork approaches in general hospital social work, developing the advantages it has in psychiatric and therapeutic community work. This is because the clientele are captive and available, there are shared experiences of illness, and educational programmes can be effectively delivered this way. Other professions also use groupwork, for example occupational therapy.

It is well established that social work help in hospital offers considerable benefits, particularly on discharge. Connor and Tibbit (1988) show that where social workers in hospital geriatric units were effectively involved in the team, patients' personal responses to the illness and treatment were taken into account better by the whole team. Also, emergencies and readmissions from home were avoided because discharge arrangements took into account the circumstances at home. Boone *et al.*'s (1981) American study in an orthopaedic department showed, in a randomised trial, that early intervention and discharge planning by social workers in every case reduced length of stay and cost of service. An American consumer survey in an urban hospital (Garber *et al.*, 1986) showed that service users saw social work as effective if they had good relationships with workers. Consumers thought that workers were more effective with interpersonal help than delivering services, especially where only one concrete service, like housing, was sought. However, users receiving only services without counselling were twice as dissatisfied. Most users would have liked to see the social worker earlier and more often. Most clients who found social workers unhelpful were self-referred or referred by other hospital staff. This points up the value of social workers carrying out their own assessment of need for their help.

McLeod (1995), summarising both her own experience and research findings, argues that multiprofessional ward meetings are not an effective means of referral for social work or other kinds of additional help, although they picked up the most serious cases in her study. The main factors were poor resources in the social services which led to avoidance of additional work, and patients being unaware of the possibilities. McCleod argues, consistent with open teamwork precepts, that patients need to have a more active role as a co-worker in the health care team.

While the interlocking organisational and professional groups suggest a systems analysis of hospital health and social care, this ignores the potential position of patients and their carers. A network analysis can help us to see where they should interact with multiprofessional teamwork.

Residential, institutional and day care

There are special characteristics of the residential and day care environment which mean that considering teamwork requires a different emphasis to the approach in other settings. However, people in other settings which require close relationships in practice can learn lessons from the residential care teamwork experience.

Clough (1982: 83–4) explains how residential and day care settings influence teamwork. Similar issues arise in hospital wards. Most practice in residential and day care takes place in public, and because residents' (residents in the following includes day centre 'attenders') whole lives are lived in the home or day care centre for the time that they are there, workers cannot put boundaries around what they have to do. It may include physical care, emotional response, therapeutic treatment and finding a lost pair of socks. Several people carry out the task, so workers are not immune from others' influence. Although several people share the task, and may have a common goal, they may not agree about the detail. Also, in most residential care, levels of skill are equated with formal status in a hierarchy, and that can lead to confusion about roles and difficulties in equal collaboration. In spite of the shared participation in the life of a home or a centre, they are often managed on shifts and communication and consistency can be hard to achieve over 24 hours, and some colleagues' work may be invisible for this reason. Also, it is possible to be in different parts of the building, and this influences and sometimes hides practice and affects colleagues' relationships. Ward (1993) expands on the skills needed to manage this situation:

● *Interdependence.* Because workers in these situations are interdependent, they need to develop skills to comment on others' work in a non-threatening way, and accept comment on their own. They have to be able to detach themselves from their own roles, to see how they interact with those of others. Managing frustration around conflicts about what to do and how to do it is also a necessary personal skill. Team members need to use open communication to foster interdependence. Fulcher (1981) usefully shows how interdependence may develop not only through personal relationships between and within work groups. It also develops through leadership and clear decision-making processes, the characteristics of the work environment, the time structure of the home or centre, members' stage of personal and skill development and their work orientation and the organisation and its policy environment. For example, whether people are on call or provide a waking service 24 hours a day affects how a residential home works and how secure it feels to residents. People at different stages of their career and personal development can contribute different things: younger people may offer enthusiasm and 'working along' with inexperienced residents, or may bring up-to-date interests to an old people's home. Older people can contribute experience of close relationships and disruption and change in their lives, which they are more likely to have experienced than younger colleagues.

● *Public practice.* Working in public means that workers have to consider the effects of what they do not only on themselves and on the individual resident but on other colleagues. Feeding back and receiving feedback on what happened can be a delicate task, but workers must commit themselves to doing it openly. Adjusting behaviour and responses by checking with colleagues as you go along can be more helpful than formal feedback sessions. It also models openness and thoughtful behaviour to residents. Ward (1993: 119) makes the point that it is patronising to residents to feel that workers must always present a 'united front'. Open discussion as you go along can be realistic and help them to understand options in different ways of behaving for themselves.

● *Multiple relationships.* Workers must not become possessive about their relationships with particular residents or colleagues. For example, Mary, a care worker in a home for elderly people, was the keyworker for a very dependent woman, who needed considerable personal care. Because Mary created a successful personal relationship which allowed her to do this with dignity and sensitivity, she began to feel a deep desire to care for and even 'rescue' her resident from other members of the staff team. This made it difficult for others to provide care when Mary was not on the shift, and meant that the resident became distressed when Mary was not there. As a result, others began to resent Mary's special relationship, and she was put under pressure to do more of the early morning and late night shifts, which adversely affected her own home life. An important point about multiple relationships in residential and day care is that, in *open* teamwork, links should extend outside the home or centre. Active work to develop such links is needed. This is something else that Mary's special relationship excluded. We need to see multiple relationships, of many different kinds, as creative and strengthening to residents' networks, not as interfering with our own role.

This does not mean to say that close personal relationships in residential and day care should be avoided. The point of these comments is to suggest that a *variety* of relationships in the network is needed. Indeed, most residential and day care centres try to establish a clear keyworker or named worker or primary nurse, who takes special responsibility for being aware of the needs of residents and plans for their care and treatment.

An important aspect of residential and day care work is communication in the team. This can be undertaken informally and continuously, as we have seen. Case recording and shared records may be particularly important in ensuring continuity over shifts and between different parts of the home or centre. However, difficulties in keeping records in different places up to date may make a multiprofessional record difficult to manage, at least until paperless computer networks are more commonplace. A variety of meetings may take place, and Ward (1993: 124) shows that it is important to be clear about different functions which may arise. He discusses meetings for business or briefing colleagues, for assessment and care-planning, for reviewing policy and resources, for providing a support group for team members, for training, for problem-solving, either about a tricky long-term issue or in an emergency, for handing over responsibility at the end of a shift and for the whole community. Supervision may also be carried out in a group, either to stimulate and provide mutual help to colleagues in their individual development or to develop and build team relationships (Atherton, 1986). The roles of different meetings must not be confused because team members may experience conflicts between the different purposes. If separate meetings cannot be held for separate purposes, different aspects of one meeting should be clearly distinguished both in the agenda-setting and management of the meeting. This might be done by setting clear purposes and time boundaries and by mechanisms such as different people chairing different parts of the meeting.

An increasingly important function of many agencies in the public sector is regulation of others, especially in the independent sector. This may also involve the evaluation of services, where they apply for grant aid, for example. Clough (1994a) explores this where it is most developed, in residential care. While the essential relationship is of an independent outsider inspecting an agency service according to set standards, there are also important elements of multiprofessional teamworking. First, there may be different professional groups involved and contributing to the agency. Second, service users and carers have a direct input to the evaluation or inspection: it is their interests which are being protected. They may need advocacy help to make their contribution effective. Third, this work is increasingly being done according to set standards or formally established criteria, both for fairness to those being inspected, to make sure that all the necessary factors are covered and to promote participation by everyone involved.

Residential and day care settings might offer the classic group-based teamwork analysis, but this neglects the role of residential and day care in linking residents with outside relationships, agencies and the community and ensuring the participation of residents in their own living arrangements. We need to develop thinking about residential care practice beyond the staff team to understand the many links it has in wider networks.

Conclusion

In this chapter, we have examined only some of the wide complexity of teams and networks involving health and social care professionals, and their users and carers. A good deal of research and practice writing exists about a variety of settings, and this gives guidance both about the problems and the possibilities for effective multiprofessional teamwork. The organisational, professional and practice context is not irrelevant, but experience in each of the many settings in which multiprofessional work is attempted suggests many lessons which are shared:

- Consider the structure of the organisational relationships, and do not try to twist complex structures into over-simplified organisational responsibilities. Accountability and effective practice often require a complex understanding of responsibilities.

- However, where conflicts in structure and accountability exist, we need a clear definition of mutual responsibilities and relationships to make teamwork effective.

- The clarity of formal definition must be backed up by informal relationships to strengthen and reinforce the formal pattern of responsibility.

- All this must be backed up by resources for communication and contact and by training. Often multiprofessional training will be useful.

Activities

See the Appendix for basic team development activities.

Evaluating the context – team project

The purpose of this team project is to define, clarify and record for supervision and team discussion the legal and organisational context of the team's work. It can be done as a team project over a period of weeks, but not too long to dissipate motivation. It can be planned and to a certain extent carried out from knowledge held within the team as part of a team event.

Stage 1: List the pieces of legislation which affect the team's main functions and their clients/patients/service users.

Stage 2: List the main pieces of national official guidance which derive from the legislation, and team's sources for information about them.

Stage 3:   List the main professional guidelines and publications which influence the team's work.

Stage 4:   List the agency guidance and policy requirements and the team's sources for information about them.

Stage 5:   Working individually from the lists, each team member rates from 1 (high) to 5 (low) the importance of each piece of legislation and guidance for them.

Stage 6:   Working as a team assess the different balances of influences on team members' work.

Stage 7:   Create pairs of team members whose work in Stage 6 suggests they have different influences *or* whose work on Stage 6 suggests that they are influenced by the same sources. Each pair is to try to identify aspects of contextual influence which create conflicts of philosophy and practice and which are mutually supportive.

Stage 8:   Work as a team on how to deal with inconsistencies, either by planning a response or raising internal awareness of situations where difficulties will arise. This may help team members be more supportive where known difficulties arise in subsequent work, and create a personal, team, professional or agency plan to seek changes.

Stage 9:   Create an information resource, for example, a notice-board, index, collection of resources, for use of students and team members in the future.

The tension grid

This activity develops Challis's (1990) analysis of policy tensions affecting SSDs, but can easily be used with other health and social care settings. The grid (Figure 7.2) adapts the terminology to be broader and includes several other possible tensions, drawn from Challis's account. There is also provision for teams to add a further tension affecting them.

Stage 1:   Each team member completes a copy of the grid giving their assessment of the balance in their team for each of the common tensions. Each puts a cross at the point marking their view of the balance between the different ends of the tension in their team. Use the scales at the side and bottom to identify the right points. Agree on the 'your choice'

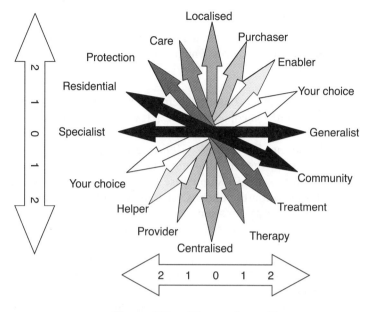

Figure 7.2   The tension grid

tension before you begin. You can add numbers to the points: 0 is a neutral point, 2 indicates a high balance towards that end.

Stage 2:   The evidence – snowball or brainstorm case examples from the past three months which show that tension affecting your work.

Stage 3:   Collect the grids and discuss differences in assessments: do they come from particular parts of the team or particular professional viewpoints?

Stage 4:   Collect, report and discuss the examples: do you all agree? Where are the divisions? Was there a way of dealing with the problems?

Stage 5:   Identify a change of practice or team organisation which could make a difference and a plan for implementing each in turn and following up on outcomes.

Evaluating the occupational groups in the team

The purpose of this activity is to help team members think about the social and occupational factors which may cause difference or similarity between them.

Stage 1:   Team members describe their own occupational group in a few words on copies of Table 7.1, according to the areas of difference set out. Use the second column for this. This is based on Sheppard's (1996) research on the factors affecting the relationships between GPs and social workers, which I summarise to provide examples in the third and fourth columns. The areas of difference may be used for any profession.

Stage 2:   Team members describe other occupational groups in the same way.

Stage 3:   Collect the tables; summarise the descriptions of groups describing themselves; then the descriptions of non-members. In both cases, if possible, integrate the descriptions so that individual views are not highlighted. Compare the two, identifying differences of view.

Stage 4:   Discuss (as a group or perhaps in rounds) factors which cause major or minor similarities and differences between the groups.

Stage 5:   Discuss differences of perception between insiders and outsiders to an occupational group; also discuss major disagreements among outsiders.

Models of collaboration

All collaboration between occupational groups and organisations builds on three elements: replacing each other, increased exchange, liaison-attachment. At the start of the activity, the extent of the team or network being considered should be agreed.

Stage 1:   Team members individually complete a copy of the diagram (Figure 7.3) for each person in the team or network being considered. Rate your side of each relationship in the open team (so it may include service users and

Table 7.1 Potential areas of difference between professions
(with GPs and social workers as examples)

Area of difference	Your profession	GPs	Social workers
Competition for same occupational territory		Total continuing health care of family in the community	Enhancing personal and family functioning in the community
Approach to teamwork		Doctor's authority, based on personal responsibility for medical decisions	Interdependence through shared authority in democratic structures
Approach to collaboration		Personal trust in known colleagues	Follows systems and structures
Frame of reference		Biophysical, with an emphasis on disease, pathology and its treatment	Social and psychological, emphasis on personal fulfilment, social integration
Model of explanation		Minimises social and psychological, favours physical explanations	Rejects pathology, medical models, favours social, psychological explanations
Types of explanation		Individual responsibility	Social, economic factors, environment
Values		Respect for life (life of patient paramount)	Respect for persons (wishes of client paramount)
Oppressive practice		Social status of doctors leads to exercising social control on conventional moralities based on informal moral authority	Awareness of social structures and economic and social oppression leads to caution in accepting moral authority and rejection of social control except in legally defined situations

Source: derived from Sheppard (1996: 66–8)

carers), and your perception of the others. 1 = a low level
of that kind of collaboration; 5 = high level.

Stage 2: Team members individually list, if possible, concrete
examples of replacement, exchange and liaison in
their relationship during the previous six months and of
possible replacements, exchanges or liaisons which might
be developed.

Stage 3: In the group, list each potential contact with the types of collaboration which have been tried, and identify people where
there are difficulties and why. Plan a programme of training
and development which would increase the amount of collaboration of different kinds with each contact.

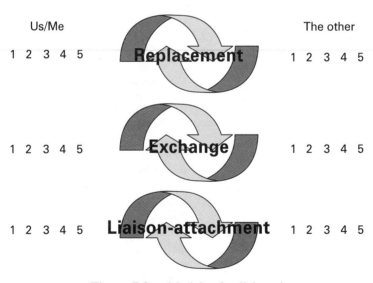

Figure 7.3   Models of collaboration

8

Teamwork and Management: Team Leaders and Others

Who leads a team when teamwork is supposed to be at least partly about equality and participation? How can you 'lead' a network which is not a structured organisation? Is leadership management? Should it be? These crucial issues are considered in this chapter. When we talk about leadership, we often confuse different ideas about or types of leadership. The first section, therefore, sorts out different ideas about leadership, distinguishes management from leadership and points to some different ways of having influence that we have already met, like consultation.

Teams probably need to incorporate several kinds of management at different times. We saw in Chapter 5 that teams are advantaged if there are multiple leaders within it for different activities. This is because they bring in from the network different contributions and they move out to the network in different directions. Looking at inter-personal roles, we also saw that, through different roles, people performed different leadership functions according to whether that kind of leadership was appropriate to the particular situation. Open teamwork means that teams need to take in complex information from their broad network and interact widely. They also need to generate ideas and energy within the team itself. Clearly multiple leadership might, therefore, be a desirable way of managing teams. The second section looks at various leadership activities in a team. It does so in such a way that a single leader can take up different roles, or different people can take up different aspects of leadership.

Every leader must have followers, managers have people who are managed. Leadership and management are statuses which imply difference from, and probably power over or influence on, others.

Ideas on leadership

Team leaders are sometimes appointed as managers in an organisation, with formal accountability within the organisation for the work of their team. Another view of leadership is that it comes from the personal character of the leader who enthuses team members with commitment to their work. Our understanding of leadership is often an uneasy mixture of these two different ideas. If you are familiar with sociological writing, you can identify Weber's ideal types of bureaucratic and charismatic authority in these ideas.

Much early writing on leadership, summarised in Stogdill (1948), was concerned to identify traits of leadership, so that people with the right traits could be selected for leadership roles.

However, the trait approach to leadership presents problems. First the studies raise questions. They are mainly about children and students in unstructured situations and cannot be applied to adults in formal organisations. Also, they did not look at whether leaders were effective, but at how they emerged from the group (Smith and Peterson, 1988). It is hard to identify who has and who does not have these traits, and to find enough people with all of them to provide leadership throughout organisations. More seriously, different organisations and situations have different needs at different times, so logically different traits and styles of leadership would be required in different circumstances. This view led to situational (Vroom and Yetton, 1973) and contingency (Fiedler, 1969) views of leadership, similar to situational and contingency views of teamwork that we met in Chapters 2 and 4. These views suggest that the situation in which leadership takes place and factors which impinge upon it affect how it is done. Empirical research in commercial and industrial settings confirms the fact that team leaders can move between different styles of leadership (Ribeaux and Poppleton, 1978: 292).

Vroom and Yetton's (1973) classic study identified five leadership styles in groups:

- *A1 autocratic* leaders decided things on their own, using existing information.

- *A2 autocratic* leaders get subordinates to find information, then make decisions based on it.
- *C1 consultative* leaders get ideas from subordinates individually, then make the decision.
- *C2 consultative* leaders explore problems and solutions with the group, then make the decision.
- *Group* leaders share the problem, discuss alternatives and try to reach a consensus, which is accepted.

Managers look at the situation, ask themselves how much group support they need, whether, if they seek group involvement, the team is likely to accept the restraints of agency policy or whether group decision-making is needed to prevent conflict. After making this assessment, they decide on a style of leadership. They follow this process in two-thirds of situations, overlooking the need to get group acceptance in one-third of situations.

Smith and Peterson (1988) propose a model of leadership which suggests that organisations are faced with many events, which have potentially multiple meanings. Leaders must choose among the meanings. Over time, the choices they make become routinised, while recognising that some actors in the situation define important and influential meanings for them. That is, their definition of the situation is more powerful with leaders than other definitions. These powerful definitions interact with the leadership's self-management, that is, their own definitions and preferences. Hunt (1991) draws together the wide range of literature which points to different aspects of leadership being important at different levels in an organisation. At the higher levels, a strategic view of a range of complex factors over a long timescale is needed. At lower levels, more detailed information about everyday activities with a shorter timescale is needed.

In summary, we can see leadership in different ways according to the organisation, its work and the level in the organisation in which the leader operates. The same is true of leadership in teams. We would expect one thing of a director of social services or the chief executive of a health trust leading a senior management team and quite another of the team leader of a community mental health team. We must see a leader as defining situations and deciding how to respond to events, taking into account influence from others, the activity involved and the need to balance achievement of the task and the need to maintain relationships.

Leading and managing in teams

Is being a team leader the same as management? Are team leadership and management incompatible? Cockburn (1990: 105) proposes that management is concerned with achieving pre-defined corporate goals. Leadership, on the other hand, he says, is about interpreting complex, perhaps conflicting, social requirements involving different groups and interests within an organisation. Both are clearly required. Leadership may be by designated or appointed team leaders, or by team members who take on a leadership role in a particular issue, either naturally or by agreement. Either way, leadership implies being responsible for, or wanting to achieve outcomes, so it therefore involves management in Cockburn's sense. Moreover, Smith's (1984) SSD study of what makes a team leader effective suggests that high personal involvement in resolving conflicts and problems in tasks and a preparedness to face and deal with conflicts led to teams which were more effective at dealing with problems as a group. So successful management came out of successful personal leadership. Leading, therefore also means managing; managing successfully also means leading.

Leadership and management are not, however, the same, although each involves the other. Current management thinking, with its concern for self-managing teams (see Chapter 1), distinguishes between three types of team leadership, outlined below. Shonk (1992: 136–9), for example, sees these types as a continuum from leadership centred on individuals and leadership centred on the team, and allies this continuum with a continuum from low to high team autonomy. However, we often use all these styles of leadership in a team at different points in its life, or as part of different processes.

- *One-on-one leadership.* Here, the leader works primarily with individuals. Team meetings might be mainly information sessions. This might be typical of a group of GPs, with a senior partner. Each carries their own professional responsibility for work with patients; leadership is a coordinating function and may include elements of coaching or professional supervision or consultation about difficult cases. The same sort of pattern was typical of social work teams of individual practitioners, in hospitals, in area teams and in probation teams before the 1970s when interest grew in teambuilding and community involvement. Where this is part of a mixture of leadership styles, it is often used for professional supervision or consultation or shared work on a difficult case.

- *Participative leadership.* The leader is 'first among equals' (or more or less equals), and takes responsibility for the team's work, while consulting with team members. This is typical of a small group of practitioners who work autonomously. In a 'mixed styles' approach, this might be used with liaison with outside agencies. One person takes the lead and perhaps most of the work, but others agree the general approach, so that if they deal with the agency, they can follow the agreed line.

- *Team leadership.* The team works together to make all its decisions, and leadership rotates or changes according to need. For example, Harrington-Mackin (1996: 39) argues against teams allowing members to opt out of being part of leadership rotation: 'It is not helpful for strong members to become stronger, leaving weak ones behind.' Shonk (1992) sees the team leader as primarily concerned with managing the boundary of the team with the wider organisation or network, whereas Zenger *et al.* (1994) see the team leader almost as a consultant to the team in maintaining and strengthening their team identity. This form of leadership might appear in a multiagency or multiprofessional team where equality of power and responsibility among the professions might need to be demonstrated explicitly. In a 'mixed styles' situation, we might use this approach to plan for a new area of work, to break the back of a difficult project, or to set new priorities.

Harrington-Mackin (1996: 40–3) suggests identifying a variety of leadership roles within the team, with a focus on different parts of the work. I have adapted some of her management terms to a less production-oriented focus:

- *Administration focus* organises budgets, schedules, meetings, timetables, rotas.

- *Quality focus* organises reviews of work, working out standards.

- *Production focus* checks whether things are done by deadlines, statutory or contracted targets are complied with, reports arrive on time.

- *Processes focus* organises communication, identifies when relationships or coordination are not working properly.

- *Training focus* organises joint and internal training projects, keeps records of training, identifies training needs.

- *Supplies and materials focus* keeps a check on consumables, office library, guidance and information.

- *Work environment focus* organises health and safety, staff room, social facilities, equipment and housekeeping generally.

- *Service user relationships focus* generates and develops relationships with user groups and other organisations or professionals related to the work.

These tasks are of different character and require different skills, so they should suit different people. An activity at the end of this chapter uses this set of focuses to develop team tasks into leadership responsibilities for allocation among members of the team. This sort of analysis can also help identify the different parts of leadership in a team manager's job. Some organisations, for example, assume that all leadership tasks are undertaken by a designated team leader and have standard job descriptions for many administrative responsibilities. This may make reallocating responsibilities among team members difficult. Team members may resist taking on tasks that '*she* is paid for'. You can never assume that you can reallocate or delegate responsibilities. Trade union agreements may prevent it or increased responsibility may lead to claims for salary improvements. This is one reason why substantially self-managing teams require a complete organisational shift. Some movement can be made by agreeing that each focus should be taken on by the team member as a representative of the group, as part of a working group or as a consultant to the team leader. Making this sort of provision can help to overcome stultification in areas where the designated team leader is weak or uninterested.

Putting this material together, we can identify several factors in leadership which should lead to effective management. These are:

- *Being open to influence.* Likert's (1961) principle of interaction influence suggests that the more open to influence leaders are, the more influence they will have, because being involved gives team and network members more commitment to the decisions made.

- *Making knowledge and understanding available.* The more team and network members understand, the more they will trust and respond to the leader. This requires judgement: not passing on all information, but targeting where there is a *need to know* and a *wish to know*.

- *Providing time and place.* This means identifying important issues and making sure there is a chance to deal with them. Also it means making space to develop and deal with the interpersonal: to build relationships and deal with problems.

- *Valuing contributions.* Influence is no good unless it works, so leaders should demonstrate that ideas are taken seriously in the team and network, not only by the leader.

- *Dealing with distrust and deference.* Everyone with authority will at times be treated with undue deference and at others with mistrust. People may think that the power and status of a designated leader will be used against their interests, or they may be too unquestioning or leave too much to the leader. Dealing with this requires awareness of people's responses to you and openness about what you are doing. Involving people helps them see that obstructions are outside the team, rather than within the leader.

- *Getting things going and chasing them up.* While the leader does not have the responsibility to do everything, it is a leader's job to start things off and make sure that people do what they agreed to do.

- *Providing support.* We noted in Chapter 1 that many people value teams because of the support that they offer. So making sure that support works well is a valued leadership role but a designated leader does not have to do it all. I look at this in more detail below.

- *Ensures group processes are considered.* Of course much of the effort in team and network interactions goes into the actual issue or case situation being faced. However, effective teams also work explicitly on the processes by which they arrive at decisions and policies, because this means that they develop their understanding of how members relate to each other and their future capacity to overcome problems jointly.

- *Making the systems efficient.* Team and network members get frustrated if the communication, record or referral systems do not work well. It smooths a lot of paths to get this sort of thing right.

Support to teams and networks

Support to workers is a crucial way of avoiding stress and burn-out and cementing team relationships. West (1994: 67) and Chandler (1996) considering community psychiatric nurses both identify three aspects of support which are needed within teams:

- *Social support and counselling from peers.* This category includes emotional support: sympathy, understanding and encouragement. It also covers helping others with practical things, such as information, doing things to help when someone is overloaded for instance, and 'appraisal' support, where discussing things helps others to understand situations they are dealing with.

- *Team conflict resolution* through teambuilding and improving communication.

- *Training and support for team members' growth and development.* This includes both making formal training regularly available on an equitable basis, developing from assessment of training needs (see Chapter 3) and planning for individuals' personal development (see Chapter 4). Three aspects may be important. Skill development helps people to develop or strengthen their abilities to do their work, job enrichment involves building up their role so that it has more variety or is more challenging and the third is planning to keep an appropriate balance between work and home life, not neglecting either to meet the needs of the other.

In addition, West emphasises the importance of:

- *Social climate.* This involves team members being polite, warm and considerate to one another, taking an interest in non-work parts of team members' lives and affirming that you value their contribution. Humour is a useful part of team life, provided it is not sarcastic or destructive. Shared social activities or recognition of important events, such as birthdays or Christmas, may also develop social climate.

Chandler, with his professional focus, stresses:

- *Supervision* (see Chapter 4), providing the opportunity for testing out ideas and personal reactions to work, rather than simply checking what has been done.

- *Leadership* involves making sure the team is developing and manages the conflicts in which it is involved in a strategic way that allows cooperation and individual work to make progress.

In open teamwork, of course, each of these potential elements of support needs to be applied not only to members of the focal group, but also to other professionals and service users and carers in the wider network.

In modern service organisations, one of the crucial problems is managing knowledge and specialisation. Peters (1992) argues that the information that most large organisations need to manage is now too extensive and complex for this to be done in a hierarchical way: instead we must operate in clusters focusing on particular issues, using specialised skills. However, he argues (p. 473) that we must still see those clusters as accountable within the organisation and to the people served. Structures for checking that accountability is maintained must be a part of any devolved organisational structure.

Øvretveit (1997: 28–31) identifies five typical management structures in multiprofessional teams:

- *Profession-managed.* Members from each profession are separately managed from their own profession. Sometimes this also means management from separate agencies or departments. In this case, managers may form a steering or consulting group or a senior management group of a multiprofessional setting, as in a hierarchical matrix structure (see Chapter 7). Alternatively, the team forms the basis of cooperation, but this is strictly informal and needs ratifying through the separate management structures. This works well enough if the team members have a good deal of autonomy in decision-making. However, we saw in Chapter 7 that the research evidence in learning disability teams was that direct single-management was more effective at getting coordination.

- *Single-manager.* Members from different professions are all managed by a team manager from one. Øvretveit (1997: 29) found this to be rare in the UK but common elsewhere. Sometimes there are professional advisers to help the manager with professional matters.

- *Joint management.* There is a team coordinator who organises work and interpersonal relations, and each professional relates to their own manager.

- *Team manager-contracted.* The team manager uses a budget to buy services from professionally managed services. This is typical of purchasing arrangement in community care services.

- *Hybrid management.* The team leader manages core staff, has joint management relationships with others and contracts others in as well.

Where professions are working together in unclear management situations, this analysis can be helpful in seeing where responsibilities lie, and identifying where accountability is uncertain (see activities). Then accountability in those unclear situations can be defined clearly each time they arise. With some experience, these efforts to work out accountability in particular cases can be codified into a policy for dealing with similar situations in the future. In this way, over time, uncertainty can be reduced.

Problems in open team management and leadership

Two problems are commonplace for team leaders. The first is managing accountability when you are sharing responsibility. Many people fear that if you share responsibility, you lose control. More senior managers worry that a team leader promoting or permitting more participation will encourage dissidence or confusion. Subordinates can feel just as worried: they fear being blamed when things go wrong or abandoned and unsupported when things get difficult. The second problem is being 'piggy-in-the-middle' between the team and the host organisation. Leaders have to interpret the host organisation's requirements to the team, and the team's needs and demands in the other direction.

Accountability

Managing in a team involves behaving differently from conventional administrative management, but it does not mean that you abdicate responsibility. After all, delegation is an accepted requirement of all organisations: if you could do everything yourself, you would not need the team. The requirement is to be clear what is and is not being delegated, and keep a check on what is done, with clear reporting back and time limits. You can enhance this with a more participative teamwork focus. Rayner (1996), for example, suggests strategies which maintain both a focus on teamwork and also your responsibility for accountability:

- Make the boundaries clear, rather than instruct people what to do. Possible boundaries are time, equipment and resource constraints, who has authority, the main principles, budgets, safety, legal limits.

- Consider others: make sure team members respect agency policies and links elsewhere.

- Build on strengths inside the team, strengthen links outside the team.

- Consensus means 'everyone can live with it', not 'everyone thinks it's the best thing to do'.

- Respect, extend and work with members' skills. Do not cut and reorganise all the time. In return, expect them to respect agreed decisions.

Rayner (1996: 144) also suggests that team problems come from three sources: leadership, focus and capability. To respond to leadership problems, increase communication and contact with the leader, plan events that will demonstrate the leader's support and increase the budget and resources, or reduce restrictions on decision-making. If focus is the problems, concentrate on team vision, boundaries, open communication, roles and establish regular meetings. If capability is the problem, increase and plan education and training for the group and individuals, see if group relations can be improved.

Being 'in the middle'

All managers are to some extent the 'link pin' between their workers and more senior managers: teamwork exacerbates the pressures. If the work team is successful, its power to define its aims and control its boundaries increases. If the management team is successful, it forms a pressure for conformity among its members. The same is true for networks: someone on the boundary between sets is always presented with conflicts of loyalty and interest.

Conceiving of 'being in the middle' as part of open teamwork helps with this position. We can see 'being in the middle' as a point within the network, connecting through power, communication and information exchange. The strength of feeling within the groups on either side of the 'point in the middle' helps in the linking process, because perhaps by doing a forcefield analysis (see Chapter 4), we can identify the factors which are pressing on us from both directions. It may be possible to see which can be passed through ourselves, as a link and which have to be contained. This reduces the stress on us because we can usually see that not everything is in conflict. Where this is the unfortunate position, we can analyse the different aspects of the conflict. Seeing relationships as a network helps to identify alternative routes for some conflicts to be worked out. Also, each team or aspect of the network can probably resolve some aspect of the conflict on its own, thus opening the way to using the 'point in the middle' to pick off another aspect of the difficulty.

For example, a team of hospital social workers came into conflict with the group of SSD managers, one of whom was the hospital social work team manager. The SSD believed that the hospital social workers were not complying with many SSD priorities, being led by medical and health service priorities. However, the team felt that successful multidisciplinary links in the hospital required fitting in with their health team colleagues and their view of the world. Conflicts arose over the transfer of cases to area teams, and pressure was put on the team leader to get his workers to 'toe the line'. However, this would have meant serious conflict with health service staff. The team dealt with this by agreeing to negotiate some protocols about discharge with their hospital colleagues, and drew in some SSD area team social workers to form a working party to take into account both sides. They thus became a better conduit of information and communication between SSD and hospital staff, instead of trying to hold the two conflicting views apart by maintaining their separateness.

Followership

Where there are leaders, there are also followers. Hillman and McKenzie (1993: 107–23) suggest that a team leader's management responsibilities can be enhanced by workers who contribute effectively to the management process. They suggest that this is helped by the following:

- *awareness* of each other's approach to social work;
- careful planning of *supervision* and the worker's contribution to it;
- not expecting constant availability, and using *time* carefully;
- working together to manage caseloads and *workloads*;
- contributing to joint *assessments* of your performance;
- using supervision and communication through the team leader to contribute to policy and organisational *change*.

This derives from field social work. Where, as in residential or day care, workers are participating in practice with their team leader, many of the same issues are still relevant. You also need a clear analysis of who does what, how responsibility is shared, and how management is done within the situation where you are working in a group with service users. You may need an agreement with service users to pull out of a situation temporarily to agree on an approach, or practise working out what you are going to do and why in public with service users present.Meetings should have a clear purpose and structure. Rayner (1996: 78–80) recommends 'meeting on the PATIO'. He means specifying purpose, agenda, timing, information needed (and that people should bring) and outcomes required.

An important aspect of the development of ideas about teamwork in social care was the growth of non-professional or paraprofessional roles in the 1970s (see Chapter 7). Most agencies began appointing assistants and associates, to carry out more routine tasks on behalf of service users. Social work agencies now employ a range of staff with different functions requiring different levels of expertise and skill. One issue in the 1970s was defining the distinction between such roles and that of social work, itself a professional group with unclear boundaries (see, for example, Barker and Briggs, 1968, 1969). Another crucial factor, emerging from early concern about the distance of professional services from ethnic minorities in American urban areas and the poverty programmes of the 1960s, was indigeneity. That is, local people were not involved in agencies that served them, so the agencies did not reflect local perspectives, did not present a local face to service users and were not involved in open teamwork with their communities.

Working with non- or paraprofessionals and volunteers requires a different approach to professional colleagues, for a variety of reasons.

First, they may not be aware of, or may not understand, matters which are commonplace to professional workers. For example, one middle-aged social work assistant once commented to me, much younger and less experienced in the ways of the world, that she could not understand why a user with arthritis was so difficult and crotchety for much of the time. I said the reason for this was that the people with arthritis were often in continuous pain, and it turned out that the assistant was not really conscious of the implications of arthritis. She knew it was the name of a disabling condition, but had never come across anyone who suffered from it seriously and thought it was a minor affair. Professionals sometimes forget, even with something that is not their speciality, that the consistency of their training gives them a breadth of coverage which ordinary experience does not offer.

Paraprofessionals also need a more concrete form of supervision, which relates directly to their existing experience, and which builds explicitly into new knowledge. It is best to help them to see how they are developing themselves in what they are doing. In open teamwork, it is helpful also to make explicit how they fit within the network and work being done.

On the other hand, it is too easy for professionals to overlook the observation and personal responses of paraprofessionals and other more junior members of the team. Reith (1998) in her discussion of inquiries into homicides by mentally ill people, notes how senior professionals discounted the observations of junior staff. They therefore did not take into account important information which would have allowed them to assess risk properly. We also sometimes discount an indigenous point of view, which would help us make decisions better if we considered it. For example, a colleague and I were dealing with a family with many problems, including the two teenage boys who were committing many motoring offences. Our approach had been to try to develop other activities for them, which involved working with cars – a conventional response, but in this case it had involved paying for their transport to a club in a nearby town. It was an area of high unemployment. The family aide, involved in practical work with the younger children, commented to us that we were giving the boys a good time, when they ought to be kept in more. We thought this a punitive approach. Later she commented that other people in the neighbourhood had said that they thought the boys should be kept more under control. A little while later, we were affected by an outbreak of motoring offences in the area, and a father took us to task about the advantages gained by the boys of the original family, over his boys who were just as interested in cars. There was a clear perception in the neighbourhood that we were rewarding bad behaviour with interesting experiences, which other families could not afford. While this probably did not lead to copycat offending, it certainly put additional pressure on the boys and their family.

Conclusion

My experience of working with SSD and health service team leaders on teamwork suggests that many of them have little opportunity to discuss the practicalities of supporting, guiding, checking and disciplining their team members. Management courses they are offered are often too strategic and focused on organisational structure to meet their needs. Teamwork training thus often turns into work on the basic problems of being a manager. This is a difficult and worrying job, and to an extent, this book's focus on teamwork does not help team managers with the whole range of problems they face.

Nevertheless, in this book, I have tried to take a practical approach to management issues in dealing with difficult staff or difficult problems, where it arose among the teamwork issues I have discussed. Such work often involves individual work with team members, and I want to re-emphasise the starting point of this book. Trying to develop teamwork is paradoxical. It is not an answer to everything. There is no one teamwork answer to anything. Teamwork is about individual and group identity within a wider organisation. Both the individual and the group must been taken account of and worked with, and the organisational context must also be fitted in. The issues explored in the last three chapters, power, structure and leadership, are crucial elements of that context to be grappled with, clarified and worked with.

In offering this book for teamworkers and team leaders to use I propose that teamwork provides a useful context in which to manage individuals' work. Where services are multiprofessional, attention to teamwork is essential. Moreover, I have proposed that *open* teamwork is crucial to modern attitudes and policies which require professionals to engage and participate with service users and carers and create a network of interactions and cooperation much wider than the traditional one-profession team and even than the multidisciplinary team. The group will not do any longer, its wider ramifications must be understood and worked with. Right down to the last paragraph before this 'Conclusion' I have been emphasising how necessary it is to involve the whole network, and how dangerous it is to miss doing so.

The reason for this is quite simply that the people that we, collectively, serve, get a much better deal from our services if we get them to work together. Behind that, we get a much more satisfying, safer and more worthwhile form of professional practice if we can co-operate with our colleagues and be alongside our users rather than on the other side of a professional divide. It is because I count the value of teamwork to service users as the most important reason for promoting teamwork, with all its difficulties, that I have given over the next chapter to some examples of the troubles and rewards of teamwork in four different settings. All these case studies in various ways emphasise the importance of service users participating and contributing to teamwork and team decisions.

Activities

See the Appendix for basic team development activities.

Developing team leadership focuses
(derived from Harrington-Mackin, 1996: 44–50)

This activity helps a team share leadership roles explicitly among its members, by looking at specific tasks which the team needs to undertake as a team and for the team's benefit, grouping them into roles for individuals to take on and developing training for those individuals. Team leaders could use it to identify, prioritise and begin to delegate different aspects of their roles.

Stage 1: Brainstorm all the tasks the team needs to undertake, as a team for the benefit of effective teamworking.
Stage 2: Categorise them into Harrington-Mackin's leadership focuses (above).
Stage 3: Identify new focuses or vary the boundaries of the existing ones.
Stage 4: Identify who does each task at present. Do leadership focuses already cluster around particular individuals?
Stage 5: Provisionally allocate team members to focuses.

Stage 6: For each task, list what a team member would need to know and be able to do and what attitudes they should have (that is, knowledge, skills and values) to carry it out in the way the team wants.

Stage 7: Members working in twos decide what each needs to learn or do differently to meet the knowledge, skills and values requirements for their focus.

Stage 8: Each member collates a list of training targets, including priorities, to meet their needs in order to be able to take on their focus adequately.

Stage 9: Identify an agreed programme of training and a programme of members taking on their focuses.

Identifying management processes

Stage 1: Each individual in a multiprofessional setting identifies a situation in which management accountability was unclear, and writes a brief description. These are prepared as a case-book of problems.

Stage 2: Pairs or threes of team members examine a case description where they were not involved, and describe which of five management types was in use: profession-managed, single-manager, joint management, team manager-contracted and hybrid management. Where it is hybrid, they describe the particular mixture involved.

Stage 3: The analysis of management type is passed to the next pair or three. Their task is to identify another management type which would have been more effective for that case, and say why it would have been more effective.

Stage 4: Report back to the group both analyses. In discussion, rate the extent to which the team uses each different management type, especially if there is a hybrid. Does the management type actually in use vary from the formal policy? How? Is there a consistent type which is recommended to be better?

Support in the team

Stage 1: Individuals assess the extent of the team's support mechanisms, in two ways, using the template in Table 8.1. First they rate the kind of support that they personally get from the team, then, they rate the general quality of support within the team.

Stage 2: Snowball discussions about the difference between what the team offers to individuals and more broadly. Do some people feel they are missing out?

Stage 3: Report back and work out what areas of support the team needs to plan for in the future.

Table 8.1   Support in the team

Categories of support a team offers its members	My rating of the support I get from the team in each category (1 = a lot, 5 = none at all)					My rating of the team's ability to provide support in each category (1 = very high, 5 = very low)				
Social support and counselling from peers	1	2	3	4	5	1	2	3	4	5
Team conflict resolution	1	2	3	4	5	1	2	3	4	5
Training and support for team members' growth and development										
skill development	1	2	3	4	5	1	2	3	4	5
job enrichment	1	2	3	4	5	1	2	3	4	5
balance between work and home	1	2	3	4	5	1	2	3	4	5
Social climate	1	2	3	4	5	1	2	3	4	5
Supervision	1	2	3	4	5	1	2	3	4	5
Leadership	1	2	3	4	5	1	2	3	4	5

9

Four Teamwork Crunches

The early twenty-first century will be crunch time for multiprofessional teamwork. Discussing its recent development in Chapter 2, I suggested that the expansion of work in three important arenas had led to our present emphasis on it: child protection, developments during the 1990s in community care and developments in community mental health. Lying behind all of these are current concerns for public safety and security. The government interprets public concern about health and social care as a worry about whether they will consistently get the best possible treatment and whether professionals are bringing services together to overcome 'Berlin walls' between different organisations. Particularly in mental health and child protection, high profile cases of failure suggest that we are not getting this right for service users who need help and protection and the public who need to feel safe and have confidence in what is being done for them. This implies better accountability for what we do and a public policy context of uncertainty about the quality, consistency and co-operativeness of our work.

The main purpose of this book has been to present concepts and practice ideas to help teamworkers in multiprofessional care examine critically and develop their work. Although I have given some case examples in the earlier chapters, in this chapter I present some more extended case studies of work in each of these crunch teamwork arenas, three of them written by specialist contributors. These are crunches, not because the cases are anything special: we have tried to present the routine issues and responses that workers will see every day in their practice. These are crunches for professionals in health and social care because if we cannot get these areas right, we will continue to forfeit public and political confidence. I think this is illustrated in the fourth crunch, which focuses on criminal justice and mental health, a central arena for the public safety issue, which I have summarised from the published report of a public inquiry. But this is not the only issue of public confidence, as Manthorpe and Bradley (community care and health care) emphasise when outlining the importance of Mrs Lewis's initial confidence in the professionals.

Each of these case studies contains resonances of the others. This is unplanned: they were all written separately without sight of the others, and have not been edited. These resonances illustrate the similarity of the issues which face us all. Some of the problems presented in William Reynolds's case (child protection) look very similar to issues which arose in the early life of Sanjay Patel (criminal justice and forensic mental health) and were not well dealt with, leading possibly to greater failure in responding to his later problems. Each of the cases shows the complex and extensive networks of professionals and family and community members who are involved in modern health and social care. The difficult relationships and the possibility that complex communications will go wrong in all these cases illustrate realistically what we are all up against and why teamwork is hard work. In particular, in the first three case studies, we can see the importance of handling meetings appropriately, especially where users are present. We must also communicate effectively with users, and not take for granted their understanding of what are to us everyday concepts, but are to them unfamiliar or confusing.

These case studies also illustrate how transferable multiprofessional practice experiences are. Manthorpe and Bradley (community care and health care), for example, point out how user attitudes interact with professional conflicts: positive expectations from users encourage us to cooperate better; mistrust breeds mistrust. As I mentioned in Chapter 7 discussing child protection, family conflicts are sometimes taken on by different professionals supporting different sides and translated into heightened conflicts between different agencies. We see this in the Reynolds case, below, too. Even in different settings, therefore, we share the same difficulties, and it is this which makes multiprofessional teamwork a valid general topic to learn about and develop: it does not require specialised knowledge of a particular setting.

Drawing on their own experience, the writers here illustrate many of the precepts drawn out in the book, but they also make important points of their own. Shah, for example, draws a useful distinction between multiprofessional teamwork and multiprofessional practice. We may have a multiprofessional team, he says, but that does not guarantee multiprofessional practice.

Child protection

Specially written for this book by Beverley Burke and Jane Dalrymple

It is a busy Monday morning. Jean, who qualified six months ago, has already taken three referrals from the referral, assessment and information team. The third referral is a family from Montserrat, a British colony on an island affected by a volcanic eruption.

William's story

William Reynolds had lived with his family in Montserrat until nearly a year ago when the volcano erupted. It was then that, along with most of his friends and relatives, he was evacuated from the island home he loved and brought to live in the middle of Liverpool in England. The family were housed in a neighbourhood with other members of their community and a Montserratian community worker was based locally to help them with resettlement issues. William went to a local school but, although other children from Montserrat attended the school, none of his old friends was there and he found it large and noisy. William had enjoyed school in Montserrat, worked hard and done well in most subjects. His mum had told him that school in England would not be very different. Montserrat is a British dependent territory and they were British citizens. But it was different. He tried to concentrate on his work in school but somehow he just could not manage it – he could not explain to his mother why this was and he always seemed to be getting told off by the class teacher. He hates it when the teacher tells his mother about his bad behaviour because he knows it upsets her. He had been brought up to behave well in school and be respectful of teachers but he could not explain what was happening to him. He knew that his mum felt humiliated when the teacher spoke to her about his behaviour because she never said anything – just listened to the teacher.

Yesterday, when his mother collected him from school and asked how he had been, the teacher went on and on about him being 'difficult'. He could sense that his mother was not only humiliated but also saddened and frustrated by hearing all these bad things about him. When they got back home her frustration turned to anger as he seemed unable to explain why he was not behaving in school and she punished him with the strap and the next morning he was punished again before they left the house. His mum had said that the beating was to remind him that he should behave when he was in school.

The investigation

The referrals are prioritised by Bill, the senior social worker. Jean is given the task of finding out additional information regarding the family. Bill likes to respond promptly to referrals from the school.

Jean initially contacts Mr Brook, the headteacher, who provides her with some basic details. He has not directly spoken to or seen William, but he has spoken to William's class teacher, Ms Taylor. Mr Brook talks as much about William's behaviour as the alleged bruising. Jean is unsure how serious the allegation might be. However, the bruising was apparently clearly visible and the fact that William had told his class teacher that his mother had beaten him seems to point to the possibility that this situation needs to be investigated.

The word 'beaten' made Jean feel uncomfortable: it was not a word she herself would normally use except in serious situations. But that was the word that William had used. Jean felt that at this stage it was important to keep an open mind. William's use of language and her understanding of his description could be checked later. Jean spoke to a colleague, who remarked that black families could come across as strong disciplinarians and that it may be a case of excessive chastisement.

After talking to her senior, Jean decides to recontact the school so that she can talk directly to Ms Taylor. Bill mentioned to Jean that the head and staff of the school had been under some pressure since several children had arrived from Montserrat. Previously, the school had been steadily reducing its numbers and a number of senior teaching staff had taken early retirement. Now, with the newly arrived children, the school was full to capacity with mainly newly qualified staff.

Jean phones the school once again and asks to speak to Ms Taylor but the school secretary puts her straight through to Mr Brook. He informs Jean that it is policy for the head of a school to make referrals on such a serious matter. As a new worker, Jean feels a little irritated with her senior for not alerting her to this as she would have been better prepared to negotiate and explain her need to talk to the class teacher. After some discussion, Mr Brook suggests that since the school is only a few minutes walk from the office it would perhaps be helpful if someone came across to discuss the matter; he indicates that this was what social workers would normally do if he phoned about a serious allegation of abuse. Mr Brook makes the point that he had taken a serious and considered decision to make a referral and felt that it was important that something was done before the end of the school day. Jean in response to this states that she is gathering information so that an informed decision about what action needs to be taken may be made and that it would help her investigation if she could talk directly with the class teacher.

While waiting for Ms Taylor to ring her, Jean contacts the department's child protection unit, the probation service, the police, health services, education welfare and the local Montserratian community worker. In between making phone calls and discussing progress made with Bill, Ms Taylor rings. At the end of the telephone conversation Jean feels concerned about Ms Taylor's responses to her questions.

Ms Taylor does not seem to have a positive word to say about William. Alarm bells begin to ring for Jean. Ms Taylor informs Jean that William is unruly and that she had been considering involving the educational psychologist. She tells Jean that in her professional opinion she had never had to teach such a difficult child. She and the head had done as much as they could to manage William's behaviour. They had kept William's mother informed about the situation and had clearly stated to her what their concerns were about William's difficult behaviour. However, she feels that Mrs Reynolds did not really understand or appreciate how serious the situation is.

Ms Taylor went on to say that she had made every effort to help not only William but also the other Montserratian children to settle in the school. In fact she had spent some time researching Montserrat, which she found interesting, and the previous day had spent the morning looking at the geography of the island and had encouraged the children to take an active part in the lesson. William was extremely difficult in this lesson. He would not concentrate and so was unable to finish any of the tasks set him. He had refused to answer any questions put to him and at one point hit a child who he claimed was annoying him. At the end of the school day, William's mother had come to collect him. Ms Taylor felt that she had to be honest with Mrs Reynolds and so had told her that William had been extremely disruptive. Mrs Reynolds, according to Ms Taylor, did not register any emotion, despite being provided with a catalogue of William's actions.

Having gathered as much information as possible from other professionals, Jean updates Bill, the senior. A discussion takes place about what action needs to be taken and who is the most appropriate person to carry out the investigation. The purpose of the initial investigation is to discover whether William has been abused and the likelihood if he remained at home of his being abused again. The question also had to be asked regarding the severity of the abuse – should William be taken into care? Jean feels that this is what Mr Brook and Ms Taylor want.

These issues are debated at length. Finally, a plan for the initial investigation is put together. It is agreed that Jean will co-work the case with Val, an experienced level three social worker.

Val discusses with Jean how they will carry out the investigation and gather information that will enable them to make an informed decision. For Val it is important to be open and honest with everyone from the start and gain the trust of the family and the other professionals. She warns Jean that sometimes professionals will say things to social workers which they are not necessarily prepared to discuss with the family. It was important therefore to ensure that William and his mother's views were heard and represented. Val also reminds Jean that it is important to listen to everyone's point of view and ensure that the views of parents in such a situation are balanced with those of the professionals. These ideas underpin the interview strategy that Val and Jean, in consultation with Bill, devise.

Prior to visiting William at the school Jean tries to phone Mrs Reynolds but gets no reply. Val and Jean decide that, after interviewing Ms Taylor and William, they will recontact Mrs Reynolds. William restates his story, he was hit by his mum with a strap when he came in from school and again that morning prior to coming to school. William states that he had been hit to make him behave in school. William is wearing a short-sleeved shirt; a belt weal could be seen on his forearm. There is no doubt that William has physical injuries and so Val and Jean decide that William should be medically examined. They phone Mrs Reynolds from the school, she agrees to meet with Val and Jean and to William's being medically examined. Val explains to Mrs Reynolds that a case conference would have to held. Although Mrs Reynolds is cooperative, Jean is unsure whether she fully understands what was going on. She is clearly distressed and appears to be overwhelmed by the situation.

The case conference

Jean feels that Val had ensured that they were well prepared for the case conference. Nevertheless, she is surprised at the large number of people there and at how difficult the case conference is. Ms Taylor did not attend but Mr Brook was there. Jean also wonders if inviting the Montserratian community worker was such a good idea as he seems to raise more questions than provide answers. William's mother is upset throughout the meeting and at times becomes angry. She seems frustrated with the meeting – she repeats on several occasions that she thought that she was acting as any good parent would. Children should be punished for behaving badly in school. In Montserrat, children were disciplined if they did not behave. Mrs Reynolds believed that what was acceptable in Montserrat was also acceptable here, after all Montserrat was a British dependent territory.

The head makes it clear that if William is to remain in his school then his behaviour would have to improve. The Montserratian community worker is unhappy about a referral to the educational psychologist; he feels that William is being pathologised and argues strongly for involving a worker from the local black youth advocacy and counselling service. Jean feels that Val's preparation gave her the confidence to manage this difficult meeting and put forward her opinion on the situation. However, in spite of this, differences of opinion prevail and this is reflected in the subsequent plan.

Jean reflects on the process, and comes to the conclusion that simply assembling the appropriate agencies does not ensure that an agreed response to the situation will emerge. The case conference demonstrates to her that the plan agreed reflects not only the differences in professional perspectives but the ability of certain individuals to articulate their concerns persuasively. Individual anxiety and agency mandates also directed the discussion. Jean wonders what Mrs Reynolds must have been thinking as she listened to the debate – no wonder Mrs Reynolds looked bewildered, confused and more unsettled as the conference went on. The differences between the professionals at times seemed to take centre stage.

After much debate the chair manages to get agreement on a way forward. The final agreed recommendations include the following:

1. William's name would not be placed on the register
2. A referral to be made to the educational psychologist

3. A referral to be made to the black youth advocacy and counselling service
4. The SSD would have keyworker responsibility.

Core group meeting

The first core group meeting to be held involves Val, Jean, the
Montserratian community worker – Keith, Mrs Reynolds, the education welfare officer and Alicia, a worker from the black advocacy and
counselling service. As the person with keyworker responsibility, Val
chairs the meeting. What a different sort of meeting this is. Val begins
by explaining that they are a working group to take forward the
agreed recommendations from the case conference. It would meet to
review the situation every three months. The meeting was an ideal
mechanism for teasing out issues and actually involving people who
are integral to the decision-making process. Mrs Reynolds and Alicia
bring a new perspective to the presenting problem and offer alternative solutions. William's mother appears more confident, having
spoken to Alicia prior to the meeting.

Ms Taylor, having missed the case conference, wants to be sure that
the core group understood how William presents at school, to the
exclusion of anything else. Alicia in response to what she saw as only
one view of William states that she had met him on three occasions
with his mother and on his own and her impression of him was that he
was a lively, engaging young person who was clearly attempting to
cope with the many changes that had occurred in the last six months
of his life. Alicia manages to move the discussion from focusing on
William's behaviour to the child protection and family support issues.
As this discussion was continuing, Jean realises that she had only
actually seen William on one occasion and this was during the initial
investigation. Alicia informs the meeting that William had enjoyed
school in Montserrat, where the classes were much smaller. Pupils
therefore received a lot more individual attention and there was much
more space for the children to move around and engage in different
activities. Ms Taylor acknowledges that classroom management is
very different when working with a group of 32 children.

William's mother is more able to participate in this smaller
meeting. She says that she had felt driven to hitting William by the
constant negative reports she had received from the school. She had
not heard anything good about William and she had no idea what his

work was like. Mrs Reynolds goes on to say that, in Montserrat, children understood that they must work hard in school. She had therefore felt humiliated by the situation and particularly in relation to how William's class teacher had spoken to her. She had also been worried that William was not learning anything. He had been a good pupil prior to moving to England and not only enjoyed school but did well at all his lessons. Mrs Reynolds felt that she had done the right thing by punishing William.

She is supported by Alicia, who manages to change the focus of the discussion so that William's needs are addressed. Since attending the case conference, Mrs Reynolds says that she had understood that things were done very differently in England. Talking with Alicia had been helpful. Alicia had not condoned what had she had done but had been prepared to listen and talk through the issues in a way that had helped her to make sense of the differences between life in Montserrat and in Liverpool.

In spite of good intentions to work from an anti-oppressive perspective, listening to the different perspectives makes Jean realise that she had been caught up in the rather robotic procedures of child protection. Practice had not always been child-focused, culturally sensitive, and in partnership. In short, William's and his mother's needs had at times been marginalised by the process of child protection.

After a long and useful discussion the group agrees that a referral to the educational psychologist is not at this stage appropriate, but that Ms Taylor would ask her for advice on classroom management techniques and working with newly arrived children. Ms Taylor suggests that it would be helpful if William's mother could come into the classroom one or two mornings a week to help with reading. Mrs Reynolds seems quite pleased that Ms Taylor thinks that she could be of some help in the classroom. Finally the group agrees that Alicia will undertake specific pieces of direct work with William and his mother.

In view of the working relationship that Alicia has established with Mrs Reynolds and William, the group agrees that she would be the primary worker. Val would retain her keyworker role but would have less contact with the family. Keith's task was to work with Mrs Reynolds, helping her to access resources within the community and thus start to build up formal and informal support networks for herself and William. Mrs Reynolds had not managed this so far because she had felt so intimidated by the contact with the school that she had been reluctant to make any further contact with official systems.

There seems to be an understanding between everyone at the core group meeting that there should be a coordinated approach to helping Mrs Reynolds and William. It was therefore important that the people concerned in assisting the family shared resources and information in a positive way. Jean now feels that the ideal of working together in order to provide an effective seamless and consistent service is perhaps attainable.

Community care and health care

Specially written for this book by Jill Manthorpe and Greta Bradley

Mrs Lewis, an 80-year-old previously fit and busy widow, enters hospital for a planned amputation – above the knee. She has discussed with her GP and consultant the likely length of stay and is told this will be about ten days. A nurse from the hospital visits her prior to admission to talk about the operation and her feelings and questions about this: she is told that a social worker will visit her both before and after the operation to discuss arrangements for going home. A wheelchair has been ordered and her daughters have arranged the kitchen so that most of what she needs is within reach. Mrs Lewis is apprehensive but trusts the professionals involved. She received great kindness from them when her husband died a year previously, having been looked after by her for some months after major cancer surgery. The neighbours will feed her cat while she is in hospital and some cousins living at a distance say they will come to visit her in hospital. Her friends from church are praying for her, she knows.

Comment

This case history looks at multiagency and multiprofessional teamwork from a service user's perspective. Users' viewpoints have generally been overlooked and their influence portrayed as negligible. Health care teamwork can present particular problems in that there are a variety of meanings attached by professionals and agencies to the notion of 'team' and a multiplicity of divides. Hospital and community have become powerful

(cont'd)

constructs in health and social services: few teams work across these boundaries. Moreover, some professionals have their origins within either setting and their alliances are firmly established. Our case history, however, focuses on the individual service user pointing out the wider network of the 'team' potentially involved at the informal level: Mrs Lewis has adult children, other relatives, neighbours and church in a strong system of support. It also points to the importance of experience: Mrs Lewis is positive about her contacts with professionals. Poor past experiences, however, can exacerbate the mistrust of professionals and cynicism.

Mrs Lewis's elder daughter takes her to hospital in her car and helps her to settle into the ward. She gives numerous personal details to Jane who describes herself as the 'named nurse' and later comes back to explain the care that she will receive before and after the operation. The nurse puts all these details in a care plan which sits at the end of the bed in a folder (Mrs Lewis reads this when the nurse has gone). Shortly afterwards, her anaesthetist comes to introduce himself and ask her questions. This is followed by a visit from the physiotherapist who discusses ways of working on breathing and post-operative care. A consultant calls briefly but has to rush away for an emergency. Then, a nurse from the operating theatre discusses more about the operation and asks further questions. Just as Mrs Lewis is drifting off to sleep, a social worker calls on her, following a telephone call from the ward, to discuss arrangements for going home. Lastly, the hospital dietician calls as she has been told by the nurse that Mrs Lewis is diabetic. She discusses her likes and dislikes and gives advice about what is suitable.

The nurses seem friendly, but they are busy. The next morning a doctor comes and explains the operation and discusses the consent form with her.

Comment

The hospital admission and discharge process for older people brings in a multiplicity of agencies and professionals. For older

(cont'd)

people, this potentially complex network may be confusing, particularly if they are feeling unwell or anxious. People do not generally understand the precise demarcations between health and social care services and the language of 'teamwork' is not always shared with non-professionals. Mrs Lewis's story illustrates a number of points at this early stage: first, the importance of preparation – her time in hospital is likely to be limited. Second, the pressures on hospital staff to manage heavy workloads – this means they are likely to rely on sources of information such as notes, but also the patient. And thirdly, the nature of the hospital – an organisation made up of specialists and subspecialisms. Mrs Lewis never encountered many of the staff involved in her operation – those in laboratories, kitchens, the blood transfusion service, the technicians, and so on...

After the operation, Mrs Lewis feels very uncomfortable and is in pain at times. She is surprised by the emotional impact of her amputation, even though the nurse had explained to her the feelings of loss that may result and she had read some helpful leaflets. From being keen to minimise her hospital stay, she is much less keen to be discharged. At night, she finds sleeping difficult and struggles to put on 'a cheerful face' for her visitors. The nurse seems reluctant to give her any sleeping pills although she sees other patients having some. The ward is very busy and the doctors appear only briefly: she has seen several doctors and many nurses. While Jane from Green Team is her 'named nurse', she is 'run off her feet' and Mrs Lewis does not like to trouble her. She worries about her lack of energy and the pain, which, she understands, is from her phantom limb. However, she knows the real problem is that her confidence has been severely shaken. Going home appears daunting but she seems to be on a conveyor belt moving too quickly towards hospital discharge.

Comment

The section above illustrates that even Mrs Lewis's own strengths, being prepared, feeling supported and having relevant information, can be affected by a disturbing event. From 'going

(cont'd)

with the flow' of discharge she becomes more fearful and anxious: the hospital staff appear too busy. The nursing team appear to her to be a group of nurses on the ward: the benefits of teamwork are not apparent to her. Hospitals can, of course, be the site of many teams and groupings: it is perhaps a mistake to see them working in synchrony. Looking at particular working practices from the user's point of view, a valuable tool is asking: 'who benefits from teamwork?' Earlier chapters in this book propose that while teamwork can stimulate group cohesion, this may further exclude service users.

One morning, after a particularly bad night, a nurse reminds Mrs Lewis that the social worker will probably be coming to see her that day. Mrs Lewis waits for this visit. Meanwhile, various tests are done and she is visited by the wheelchair service assessor, someone from the hospital chaplaincy service, her son-in-law on his lunch break and another patient who shares a mutual friend. By the time the social worker arrives, the nurses are helping domestic staff to clear away lunch and many patients are sleeping. Mrs Lewis's named nurse is on her day off but another nurse is her named nurse for the shift. Mrs Lewis is dozing in bed when the social worker speaks softly to her to let her know she is there. She tells her that a 'home visit' has been arranged but she will be back later to sort out the details. Mrs Lewis cries when she is left as she thinks a home visit is to an old person's home... she feels that her wishes count for nothing... her leg hurts.

Comment

Mrs Lewis has now been seen by many teams or their representatives. Included here is the notion that for many people, family support itself can be seen as a 'team' with certain tasks negotiated and responsibilities allocated (many argue that gender is a major determinant here). The crucial 'home visit' will be one means of collecting information to share among a range of professionals but also with Mrs Lewis and her family. Here we can see a team assembling around a particular focus each intending to contribute specialist advice and to cover discrete

(cont'd)

areas. In this classic form, teamwork provides more than the sum of its parts by giving professionals the opportunity to work together and reflect on each other's contribution. While in this case, the home visit does not take place, as a focus it is often invested with importance. Users can find this potentially daunting or emotionally charged.

On the next ward round, the doctor enquires if Mrs Lewis has seen his social work colleagues or the occupational therapist. He says he is concerned about the results of the tests. Mrs Lewis is taken aback by his suggestion that a period in residential care is going to be 'just the job'. She worries about this over lunchtime and asks her named nurse to contact the social worker to ask her to visit again. She thought the social worker was arranging for her to go home but someone seems to be arranging residential care for her behind her back. She decides to give her handbag and her bank books to her daughters when they visit. That afternoon, the lady in the bed opposite come to say goodbye: she is going into a home. Mrs Lewis feels betrayed, cross and rather frightened. She is rather abrupt with the nursing staff and can see them chatting together when they should be getting on with helping the patients. The nurse says she is going to be discussed at the next MDT with care management so she does not need to worry. Mrs Lewis does – she does not know what MDT or care management mean.

Comment

We illustrate here the way in which many users become the source of information about themselves, an experience which probably accords with readers' memories. It is Mrs Lewis who knows whom she has seen or not. For some with, say, memory impairment, the source of such expertise may be located in family members. We also illustrate the potential for misunderstanding, particularly acute when jargon and professional language are used casually or in haste without thinking that lay people do not understand or share their meanings.

(cont'd)

The next morning, now some days after the operation, Mrs Lewis is told that the multidisciplinary team (MDT) is meeting that morning. She asks if she can attend to hear what is being said about her: the nurse says she can 'of course' and wheels her into the meeting where she finds she recognises some of the people present. The meeting is less daunting than she feared as someone introduces everybody and asks her for her views. She declares that she wants to go home and definitely does not want to go into an old people's home. There is discussion about packages of care, MDT assessment, risk assessment, resource constraints, eligibility criteria and appliances and a host of other things that she cannot always hear or understand, but the nurse says she will go over everything with her afterwards. She is immensely relieved that some people at the meeting seem to think she can go home, but rather concerned that the doctor keeps referring to residential care. She wonders if he is really in charge and whether the rest of the staff will just do as he says.

Comment

The meeting is an important focus and it is useful to consider its potential impact on individuals. Language and setting are ways of communicating to users either that this is 'professional business' or that there is an opportunity to make choices and develop plans. Preparation and information are important ways of empowering users. Equally, some 'voices' at the meeting may be more powerful than others. In what way are professionals trained to develop skills in argument; how do they learn about negotiation? Professional education may need to develop frameworks for oracy.

Mrs Lewis thinks about the meeting over lunch. She realises she will have to work on the staff who seem to be supporting her wish to go home. She thinks about ways in which she can influence them and asks the nurse to go over all the problems that other people raised. One issue they discuss is the occupational therapist's view that she needs to wait for certain alterations in her home, and for agreement about paying for them. The nurse agrees to contact the social worker again to go over the financial issues which were only briefly covered in the meeting. Mrs Lewis asks the social worker to be realistic about what can or cannot happen: she knows that the doctors are nearly ready to discharge her. The social worker says a chair-lift 'is rather difficult because of resources'. Mrs Lewis decides to go over what alternatives exist with the occupational therapist and asks that she visit her quickly. At this meeting, they go over all the points which concern the occupational therapist and Mrs Lewis agrees, reluctantly, to move her bed downstairs and to use a commode.

She goes to sleep in a better frame of mind, hoping to go home next day – which she does.

Comment

This case ends on a positive note, emphasising the potential for users to act assertively. She draws the professionals together and clarifies matter of concern. We end this illustration not expecting that all users will have to take on such coordinating work themselves, or that they will be able to. Readers can see, however, that Mrs Lewis had considerable resources: she had time, she was clear about her values and preferences and she was able to make decisions. Such abilities may assist all of us to working with the complexities of teams around leaving hospital.

Community mental health settings

Specially written for this book by Mansoor Shah

> The physician, himself a member of the dominating class, judges that the individual does not fit into an environment that has been engineered and is administered by other professionals (Illich, 1976).

Illich's assertion demonstrates his concern about the mechanistic philosophy of health care. This is still very much an issue today: users of mental health services have been striving to achieve a greater voice in the development and running of mental health services.

In this context is multiprofessional *practice* different from the multiprofessional *team*? Probably, each is the product of the other but the roles and responsibilities of each professional involved can be distinctive. In mental health settings this may suggest that multiprofessional practice arises where practitioners with different professional training work with more than one agency on a regular basis to provide services and provisions to service users in their locality. This may include approved social workers, community psychiatric nurses, hospital doctors, occupational therapists, hospital nursing staff, general practitioners, clinical psychologists and other professionals as well as those from the voluntary and private sectors.

It is often said that good practice is evident when there are good working relations between all the caring professionals. The professional boundaries and culture sometimes inhibit such relationships. There is mistrust or a concern that perpetuates the myth of what constitutes professional boundaries. Some feel threatened by it. Some are afraid to even question the other because of the differing power relationships that exist, for example between the doctors and the nursing staff. Bradbury (1996) suggests a number of ways to set about breaking down the barriers. One of her key points is that team members should be flexible and should avoid professional protectionism by taking on generic roles. The NHS and Community Care Act 1990 places duties on local authorities to consult with other agencies including collaboration between agencies, which was already in existence under the NHS Act 1977. Section 117 of the Mental Health Act 1983 is the ultimate legal basis for the care programme approach for patients detained under section 3, 37, or transferred to a hospital under sections 47 or 48.

In practice this legislative and policy basis has had little or no impact on how the various professionals in these agencies actually work together. There remains difficulty in translating policy into practice because professionals do not have clear and shared definitions of what they perceive the legislation to be. For example, *consultation* has been a crucial word in the NHS and Community Care Act 1990, and has been given status as the main tool in creating community care services, which are supposed to be user-led. Definitions of consultation are open to different interpretations and result in an incoherent social care model of community care services for the user. There is a history of mistrust and unequal power relationships between the providers and users of services. This is further emphasised by users' perceptions that their needs are consistently placed on the periphery rather than being central to the whole assessment procedure.

Community mental health teams (see Chapter 7) might be a forum where the difficulties and opportunities in effective collaboration in community care are particularly evident. But how effective are they in their relationships with service users? Are they the cornerstones of good quality provision? Would community mental health teams require effective targeting, the provisions of relevant services appropriate team composition, adequate resources and measures to maintain effective collaboration among staff and service users?

To address the above questions the following case scenario will represent a number of issues, which will seek to demonstrate the process of multidisciplinary practice.

Case example

Danny is about 18 years old and of mixed (Anglo-Asian) race. He is compulsorily admitted into hospital under section 2 of the Mental Health Act 1983 and after further psychiatric assessment is detained under section 3 for treatment. He is diagnosed as suffering from schizophrenia. Danny's keyworker, a social worker, is informed by a member of the nursing staff that he suspects that Danny is abusing drugs. The keyworker has his first contact with Danny at the ward round where he has been an inpatient for the last three weeks. A ward round can be quite threatening due to the presence of the clinical team comprising ward nursing staff, social workers, doctors, community psychiatric nurses and occupational therapists. At the ward meeting, Danny is friendly and under the circumstances seems confident with himself. The purpose of the meeting is to initiate a care plan for Danny. The consultant psychiatrist dominates the meeting and reflects the power and status of her position by chairing the meeting and controlling the content of what is said and by whom. One of the outcomes of this meeting is that Danny is informed about his diagnosis and that he will remain sectioned. Danny clearly states that he does not want to remain in hospital, wants to go home and does not agree with the diagnosis of schizophrenia, which he has been labelled with. He does his best to convince the consultant to discharge him or consider alternative treatments to depot injections (that is, where medication is released over a long period in the body).

At this point there is no further consultation with the other professionals present, especially the newly appointed keyworker. The ward meeting concludes by the consultant asking Danny to return to the ward.

After Danny left the room the keyworker was concerned that nobody at the meeting had discussed the possibility of Danny abusing drugs which may have implication on his diagnosis. The keyworker therefore feels that it is important to ask for clarification about Danny's diagnosis. Initially this question is received with complete silence and is then followed by the consultant requesting the key-worker to speak to her after the meeting in private.

Clearly, this is an example of how a multiprofessional team failed to engage within a multiprofessional practice framework. This case recognises both the need for shared agreement and ownership by the team, of the contents and issues for discussion in the ward meeting as well as the centralisation of the user's needs. Figure 9.1 represents some of the issues identified in the case scenario which hindered good multiprofessional teamworking in practice.

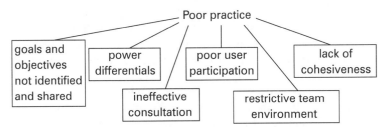

Figure 9.1 Sources of poor practice in multiprofessional teamwork

To achieve effective collaboration between and among members of a multiprofessional team, we need to identify what in this situation would have been helpful. This brings the discussion back to the need for clarification of definitions about multiprofessional practice and a multiprofessional team. One may argue that the former is an effective outcome of the latter because this suggests that the team evolves over time but is shaped and directed by each individual member having shared control. This is administered through the coordination of information, which assists the personal development skills of each team member and reinforces the dynamics of the team. Each team member feels that his or her contribution is valued and respected; while at the same time open to constructive criticism. This can only be achieved by creating a safe and acceptable working team environment.

The success of a cohesive and productive multiprofessional team should be measured in relation to how well the user has been involved in the consultation process. In the case scenario, there was neglect of the user's perspective which was reinforced by team members not having access to the full circumstances of the individual concerned.

The ward meeting was constrained by the overwhelming power differential created by the presence and the status of the consultant. Furthermore, this case gives a vivid presentation of how the definition of multiprofessional practice can be distorted by an examination of the role various agencies undertake as part of working in a multidisciplinary way, placing the emphasis on the representation of the agency and not the individual role of the professional as part of the multidisciplinary team. This is captured in the phrase 'overcoming hierarchies', that is, professional boundaries have no place in a multiprofessional team which seeks to realise its full potential by working within a multiprofessional practice framework. A positive sense of belonging to a team and clarity about its role are likely to be central to its long-term viability. Clarity about accountability and responsibility within teams, effective relationships with primary care and the need for collaborative commissioning, strategy development, and training initiatives are also recommended as an organisational basis for multiprofessional teamwork and practice.

If we now reconsider the case scenario to integrate the principles of what has been described as good multidisciplinary teamworking the case scenario should read as follows. The changes made are in italics.

Case example revisited

Danny is about 18 years old and of mixed (Anglo-Asian) race. He is compulsorily admitted into hospital under section 2 of the Mental Health Act 1983 and later after further psychiatric assessment is detained under section 3 for treatment. He is diagnosed as suffering from schizophrenia. Danny's keyworker, a social worker *and other members of the ward team* are informed by a member of the nursing staff that he suspects that Danny is abusing drugs. The keyworker has his first contact with Danny at the ward round where he had been an inpatient for the last three weeks. A ward round can be quite threatening due to the presence of the clinical team comprising of ward nursing staff, social workers, doctors, community psychiatric nurses and occupational therapists.

Before Danny is asked to enter the ward meeting, everyone present has an opportunity to discuss how they were going to work together and what issues they need to address and why. Up-to-date information about Danny is shared and discussed. Where there was evidence of misinterpretation of the perceived facts, team members are encour-

aged to challenge and explore constructively how this information should be used in the meeting. It is agreed that the team had established a consensus on the definition of the care package being offered to Danny. At the ward meeting *the information is shared with Danny.* The purpose of the meeting is to initiate a care plan for Danny *and he is given the opportunity to articulate his needs and concerns. To assist the team discussion, it is agreed that this meeting should be chaired by the keyworker and that at any subsequent ward meetings the role of chair would be rotated.* One of the shared decisions of this meeting is that Danny is informed about his diagnosis and that he will remain sectioned. Danny clearly states that he does not want to remain in hospital, wants to go home and does not agree with the diagnosis of schizophrenia, which he had been labelled with. He does his best to convince the consultant to discharge him or consider alternative treatments to depot injections.

At this point *further discussions take place between all members of the ward team.* The ward meeting concludes by the team *reassuring Danny that all of his circumstances have been considered and it is still felt that he should remain on the ward. After Danny leaves the room the keyworker was pleased that the meeting had taken into account the possibility of Danny abusing drugs which may have implications on his diagnosis.* The keyworker therefore felt it was important to ask for clarification about Danny's diagnosis. *This comment was constructively* received.

Criminal justice and public safety

On 2 February 1995, a combination probation order was made on Sanjay Patel (Leicestershire Health Authority, 1998), for offences committed in 1994. The order was for one year's probation and 40 hours of community service under the Criminal Justice Act 1991. Soon after that, a custodial sentence of five months in a young offenders' institution was imposed for later offences, so the order lapsed. Sanjay was released on 19 May 1995, and a probation officer supervised the licence which terminated on 18 August 1995.

Sanjay had previously been in care. There is evidence of some history of neglect and physical and emotional abuse as a child, but the details have been lost because he moved from his parents' home to his grandparents, and lost contact with his parents. He was referred from primary school to a child guidance clinic because of naughty behaviour and urinary incontinence, but the referral did not take place. He was excluded from two later primary schools because of very disturbed behaviour. He made some progress at a school for emotionally and behaviourally disturbed children. A psychologist recommended specialist counselling to help with family problems, but it did not happen. The problems identified were of low self-esteem, and the probable consequence of self-harming behaviour. He was having difficulty coping with early life experiences which had meant the loss of contact with both parents. He had a 'profound sense of having been abandoned' (Leicestershire Health Authority, 1998: 12).

However, no psychiatric referral was made until June 1992. Sanjay was diagnosed as having a conduct disorder and was seen nine times, out of 12 appointments offered. He was discharged from psychiatric care when he moved to a vocational and social skills training centre for young adults, but the psychiatrist recommended that he should be found psychiatric help, if necessary, near the place he moved to. This was not followed up, and care programme approach case conferences did not take place, because it was unclear whether this procedure applied to young people. Later, the DoH (1996b: Annex) issued guidance to say that it was. The SSD social worker responsible for people leaving care was notified of the psychiatric discharge by telephone.

Sanjay had been accommodated by the SSD at his request and that of his grandparents after several delinquent episodes in November 1991. He was placed with foster parents, but this broke down when he accused them of introducing him to drug-taking. He was placed with another foster parent: this broke down in August 1992 after a series of incidents. Nonetheless, Sanjay formed a strong emotional bond with her and continued to confide in her and help care for her children.

During this time, as a result of several offences, Sanjay was placed on a supervision order with a condition of intermediate treatment: a programme of skill development supervised by a specialist social worker. When he went to the vocational and social skills training centre, he was provided with a supported living arrangement. He was supported by a leaving care team of specialist social workers. He lived in a variety of accommodation, including various hostels. He was excluded from many, and eventually from the training centre, after a variety of incidents there and elsewhere, including threats to 'wreck' it. The training centre had a liaison psychiatrist, but did not regard Sanjay as mentally ill, had not received information about the previous psychiatric treatment with its suggestion of follow-up if required, and may have assumed that the 'intermediate treatment' implied more medical intervention than it did.

When the probation service took up their supervision, the leaving care team continued their involvement, but did not pass on all the detail of the disturbed history. There was no protocol for handing over cases from the SSD to probation. Probation officers and social workers witnessed several violent incidents. On one occasion in July 1995, Sanjay was punched on the jaw by someone he was trying to rob, and attended Leicester Royal Infirmary, where he assaulted a doctor. Subsequently, he went to the probation office, was verbally abusive to staff and damaged the office. His girlfriend said he had hit her with a baseball bat. These matters were reported to the police, and Sanjay was remanded in custody, being bailed eventually at the end of July. The probation service decided at that point not to offer voluntary after-care when the licence finished in August 1995. There were repeated incidents of inappropriate and sometimes violent behaviour.

On 4 October 1995, Sanjay called at the SSD leaving care team office to complain about the Benefits Agency, and was offered help to appeal. He was dissatisfied with this, became abusive and threatening, left the office and assaulted a man using the public phone near by. This was reported to probation, but not to the police, because the man was unknown, did not make a complaint and the incident seemed to insubstantial.

On 10 October 1995, there were a number of vexatious incidents between Sanjay, members of the public and his girlfriend during the day. He was out with his girlfriend in the evening, having consumed a considerable quantity of alcohol. Sanjay seems to have believed that Mr Patrick Cullen insulted his girlfriend, and he killed him.

The Report of the Inquiry into Sanjay's case comments:

the Probation Service now recognises that the work carried out with Sanjay was in response to a series of crises rather than involving planned, proactive, strategic management of a multifaceted case. Such a review could have resulted in a recommendation for an opinion from a forensic psychiatrist at this stage. The approach that was taken blinded those involved to underlying mental health issues and also prevented them from seeing Sanjay as anything other than a 'run-of-the-mill' case. Good practice should have indicated the need for a strategic multidisciplinary team review and a more formal assessment of the risks presented. This could have included referral to the psychiatric panel discussion provided by a local forensic psychiatrist in one of the Probation Service Offices. Facilities for multi-disciplinary reviews are now in place.

I have described the Probation Service involvement in Sanjay's case, in a political context in which the Probation Service is moving towards closer relationships with the criminal justice system and away from involvement in health and social care services. I do so to illustrate that, even if the major focus of the service is on the punishment, control and prevention of offending, this will necessarily continue to involve participation in and understanding of the wide range of care provision. People do not just arrive ready-made as offenders, and in this case, we can see a steadily escalating series of events in an unfortunate life, which led to disaster. Sanjay was, perhaps, a marginal case for the Probation Service: they never really got going with the combination order. The short licence was marred by unfortunate incidents, and so not pursued. And yet, if multiprofessional work had been effective, the Service might have been alerted to the wider issues. Also, the system has to be available: multidisciplinary reviews were introduced later, probably partly as a consequence of the experience of Sanjay's case.

Not only the Probation Service, whatever it becomes, but also any public service can find itself involved in a complex human life with a long history of attempts to deal with the problems arising in that life by a variety of public, voluntary and private agencies, and individuals such as the foster mother. The services and the community involvement are a complex network, just as we see in Sanjay's case. Good work is done, just as in Sanjay's case. Not every opportunity is followed up, perhaps due to resources, just as in Sanjay's case. Every service, whether centrally involved or apparently marginal, can make a difference to the outcome. We can see in this case that the long parade of misfortunes that characterises the lives of many social work clients, offenders helped by the probation service, many patients of health care services and some users of all public services.

The unfortunate consequences of Sanjay's life and experiences illustrate only too clearly the need for effective multiprofessional work. Here, there was a need to act preventively and early, for systems that facilitated collaboration, and for every professional, every volunteer, every member of a community to be listened to, participate and influence the outcome of care services' interventions in human lives. We have to make that work. Sanjay may eventually be released, after multiprofessional treatment, to multiprofessional supervision. His unfortunate history – its good work and its lost opportunities – and his likely future needs make it only too clear why teamwork is a vital part of all multiprofessional health and social care.

Appendix on Team Development Activities

Most chapters of this book offer activities on team issues for teams to work collectively. The reason for this is that many team development guides propose working on team development issues away from everyday work. Activities are often used for this. This is because they are neutral on the hot, controversial or worrying topics of the team. Also, they put boundaries round particular aspects of the team's work that you want to develop. Otherwise, it can be hard to disentangle one issue the team faces from the whole complexity of what you are doing.

However, there are disadvantages to using team development activities. Because they may deal with processes and issues separately from the work of the team, some people find them over-theoretical, and some may feel they concentrate on personalities, rather than the team's real work. Some people (especially men, who may become competitive) may enjoy the 'games-playing' aspects and others (often, in particular, women) are turned off by this. So it is important to get consent (not just acquiescence) to working in this way. Many teams prefer to include strong elements of real work and issues in team activities. Some activities offer outward-bound or non-work-relevant activities, intended to get people to bond with each other. However, it is often unclear what to do with the bonding if it is achieved. Also, if bonding does not work, people still have to work together. Therefore, this book's activities focus on the immediately useful and practical.

The activities in this Appendix are conventional, widely used, adaptable activities. They may be used to create new activities to cover any issues which might arise in a team, to add to the specific activities in this book or others – see 'Further Reading'. Adapting and building up activities precisely relevant to the team's focus is often better than following set activities which are not quite relevant. Although these are the main generalised activities that team development activities use, there are other well-known exercises in this book, for example, the Johari window (Chapter 3) and forcefield analysis (Chapter 4).

Briefing and debriefing

As with all training activities, participants must be briefed before they start and debriefed at the end, so that potential difficulties are dealt with. Briefing and debriefing is not about telling people what to do, but helping them to *participate comfortably and safely* in the activity, so that they end up feeling good about the organiser, their colleagues and themselves, even if this particular activity does not do much for them personally.

Stage 1:   Participants should, at least, be informed about the purpose of the activity and an outline of what will happen and how they will participate. Ideally they should have the opportunity of participating in defining its purpose and content, or in deciding that the event of which the activity is a part should take place, what it should contribute to the team and how it might help them.

Stage 2:   Participants should be given a moment to consider the discussion about purpose and content, and perhaps asked to note down any thoughts they have about it. Then they are asked if they have any questions or comments to make at this stage.

Stage 3:   It may be useful to allow people to make a round or two (see below) to ask questions and to say what they expect to gain from the activity.

Stage 4:   Then give specific instructions to set the activity going and set the time limit. Check that members have understood them, inviting anyone to raise a question if, as they go along, they are unclear about what to do. Warn people a few moments before the time limit is reached.

Stage 5:   After the activity, *particularly if it has involved a role play*, people need to come out of their participation in the activity and reassume their normal role in which they take into account a range of aspects of their situation, not just the defined situation of the activity. They need to be able to express any experiences that the activity generated in them. A question might be: 'what did you find particularly easy and difficult in the activity?'

Stage 6:   Another approach may be to allow people to make a round about things that they learned or bad and good (always finish with the good) aspects of the experience.

Icebreaking

Most group facilitation guidance recommends undertaking ice-breaking activities to shift people's focus into the event and away from their everyday concerns and to start people off with a group, rather than personal focus. Part of the reason for this is so that people can get to know each other. Some work groups are impatient with this sort of activity: they have an agenda and want to get on. However, it is necessary to warm up. I often start with a relatively undemanding and enjoyable activity, such as drawing a map of the team territory or writing a list of team members (see 'Activities' in Chapter 5). This may make participants aware that they do not know each other as well as they thought, or that they do share perceptions, each of which is helpful in its way. Other possibilities are:

What's my line? – People are asked to mime their favourite non-work activity and others have to guess.

Boxing troubles – Each person is asked to tell the group about the main thing that is concerning them as they come to the event, write it down and put it in an envelope, which the team puts in a box. At the end of the event, everyone retrieves their 'trouble' and says if there is anything in the event which has helped them with it and how this happened. Alternatively, people may keep an entirely personal problem in their box: they can say whether and how the event helped, without revealing their problem.

Rounds

Rounds give participants the opportunity to respond to the experience they have taken part in and indicate any issues that they want to raise.

One useful way of doing so is to ask each participant in turn to answer a question about their response to the activity – to go 'round' the group. Generally people should be asked for positives. In many cases, participants find the positives are the most difficult thing to offer. The rules are that no personal comment is to be made about another person (I give an exception below), that people should talk about themselves, be specific, be concrete, no negatives without positives to go with them. Nobody is allowed to 'pass'.

You can have rounds of questions, expectations, things learned, things still to learn, bad and good parts *for them* of the experience.

If there has been a lot of conflict, one useful round, which breaks the rule on no personal comment about others, is to ask everyone to say something they value about the person on their left or something they contributed to the event.

Snowballing

Snowballing enables members of a group to consider their own personal reaction to an issue or problem in relative safety, to check their reactions with others, but without disclosing more than they want to a large group. It also allows opinions and ideas to be collected and conveyed to the large group in a way which reinforces underconfident group members and restrains the influence of the overconfident.

Stage 1: Each group member is asked to write down privately their response to a specific question, problem or issue. This may be prepared in advance (for example notice is given the day before, or at the previous team meeting).

Stage 2: The private response, or a part of it which the team member feels comfortable in sharing, is shared with one other team member in a pair. If there is an uneven number, make one threesome. Do not allow anyone to sit out. The pair/threesome should create an agreed statement covering both their points/reactions. More general discussion is permitted in the pair/threesome, to allow team members to try out ideas, which might then be added in to the statement.

Stage 3: The statements are read out to, or written down on flipchart paper, or typed for circulation to the whole team, which can discuss the ideas/reactions.

Brainstorming and filtering

Brainstorming stimulates creativity by allowing ideas to be put forward for consideration by the team without the inhibitions of a formal meeting or rational discussion. Filtering turns the results of a brainstorm into something useable. This second process is important. Kaner *et al.* (1996: 4–20) show how getting ideas out of a group can lead to people going off at tangents. Brainstorming offers an explicit process of divergent thinking (getting the ideas out) and filtering builds on convergent thinking (sorting them out and honing them down). In the middle, you may have a 'groan zone', in which there is a lot of confusion and argument. It is better to acknowledge that this might happen: this shows that you have got the ideas out and are not trying to be convergent too soon. Filtering pulls things together, and allows you to close off the process.

Stage 1: Identify a specific problem or issue that requires creative ideas.

Stage 2: Appoint a scribe to write down ideas on a flip chart or chalkboard. No discussion or criticism of ideas is allowed, and all ideas are encouraged even if they seem crazy or they are jokes, because later filtering can be used to weed out things that might not work or to develop the germ of an idea. Jokes rely on incongruity and can be particularly creative sources of ideas which can be developed. Repetition or slightly different developments of an idea are also valuable. Tell the scribe to write down everything, or at least a reminder of each point for further discussion.

Stage 3: *Either* let people call out ideas, within a time limit, *or* go round each person in turn for an idea. People are allowed to pass. Go round again until no more ideas come out.

Stage 4: Appoint a new scribe – the first will be exhausted and sharing participation round is useful. Organise the ideas into relevant groups, if necessary. Filter ideas according to a set of filters (perhaps about four criteria) agreed beforehand. Typical filters are (Kelly, 1994: 21): cost, timescale, availability of resources, good fit with values or present work practices, creative change, impact on service users, resistance or acceptability of the idea to team, or other powerful people (for example managers), practicality, people's willingness to experiment. This is the point at which you may get to the 'groan zone'.

Stage 5: *Either* cross out ideas which do not meet the requirements of particular filters, and pick the ideas which still remain *or* tick each idea which meets the requirements of each filter, and pick the ideas which achieve the most ticks.

Further Reading

Multiprofessional work in health and social care

All of these books are referred to in the text and appear in the Bibliography, but I list them here, with some comments, to offer a guide to fairly extensive modern works on multiprofessional practice in different health and social care settings.

Fatout, M. and Rose, S. R. (1995) *Task Groups in the Social Services*, Thousand Oaks, CA: Sage.

While this book has some material on multiprofessional work in general, its strength is a focus on groupwork, and in particular on decision-making processes in groups.

Garner, H. G. and Orelove, F. P. (eds) (1994) *Teamwork in Human Services: Models and Applications across the Life Span*, Boston, MA: Butterworth-Heinmann.

An American collection whose assets are articles from a wide range of fields under-represented in other collections, including early years intervention with disabled children, learning disabilities, residential child care, medical settings, people with disabilities and older people.

Hornby, S. (1993) *Collaborative Care: Interprofessional, Interagency and Interpersonal*, Oxford, Blackwell.

A single-author work from someone with a psychotherapy background. It has a very strong focus on the individual client as the centre of work, and extended discussion of identity, role and boundary problems, using a psychodynamic perspective.

Leathard, A. (ed.) (1994) *Going Inter-Professional: Working together for Health and Welfare*, London: Routledge.

A good range of articles, with strength on training, from a network of writers associated with the *Journal of Interdisciplinary Care*, South Bank University and the Marylebone Centre Trust. While it comes mainly from a health care perspective, these origins connote an emphasis on holistic health care, rather than a concern with health service structures on medical practice.

Loxley, A. (1997) *Collaboration in Health and Welfare: Working with Difference*, London: Jessica Kingsley.

A briefer work than the others, from a very experienced trainer and medical social worker, which integrates policy, ideology and conceptual work on the differences between health and social care.

Øvretveit, J. (1993) *Coordinating Community Care: Multidisciplinary Teams and Care Management*, Buckingham: Open University Press.

Øvretveit's work in health and social care (for more see the Bibliography) is extensively researched through consultancy work, and this book brings together a vivid sense of practical management problems, with a good understanding of management issues.

Soothill, K., Mackay, L. and Webb, C. (eds) (1995) *Interprofessional Relations in Health Care*, London: Arnold.

Another good range of articles with a strong base in researched case studies, with a good emphasis on training and issues of management and professionalisation. It includes a concern for the patient's perspective.

Watkins, M., Hervey, N., Carson, J. and Ritter, S. (eds) (1996) *Collaborative Community Mental Health Care*, London: Arnold.

An extensive collection of articles from a variety of different professional viewpoints is strongly based on practical experience and research evidence and with a focus on mental health care.

Practical books on team development

These books offer sources for activities and practical guidance on working in team development.

Gawlinski, G. and Graessle, L. (1988) *Planning Together: the Art of Effective Teamwork*, London, Bedford Square Press.

Excellent collection of team development activities, focused on the needs of voluntary organisations. Very good on strategy, mission, values and planning.

Kaner, S., Lind, L., Toldi, C., Fisk, S. and Berger, D. (1996) *Facilitator's Guide to Participatory Decision-Making*, Gabriola Island, BC, Canada: New Society.

A very practical, comprehensive guide to helping groups and teams make decisions in a participative way, based on a well-thought-out model of democratic decision-making. Any team or group leader can learn mountains of practical skills from this excellent book.

Merry, U. and Allerhand, M. E. (1977) *Developing Teams and Organizations: a Practical Handbook for Managers and Consultants*, Reading, MA: Addision-Wesley.

I still find this book useful for a very wide range of activities, which also includes descriptions of the basic forms of teamwork development activities.

Nilson, C. (1993) *Team Games for Trainers*, New York: McGraw-Hill.

A hundred activities, from a management perspective, with overhead projector slides and graphics for copying. They focus on participation. You can also adapt them. I find some of the questionnaires a bit naive in expecting people to disclose the things they ask. However, I think that about lots of personal assessment questionnaires. I prefer open-ended sentence-completion questionnaires for this purpose, as in Chapter 3.

Pritchard, P. and Pritchard, J. (1994) *Teamwork for Primary and Shared Care: a Practical Workbook* (2nd edn), Oxford: Oxford University Press.

Many useful activities based on primary health care teams, which can be adapted to many multiprofessional settings. Based on a coherent model of team development which focuses on goals and tasks first, followed by interprofessional relationships, evaluation and then wider contexts of practice.

Bibliography

Abramson, J. S. and Mizrahi, T. (1996) 'When social workers and physicians collaborate: positive and negative interdisciplinary experiences', *Social Work*, **41**(3): 270–81.

Adair, J. (1986) *Effective Teambuilding* (London: Pan).

Allan, M., Bhavnani, R. and French, K. (1992) *Promoting Women: Management Development and Training for Women in Social Services Departments* (London: HMSO).

AMA (1994) *Special Child: Special Needs: Services for Children with Disabilities* (London: AMA).

Atherton, J. S. (1986) *Professional Supervision in Group Care: A Contract-based Approach* (London: Tavistock).

Austin, M. J. (1978) *Professionals and Paraprofessionals* (New York: Human Sciences Press).

Axelrod, R. (1984) *The Evolution of Cooperation* (New York: Basic Books).

Bamford, T. (1982) *Managing Social Work* (London: Tavistock).

Barclay Report (1982) *Social Workers: Their Role and Tasks* (London: Bedford Square Press).

Barker, R. L. and Briggs, T. L. (1968) *Differential Use of Social Work Manpower: An Analysis and Demonstration Study* (New York: National Association of Social Workers).

Barker, R. L. and Briggs, T. L. (1969) *Using TEAMS to Deliver Social Services* (Syracuse, NY: Division of Continuing Education and Manpower Development, Syracuse University School of Social Work).

Bayley, M., Parker, J. P., Seyd, R. and Tennant, A. (1987) *Practising Commuity Care: Developing Locally-based Practice* (Sheffield: Social Services Monographs: Research in Practice).

Beecher, W. (ed.) (1988) *Directory of Community Social Work Initiatives in Scotland* (London: National Institute for Social Work).

Belbin, R. M. (1981) *Management Teams: Why they Succeed or Fail* (London: Heinemann).

Belbin, R. M. (1993) *Team Roles and Work* (London: Butterworth-Heinemann).

Benne, K. D. and Skeats, P. (1948) 'Functional roles of group members', *Journal of Social Issues,* **4**(2): 41–9.

Benson, J. K. (1982) 'A framework for policy analysis' in Rogers, D., Whitten, D. and associates (eds) *Interorganizational Coordination* (Ames, Iowa: Iowa State University Press).

Berger, M. (1996) *Cross-Cultural Team Building: Guidelines for More Effective Communication and Negotiation* (Maidenhead: McGraw-Hill).

Berkman, L. F. (1985) 'The relationship of social networks and social support to morbidity and mortality', in Cohen, S. and Syme, S. L. (eds) *Social Support and Health* (Orlando, FL: Academic Press).

Blake, R. and Mouton, J. (1964) *The Managerial Grid* (Houston: Gulf).

Boone, C. R., Coulton, C. J. and Keller, S. M. (1981) 'The impact of early and comprehensive social work services on length of stay', in Davidson, K. W. and Clarke, S. S. (eds) (1990) *Social Work in Health Care: A Handbook for Practice, Part II* (New York: Haworth): 539–49.

Bowling, A. (1981) *Delegation in General Practice: A Study of Doctors and Nurses* (London: Tavistock).

Bradbury, N. (1996) *Joint Working: Why is it so Difficult?* (Birmingham: North Birmingham Mental Health Trust).

Bradley, K. and Hill, S. (1983) 'After Japan: the quality circle transplant and productive efficiency', *British Journal of Industrial Relations*, 21(3): 68–82.

Brill, N. I. (1976) *Teamwork: Working Together in the Human Services* (Philadelphia, PA: Lippincott).

Bruce, N. (1980) *Teamwork for Preventive Care* (Chichester: Research Studies Press).

Bryar, R. and Bytheway, B. (eds) (1996) *Changing Primary Health Care: The Teamcare Valleys Experience* (Oxford: Blackwell).

Buckle, J. (1981) *Intake Teams* (London: Tavistock).

Burell, K. and Lindström, K. (1987) *Teamview: A Teambuilding Programme* (Original Swedish edn, 1985) (Hove: Pavilion).

Burke, P. (1987) 'Client problems and social work responses', in Wedge, P. (ed.) *Social Work: A Second Look at Research into Practice* (Birmingham: BASW), pp. 46–53.

Burke, P. C. (1990) 'The fieldwork team response: an investigation into the relationship between client categories, referred problems and outcome' *British Journal of Social Work*, 20(5): 469–82.

Burton, M. and Kagan, C., with Clements, P. (1995) *Social Skills for People with Learning Disabilities: A Social Capability Approach* (London: Chapman & Hall).

Bywaters, P. (1986) 'Social work and the medical profession – arguments against unconditional collaboration', *British Journal of Social Work*, 16(4): 661–77.

CAIPE (1992) 'A national survey that needs to be repeated', *Journal of Interprofessional Care*, 6(1): 65–71.

Cannan, C. and Warren, C. (eds) (1997) *Social Action with Children and Families: A Community Development Approach to Child and Family Welfare* (London: Routledge).

Caplan, G. (1974) *Support Systems and Community Mental Health: Lectures in Concept Development* (New York: Behavioral Publications).

Caplan, G. and Caplan, R. B. (1993) *Mental Health Consultation and Collaboration* (San Francisco: Jossey-Bass).

Caplan, G. and Killilea, M. (eds) (1976) *Support Systems and Mutual Help: Multidisciplinary Explorations* (New York: Grune & Stratton).

Case, S. S. (1994) 'Gender differences in communication and behaviour in organisations', in Davidson, M. J. and Burke, R. J. (eds) *Women in Management: Current Research Issues* (London: Paul Chapman), pp. 144–67.

Casto, M. (1994) 'Inter-professional work in the USA – education and practice', in Leathard, A. (ed.) *Going Inter-Professional: Working Together for Health and Welfare* (London: Routledge), pp. 188–205.

Challis, L. (1990) *Organising Public Social Services* (London: Longman).

Chandler, J. (1996) 'Support for community psychiatric nurses in multidisciplinary teams: an example', in Watkins, M. *et al.*, *Collaborative Community Mental Health Care* (London: Arnold), pp. 292–306.

Chang, R. Y. (1995a) *Success Through Teamwork: A Practical Guide to Interpersonal Team Dynamics* (London: Kogan Page).

Chang, R. Y. (1995b) *Building a Dynamic Team: A Practical Guide to Maximising Team Performance* (London: Kogan Page).

Clark, N. (1994) *Team Building: A Practical Guide for Trainers* (London: McGraw-Hill).

Clough, R. (1982) *Residential Work* (London: Macmillan).

Clough, R. (ed.) (1994a) *Insights in Inspection: The Regulation of Social Care* (London: Whiting and Birch).

Clough, R. (1994b) 'Putting inspections into effect', in Clough, R. (ed.) *Insights into Inspection: The Regulation of Social Care* (London: Whiting and Birch): 117–43.

Cockburn, J. (1990) *Team Leaders and Team Managers in Social Services* (Norwich: University of East Anglia Social Work Monographs).

Colenso, M. (1997) *High Performing Teams... in Brief* (Oxford: Butterworth-Heinemann).

Collins, A. H. and Pancoast, D. L. (1976) *Natural Helping Networks: A Strategy for Prevention* (New York: National Association of Social Workers).

Connor, A. and Tibbet, J. E. (1988) *Social Workers and Health Care in Hospitals: A Report from a Research Study by the Central Research Unit for Social Work Services Group, Scottish Office* (Edinburgh: HMSO).

Corney, R. H. (1982) 'Health visitors and social workers', in Clare, A. W. and Corney, R. H. (eds) *Social Work and Primary Health Care* (London: Academic Press), pp. 133–9.

Corney, R. (1993) 'Studies of the effectiveness of counselling in general practice', in Corney, R. and Jenkins, R. (eds) *Counselling in General Practice* (London: Routledge), pp. 31–44.

Corney, R. H. and Clare, A. W. (1983) 'The effectiveness of attached social workers in the management of depressed women in general practice', *British Journal of Social Work*, **13**(1): 57–74.

Corre, G. (1993) 'Multidisciplinary mental health work in East Birmingham', *Social Services Research*, (3): 1–5.

CPA (1996) *A Better Home Life: A Code of Good Practice for Residential and Nursing Home Care* (London: Centre for Policy on Ageing).

Culhane, M. (1996) 'Integrating hospital and community services', in Watkins, M., Hervey, N., Carson, J. and Ritter, S. (eds) *Collaborative Community Mental Health Care* (London: Arnold), pp. 25–40.

Dalley, G. (1989) 'Professional ideology or organisational tribalism? The health service–social work divide', in Taylor, R. and Ford, J. (eds) *Social Work and Health Care* (London: Jessica Kingsley), pp. 102–17.

Darvill, G. and Munday, B. (eds) (1984) *Volunteers in the Personal Social Services* (London: Tavistock).

David, T. (1994) *Working Together for Young Children: Multiprofessionalism in Action* (London: Routledge).

Day, P., Rhodes, V. and Truefitt, T. (1978) 'Priorities and an area team', *Social Work Today*, **10**(7): 22–3.

Deeprose, D. (1995) *The Team Coach: Vital New Skills for Supervisors and Managers in a Team Environment* (New York: American Management Association).

DHSS (1976) *Priorities for Health and Personal Social Services in England: A Consultative Document* (London: HMSO).

DHSS (1978) *Social Services Teams: A Practitioner's View* (London: HMSO).

Dingwall, R. (1980) 'Problems of teamwork in primary care', in Lonsdale, S., Webb, A. and Briggs, T. (eds) *Teamwork in Personal Social Services and Health Care* (London: Croom Helm), pp. 111–37.

Dingwall, R., Eekelaar, J. and Murray, T. (1983) *The Protection of Children* (Oxford: Blackwell).

DoH (1990) *Care Programme Approach (CPA) for People with a Mental Illness Referred to Specialist Psychiatric Services* (HC(90)23/LASSL(90)11) (London: DoH).

DoH (1991) *Welfare of Children and Young People in Hospital* (London: HMSO).

DoH (1996a) *Building Bridges: A Guide to Arrangements for Inter-agency Working for the Care and Protection of Severely Mentally Ill People* (London: DoH).

DoH (1996b) *Collaborative Practice in Action* HSG(96)6 (London: DoH).

DoH/Welsh Office (1993) *Code of Practice: Mental Health Act, 1983* (London: HMSO).

Donnellon, A. (1996) *Team Talk: The Power of Language in Team Dynamics* (Boston, MA, Harvard Business School Press).

Douglas, R., Ettridge, D., Fearnhead, D., Payne, C., Pugh, D. and Sowter, D. (1988) *Helping People Work Together: A Guide to Participative Working Practices* (London: National Institute for Social Work).

Dunnell, K. and Dobbs, J. (1982) *Nurses Working in the Community: A Survey Carried out on Behalf of the Department of Health and Social Security in England and Wales in 1980* (London: HMSO).

Durfee, M. and Tilton-Durfee, D. (1995) 'Multiagency child death review teams: experience in the United States', *Child Abuse Review,* **4**: 377–81.

Dyer, W. G. (1987) *Team Building: Issues and Alternatives* (2nd edn) (Reading, MA: Addison-Wesley).

Dyer, W. G. (1995) *Team Building: Current Issues and New Alternatives* (3rd edn) (Reading MA: Addison-Wesley).

Eisenhardt, K. M., Kahwajy, J. L. and Bourgeois, L. J. (1997) 'How management teams can have a good fight', *Harvard Business Review,* **75**(4): 77–85.

Ellis, R. and Whittington, D. (1993) *Quality Assurance in Social Care: A Handbook* (London: Arnold).

Ellis, R. and Whittington, D. (1998) *Quality Assurance in Social Care: An Introductory Workbook* (London: Arnold).

Fagin, L. (1996) 'Teamwork among professionals involved with disturbed families', in Watkins, M. *et al.* (eds) *Collaborative Community Mental Health Care* (London: Arnold), pp. 4–24.

Fatout, M. and Rose, S. R. (1995) *Task Groups in the Social Services* (Thousand Oaks, CA: Sage).

Fiedler, F. E. (1965) 'Leadership – a new model', in Gibb, C. A. (ed.) (1969) *Leadership: Selected Readings* (Harmondsworth: Penguin), 230–41.

Filley, A. C. (1975) *Interpersonal Conflict Resolution* (Glenview, IL: Scott Foreman).

Fisher, M., Newton, C. and Sainsbury, E. (1984) *Mental Health Social Work Observed* (London: Allen & Unwin).

Fox, S. and Dingwall, R. (1985) 'An exploratory study of variations in social workers' and health visitors' definitions of child mistreatment', *British Journal of Social Work,* **15**(5): 467–77.

French, J. R. P. and Raven, B. H. (1959) 'The bases of social power', in D. Cartwright and A. Zander (eds) (1974) *Group Dynamics: Theory and Research* (3rd edn) (London: Tavistock), pp. 259–69.

Fulcher, L. C. (1981) 'Team functioning in group care', in Ainsworth, F. and Fulcher, L. C. (eds) *Group Care for Children: Concept and Issues* (London: Tavistock).

Fuller, R. and Tulle-Winton, E. (1996) 'Specialism, Genericism and others: does it make a difference? A study of social work services to elderly people', *British Journal of Social Work,* **26**(5): 679–98.

Furniss, T. (1991) *The Multiprofessional Handbook of Child Sexual Abuse* (London: Routledge).

Garber, L., Benner, S. and Litwin, D. (1986) 'A survey of patient and family satisfaction with social work services', in Davidson, K. W. and Clarke, S. S. (eds) (1990) *Social Work in Health Care: A Handbook for Practice,* Part II (New York: Haworth), pp. 641–52.

Garner, H. (1994) 'Critical issues in teamwork' in Garner, H. G. and Orelove, F. P. *Teamwork in Human Services: Models and Applications across the Life Span* (Boston, MA: Butterworth-Heinemann), pp. 1–18.

Garner, H. G. and Orelove, F. P. (1994) *Teamwork in Human Services: Models and Applications across the Life Span* (Newton, MA: Butterworth-Heinemann).

Gawlinski, G. and Graessle, L. (1988) *Planning Together: The Art of Effective Teamwork* (London: Bedford Square Press).

Gibbons, J., Conroy, S. and Bell, C. (1995) *Operating the Child Protection System* (London: HMSO).

Goble, R. (1994) 'Multi-professional education in Europe: an overview', in Leathard, A. (ed.) *Going Inter-Professional: Working Together for Health and Welfare* (London: Routledge), pp. 175–87.

Goldberg, E. M. and Warburton, R. W. (1979) *Ends and Means in Social Work: The Development and Outcome of a Case Review System for Social Workers* (London: Allen & Unwin).

Goodstein, L. D. (1978) *Consulting with Human Service Systems* (Reading, MA: Addison-Wesley).

Hadley, R. and Hatch, S. (1981) *Social Welfare and the Failure of the State: Centralised Social Services and Participatory Alternatives* (London: Allen & Unwin).

Hadley, R. and McGrath, M. (eds) (1980) *Going Local: Neighbourhood Social Services* (London: Bedford Square Press).

Hadley, R. and McGrath, M. (1984) *When Social Services are Local: the Normanton Experience* (London: Allen & Unwin).

Hall, A. (1975) 'Policymaking: more judgement than luck', *Community Care,* 6 August: 16–18.

Handy, C. (1985) *Understanding Organisations* (Harmondsworth: Penguin).

Harrington-Mackin, D. (1996) *Keeping the Team Going: A Tool Kit to Renew and Refuel your Workplace Teams* (New York: American Management Association).

Harrison, L. and Thistlethwaite, P. (1993) 'Care management in a primary health care setting: pilot projects in East Sussex', in Randall Smith, Lucy Gaster, Lyn Harrison, Linda Martin, Robin Means and Peter Thistlethwaite *Working Together for Better Community Care* (Bristol: School for Advanced Urban Studies), pp. 53–82.

Hatfield, B., Huxley, P. and Mohamad, H. *et al.* (1993) 'The support networks of people with severe, long-term mental health problems', *Practice,* **6**(1): 25–40.

Health Advisory Service (1995) *Place in Mind: Commissioning and Providing Mental Health Services for People who are Homeless* (London: HMSO).

Henderson, P. (1995) *Children and Communities* (London: Pluto).

Hendry, E. (1995) 'The inter-agency child protection trainer – a developing role', *Child Abuse Review,* **4**: 227–9.

Hillman, J. and McKenzie, M. (1993) *Understanding Field Social Work* (Birmingham: Venture).

Holder, D. and Wardle, M. (1981) *Teamwork and the Development of a Unitary Approach* (London: Routledge and Kegan Paul).

Holdsworth, N., MacDonald, F. and Paxton, R. (1995) 'Working with primary care teams on mental health research projects: motivation and facilitation', *Journal of Mental Health,* **4**: 395–402.

Home Office (1988) *The Investigation of Child Abuse* (Circular 52/1988) (London: Home Office).

Home Office/DoH (1995) *Mentally Disordered Offenders: Inter-agency Working* (London: Home Office/DoH).

Home Office, DoH, DES and Welsh Office (1991) *Working Together under the Children Act 1989: A Guide to Arrangements for Inter-agency Co-ordination for the Protection of Children from Abuse* (London: HMSO).

Hornby, S. (1993) *Collaborative Care: Interprofessional, Interagency and Interpersonal* (Oxford: Blackwell).

Horwitz, J. J. (1970) *Team Practice and the Specialist* (Springfield, IL: Charles C. Thomas).

Hunt, J. G. (1991) *Leadership: A New Synthesis* (Newbury Park, CA: Sage).

Huntington, J. (1981) *Social Work and General Medical Practice* (London: Allen & Unwin).

Illich, I. (1976) *Limits to Medicine: Medical Nemesis: The Expropriation of Health* (Harmondsworth: Penguin).

Jeffreys, M. (1986) 'Professional team roles', in Shepherd, M., Wilkinson, G. and Williams, P. (eds) *Mental Illness in Primary Care Settings* (London: Tavistock), pp. 93–103.

Jerome, P. J. (1995) *Re-Creating Teams During Transitions: A Practical Guide to Optimizing Team Performance During Changing Times* (London: Kogan Page).

Jones, R. V. H. (1986) *Working Together – Learning Together* (Occasional Paper 33) (London: Royal College of General Practitioners).

Kakabadse, A. (1982) *Culture of the Social Services* (Aldershot: Gower).

Kane, R. (1975a) 'The interprofessional team as a small group', in Davidson, K. W. and Clarke, S. S. (eds) (1990) *Social Work in Health Care: A Handbook for Practice,* Part 1 (New York: Haworth), pp. 277–93.

Kane, R. A. (1975b) *Interprofessional Teamwork* (New York: Syracuse University School of Social Work, Manpower Monograph No. 8).

Kane, R. A. (1980) 'Multi-disciplinary teamwork in the United States: trends, issues and implications for the social worker', in Lonsdale, S., Webb, A. and Briggs, T. L. (eds) *Teamwork in the Personal Social Services and Health Care: British and American Perspectives* (London: Croom Helm), pp. 138–51.

Kaner, S., Lind, L., Toldi, C., Fisk, S. and Berger, D. (1996) *Facilitator's Guide to Participatory Decision-Making* (Gabriola Island, BC, Canada: New Society).

Katzenbach, J. R. and Smith, D. K. (1993) *The Wisdom of Teams: Creating the High-Performance Organization* (Boston, MA: Harvard Business School Press).

Kelly, P. K. (1994) *Team Decision-Making Techniques* (London: Kogan Page).

King, D. (1991) *Moving on from Mental Hospitals to Community Care: A Case Study of Change in Exeter* (London: Nuffield Provincial Hospitals Trust).

Knoke, D. and Kuklinski, J. H. (1982) *Network Analysis* (Beverly Hills: Sage).

Leathard, A. (1994) 'Inter-professional development in Britain: an overview', in Leathard, A. (ed.) *Going Inter-Professional: Working Together for Health and Welfare* (London: Routledge), pp. 3–35.

Leicestershire Health Authority (1998) *Report of the Independent Inquiry into the Treatment and Care of Sanjay Kumar Patel* (Chair: Professor Herschel Prins) (Leicester: Leicestershire Health Authority).

Leigh, A. and Maynard, M. (1995) *Leading Your Team: How to Involve and Inspire Teams* (London: Nicholas Brealey).

Lewis, J. W. (1975) 'Management team development: will it work for you?' *Personnel,* **52**(July-August): 11–25.

Likert, R. (1961) *New Patterns of Management* (New York: McGraw-Hill).

Lindström, K.(1987) *Team Skills* (Original Swedish publication, 1984) (Management Learning Resources).

Lipnack, J. and Stamps, J. (1993) *The TeamNet Factor: Bringing the Power of Boundary Crossing into the Heart of Your Business* (Essex Junction, VT: Oliver Wight).

Lloyd, S. and Burman, M. (1996) 'Specialist police units and the joint investigation of child abuse', *Child Abuse Review,* **5**(1): 4–17.

Loxley, A. (1997) *Collaboration in Health and Welfare: Working with Difference* (London: Jessica Kingsley).

Lundy, J. L. (1994) *Teams: Together Each Achieves More Success: How to Develop Peak Performance for World-Class Results* (Chicago, IL: Dartnell).

McCleod, E. (1995) 'Patients in interprofessional practice', in Soothill, K. *et al. Interprofessional Relations in Health Care* (London: Arnold).

McDougall, M. (1996) 'Using human resources development to progress women into management' in Briley, S. (ed.) *Women in the Workforce: Human Resource Development Strategies into the Next Century* (Edinburgh: HMSO): 14–22.

McGeough, P. (1995) *Team Briefing: A Practical Handbook* (London, Industrial Society).

McGrath, M. (1991) *Multi-disciplinary Teamwork: Community Mental Handicap Teams* (Aldershot: Avebury).

McGregor, D. (1960) *The Human Side of Enterprise* (New York, McGraw-Hill).

McIntosh, J. and Dingwall, R. (1978) 'Teamwork in theory and practice', in Dingwall, R. and McIntosh, J. (eds) *Readings in the Sociology of Nursing* (London: Churchill Livingstone).

McIntosh-Fletcher, D. (1996) *Teaming by Design: Real Teams for Real People* (Chicago, IL: Irwin).

Maddux, R. B. (1996) *Team Building: An Exercise in Leadership* (2nd edn) (London: Kogan Page).

Maguire, L. (1991) *Social Support Systems in Practice: A Generalist Approach* (Silver Spring, MD: National Association of Social Workers).

Marchington, M. (1992) *Managing the Team: A Guide to Successful Employee Involvement* (Oxford: Blackwells).

Margerson, C. J. and McCann, D. (1995) *Team Management: Practical New Approaches* (2nd edn) (Oxford: Management Books).

Marriotti, J. L. (1996) *The Power of Partnerships: The Next Step: Beyond TQM, Reengineering and Lean Production* (Cambridge, MA: Blackwells).

Maslow, A. (1970) *Motivation and Personality* (2nd edn) (New York: Harper & Row).

Mayo, E. (1933) *The Human Problems of an Industrial Civilisation* (Boston: Division of Research, Graduate School of Business Administration, Harvard University).

Merry, U. and Allerhand, M. E. (1977) *Developing Teams and Organizations: A Practical Handbook for Managers and Consultants* (Reading, MA: Addison-Wesley).

Metropolitan Police and Bexley London Borough (1987) *Child Sexual Abuse: Joint Investigative Project* (London: HMSO).

Middleton, L. (1992) *Children First: Working with Children and Disability* (Birmingham: Venture).

Mistral, W. and Velleman, R. (1997) 'CHMTs: the professionals' choice?' *Journal of Mental Health,* **6**(2): 125–40.

Morgan Report (1991) *Safer Communities: The Local Delivery of Crime Prevention Through the Partnership Approach* (London: Home Office Standing Conference on Crime Prevention).

Morrall, P. A. (1997) 'Lacking in rigour: a case study of the professional practice of psychiatric nurses in four community mental health teams', *Journal of Mental Health,* **6**(2): 173–9.

Mullender, A. (1996) *Rethinking Domestic Violence: The Social Work and Probation Response* (London: Routledge).

Myers, J. and Cooper, B. (1996) 'Creating and sustaining an inter-agency training pool', *Child Abuse Review,* **5**: 289–93.

Nadel, S. F. (1957) *The Theory of Social Structure* (London: Cohen and West).

Nilson, C. (1993) *Team Games for Trainers* (New York: McGraw-Hill).

Oakland, J. S. (1999) *Total Organizational Excellence: Achieving World-class Performance* (Oxford: Butterworth-Heinemann).

Onyett, S. and Ford, R. (1996) 'Multidisciplinary community teams: where is the wreckage', *Journal of Mental Health,* **5**(1): 47–55.

Orelove, F. P. (1994) 'Transdisciplinary teamwork', in Garner, H. G. and Orelove, F. P. *Teamwork in Human Services: Models and Applications across the Life Span* (Newton, MA: Butterworth-Heinemann), pp. 37–59.

Øvretveit, J. (1992) *Therapy Services: Organisation, Management and Autonomy* (Reading: Harwood).

Øvretveit, J. (1993) *Coordinating Community Care: Multidisciplinary Teams and Care Management,* Buckingham: Open University Press.

Øvretveit, J. (1997) 'How to describe interprofessional working', in Øvretveit, J., Mathias, P. and Thompson, T. (eds) *Interprofessional Working for Health and Social Care* (London: Macmillan), pp. 9–33.

Owen, H. (1996) *Creating Top-Flight Teams* (London: Kogan Page).

Pappas, V. C. (1994) 'Interagency collaboration: an interdisciplinary approach', in Garner, H. P. and Orelove, F. P. (eds) *Teamwork in Human Services: Models and Applications Across the Life Span* (Boston, MA: Butterworth-Heinemann), pp. 60–85.

Parker, G. M. (1990) *Team Players and Teamwork: The New Competitive Business Strategy* (San Francisco: Jossey-Bass).

Parsloe, P. (1981) *Social Services Area Teams* (London: Allen and Unwin).

Patmore, C. and Weaver, J. (1991) *Community Mental Health Teams: Lessons for Planners and Managers* (London: Good Practices in Mental Health).

Paxton, R. (1995) 'Goodbye community mental health teams – at last', *Journal of Mental Health,* **4**: 331–4.

Payne, C. and Scott, T. (1982) *Developing Supervision of Teams in Field and Residential Social Work – Part 1* (London: National Institute for Social Work).

Payne, M. (1979) *Power, Authority and Responsibility in Social Services: Social Work in Area Teams* (London: Macmillan).

Payne, M. (1982) *Working in Teams* (London: Macmillan).

Payne, M. (1993) *Linkages: Networking in Social Care* (London: Whiting & Birch).

Payne, M. (1995) *Social Work and Community Care* (London: Macmillan).

Pence, D. and Wilson, C. (1994) *Team Investigation of Child Sexual Abuse: The Uneasy Alliance* (Thousand Oaks, CA: Sage).

Peters, T. (1992) *Liberation Management: Necessary Disorganization for the Nanosecond Nineties* (London: Macmillan).

Peters, T. J. and Waterman, R. H. (1982) *In Search of Excellence* (New York: Harper and Row).

Pietroni, P. C. (1992) 'Towards reflective practice – the languages of health and social care', *Journal of Interprofessional Care,* **6**(1): 7–16.

Pietroni, P. (1994) 'Interprofessional teamwork: its history and development in hospitals, general practice and community care (UK)', in Leathard, A. (ed.) *Going Inter-Professional: Working Together for Health and Welfare* (London: Routledge), pp. 77–89.

Platt, S., with Piepe, R. and Smyth, J. (1988) *Teams: A Game to Develop Group Skills* (Aldershot: Gower).

Plovnik, M., Fry, R. and Rubin, I. (1975) 'New developments in OD Technology: programmed team development', *Training and Development Journal,* 4 April.

Pritchard, P. and Pritchard, J. (1994) *Teamwork for Primary and Shared Care: A Practical Workbook* (2nd edn) (Oxford: Oxford University Press).

Quick, T. L. (1992) *Successful Team Building* (New York: American Management Association).

Rawson, D. (1994) 'Models of inter-professional work: likely theories and possibilities', in Leathard, A. (edn) *Going Inter-Professional: Working Together for Health and Welfare* (London: Routledge), pp. 38–63.

Ray, D. and Bronstein, H. (1995) *Teaming Up: Making the Transition to a Self-directed Team-based Organization* (New York: McGraw-Hill).

Rayner, S. R. (1996) *Team Traps: Survival Stories and Lessons from Team Disasters, Near-misses, Mishaps and Other Near-death Experiences* (New York: Wiley).

RCGP (1985) *What Sort of Doctor? Assessing Quality of Care in General Practice* (London: Royal College of General Practitioners).

Redman, W. (1996) *Facilitation Skills for Team Development* (London: Kogan Page).

Reith, M. (1998) *Community Care Tragedies: A Practice Guide to Mental Health Inquiries* (Birmingham: Venture).

Rhodes, R. A. W. (1986) *The National World of Local Government* (London: Allen and Unwin).

Ribeaux, P. and Poppleton, S. E. (1978) *Psychology and Work: An Introduction* (London: Macmillan).

Robertson, S. (1989) 'Groupwork in general hospitals', in Taylor, R. and Ford, J. (eds) *Social Work and Health Care* (London: Jessica Kingsley), pp. 118–30.

Rushmer, R. (1997) 'What happens to the team during teambuilding? Examining the change process that helps to build a team', *Journal of Management Development*, **16**(5): 316–27.

Ryrie, I., Hellard, L., Kearns, C., Robinson, D., Pathmanathan, I. and O'Sullivan, D. (1997) 'Zoning: a system for managing case work and targeting resources in community mental health teams', *Journal of Mental Health*, **6**(5): 515–23.

Saul, P. (1991) *Strategic Team Leadership: Creating Winning Teams for the 1990s* (Sydney: McGraw-Hill).

Savio, M. (1996) 'Community care and inter-professional relationships: community psychiatric nursing in Britain and Italy', *Social Work in Europe*, **3**(3): 1–11.

Schein, E. H. (1969) *Process Consultation: the Role in Organization Development* (Reading, MA: Addison-Wesley).

Schein, E. H. (1988) *Process Consultation*, Volume 1: *Its Role in Organization Development* (2nd edn) (Reading, MA: Addison-Wesley).

Schein, E. H. (1999) *Process Consultation Revisited: Building the Helping Relationship* (Reading, MA: Addison-Wesley).

Schindler, R. and Brawley, E. A. (1987) *Social Care at the Front Line: A Worldwide Study of Paraprofessionals* (New York: Tavistock).

Scott, J. (1991) *Social Network Analysis: A Handbook* (London: Sage).

Seed, P. (1990) *Introducing Network Analysis in Social Work* (London: Jessica Kingsley).

Shaw, I. (1994) *Evaluating International Training* (Aldershot: Avebury).

Shepherd, G. (1995) 'Care and control in the community', in Crichton, J. (ed.) *Psychiatric Patient Violence: Risk and Response* (London: Duckworth), pp. 111–26.

Sheppard, M. (1992) 'Contact and collaboration with general practitioners: a comparison between social workers and community psychiatric nurses', *British Journal of Social Work*, **22**(4): 491–536.

Sheppard, M. (1996) 'Primary health care: roles and relationships', in Watkins, M. *et al.* (eds) *Collaborative Community Mental Health Care* (London: Arnold), pp. 58–77.

Shonk, J. H. (1992) *Team-based Organizations: Developing a Successful Team Environment* (Homewood, IL: Business One Irwin).

Simon, D. (1991) 'Case-swop: a co-working structure', *Practice*, **5**(2): 160–9.

Smale, G. (1996) *Mapping Change and Innovation* (London: HMSO).

Smale, G., Tuson, G., Cooper, M., Wardle, M. and Crosbie, D. (1988) *Community Social Work: A Paradigm for Change* (London: National Institute for Social Work).

Smith, P. B. (1984) 'Social service teams and their managers', *British Journal of Social Work*, **16**(6): 601–13.

Smith, P. B. and Peterson, M. F. (1988) *Leadership, Organizations and Culture: An Event Management Model* (London: Sage).

Soothill, K., Mackay, L. and Webb, C. (eds) (1995) *Interprofessional Relations in Health Care* (London: Arnold).

Spencer, J. and Pruss, A. (1992) *Managing Your Team: How to Organise People for Maximum Results* (London: Piatkus).

Steinberg, D. (1989) *Interprofessional Consultation: Innovation and Imagination in Working Relationships* (Oxford: Blackwell).

Stogdill, R. M. (1948) 'Personal factors associated with leadership', in Gibb, C. A. (ed.) (1969) *Leadership: Selected Readings* (Harmondsworth: Penguin), pp. 91–133.

Stones, C. (1994) *Focus on Families: Family Centres in Action* (Basingstoke: Macmillan).

Storrie, J. (1992) 'Mastering interprofessionalism – an inquiry into the development of master programmes with an interprofessional focus', *Journal of Interprofessional Care*, **6**(3): 253–60.

Streeck, W. and Schmitter, P. C. (1985) 'Community, market, state – and associations? The prospective contribution of interest governance to social order', in Thompson, G., Frances, J. Levačič, R. and Mitchell, J. (eds) *Markets, Hierarchies and Networks: The Coordination of Social Life* (London: Sage), pp. 227–41.

SWSG (Social Work Services Group) (1988) *Child Abuse: An Action Programme* (SWSG Circular 9/1988) (Edinburgh: Scottish Office).

Syer, J. D. and Connolly, C. (1996) *How Teamwork Works: The Dynamics of Effective Team Development* (London: McGraw-Hill).

Thompson, J. L. (1997) *Strategic Management: Awareness and Change* (3rd edn) (London: International Business Press).

Thompson, N., Stradling, S., Murphy, M. and O'Neill, P. (1996) 'Stress and organisational culture', *British Journal of Social Work*, **26**(5): 647–65.

Trevillion, S. (1988) 'Conferencing the crisis: the application of network models to social work practice', *British Journal of Social Work*, **18**(2): 298–308.

Trevillion, S. (1992) *Caring in the Community: A Networking Approach to Community Partnership* (London: Longman).

Tuckman, R. W. (1965) 'Developmental sequence in small groups', *Psychological Bulletin* **63**(6): 384–99.

Twinn, S. and Cowley, S. (eds) (1992) *The Principles of Health Visiting: A Re-examination* (London: UK Standing Conference on Health Visitor Education).

Vaughan, P. J. and Badger, D. (1995) *Working with Mentally Disordered Offenders in the Community* (London: Chapman & Hall).

Vickery, A. (1977) *Caseload Management* (London: National Institute for Social Work).

Vroom, V. H. and Yetton, P. H. (1973) *Leadership and Decision-making* (Pittsburgh, PA: University of Pittsburgh Press).

Walton, R. E. (1987) *Managing Conflict: Interpersonal Dialogue and Third-party Roles* (2nd edn) (Reading, MA: Addison-Wesley).

Ward, A. (1993) *Working in Group Care: Social Work in Residential and Day Care Settings* (Birmingham: Venture).

Wasserman, S. and Faust, K. (1994) *Social Network Analysis: Methods and Applications* (Cambridge: Cambridge University Press).

Watkins, M., Hervey, N., Carson, J. and Ritter, S. (eds) (1996) *Collaborative Community Mental Health Care*, London: Arnold.

Waterhouse, L. and Carnie, J. (1990) *Child Sexual Abuse: The Professional Challenge to Social Work and Police: Report to the Social Work Services Group* (Edinburgh: Scottish Office Research Unit Papers).

Webb, A. L. and Hobdell, M. (1980) 'Co-ordination and teamwork in the health and personal social services', in Lonsdale, S., Webb, A. and Briggs, T. L. (eds) *Teamwork in the Personal Social Services and Health Care: British and American Perspectives* (London: Croom Helm).

Wells, J. S. G. (1997) 'Priorities, "street-level bureaucracy" and the community mental health team', *Health and Social Care in the Community*, **5**(5): 333–42.

Wenger, G. C. (1994) *Understanding Support Networks and Community Care: Network Assessment for Elderly People* (Aldershot: Avebury).

Werbner, P. (1988) 'Taking and giving: working women and female bonds in a Pakistani immigrant neighbourhood', in Westwood, S. and Bhachu, P. (eds) *Enterprising Women: Ethnicity, Economy and Gender Relations* (London: Routledge), pp. 177–202.

West, M. A. (1994) *Effective Teamwork* (Leicester: British Psychological Society).

Whittington, C. (1983) 'Social work in the welfare network', *British Journal of Social Work*, **13**(3): 265–86.

Wilson, G. (1995) *Self-Managed Team Working: The Flexible Route to High-Performance* (London: Pitman).

Wilson, P. (1996) *Empowering the Self-Directed Team* (Aldershot: Gower).

Wolfenden Committee (1978) *The Future of Voluntary Organisations* (London: Croom Helm).

World Health Organization (1984) *Glossary of Terms Used in the 'Health for All' Series No. 1–8* (Geneva: WHO).

Zenger, J. H., Musselwhite, E., Hurson, K. and Perrin, C. (1994) *Leading Teams: Mastering the New Role* (Homewood, IL: Business One Irwin).

Author Index

A

Abramson, J. S. 159
Adair, J. 6, 31, 70, 116–18
Allan, M. 76–7, 83
Allerhand, M. E. 60, 78–80, 103, 106
AMA 180
Atherton, J. S. 194
Austin, M. J. 176
Axelrod, R. 28

B

Badger, D. 185
Bamford, T. 176
Barclay Report 176
Barker, R. L. 213
Bayley, M. 176
Belbin, R. M. 119–23
Bell, C. 179
Benne, K. D. 117–18
Benner, S. 190
Benson, J. K. 15
Berger, D. 160–2
Berger, M. 36
Berkman, L. F. 17
Bhavnani, R. 76–7, 83
Blake, R. 31–2
Boone, C. R. 190
Bourgeois, L. J. 148–9
Bowling, A. 181
Bradbury, N. 235
Bradley, K. 34
Brawley, E. A. 176
Birggs, T. L. 213
Brill, N. I. 6, 69, 70, 114–15, 118–19, 125, 136
Bronstein, H. 35
Bruce, N. 182
Bryer, R. 181
Buckle, J. 176
Burell, K. 69–70
Burke, P. C. 88
Burman, M. 10, 179
Burton, M. 158
Bytheway, B. 181
Bywaters, P. 29

C

Cannan, C. 180
Caplan, G. 16–17, 94
Caplan, R. B. 16
Carnie, J. 179
Case, S. S. 82
Casto, M. 186

Centre for Policy on Ageing (CPA) 127
Challis, L. 177, 196–7
Chandler, J. 208-9
Chang, R. Y. 52–3, 150–1, 154–5
Clark, N. 114, 122
Clements, P. 158
Clough, R. 10, 191–2, 194
Cockburn, J. 176, 204
Colenso, M. 7, 35, 52–3
Collins, A. H. 16
Connolly, C. 7, 70, 122
Connor, A. 190
Conroy, S. 179
Cooper, B. 187
Cooper, M. 176
Corre, G. 183
Corney, R. H. 90, 182
Coulton, C. J. 190
Cowley, S. 180
Crosbie, D. 176
Culhane, M. 184

D

Dalley, G. 182
Darvill, G. 177–8
David, T. 10, 180
Day, P. 88
Deeprose, D. 34
DES 187
DHSS 176, 181
Dingwall, R. 90, 181
Dobbs, J. 181
DoH 10, 180, 185–6 187, 240
Donnellon, A. 95, 111–12, 157
Douglas, R. 23
Dunnell, K. 181
Durfee, M. 10
Dyer, W. G. 30

E

Eekelaar, J. 90
Eisenhardt, K. M. 148–9
Ellis, R. 75
Ettridge, D. 23

F

Fagin, L. 184
Fatout, M. 7
Faust, K. 11–15, 155–6
Fearnhead, D. 23

Fiedler, F. E. 202
Filley, A. C. 149–50
Fisher, M. 183
Fisk, S. 160–2, 247
Ford, R. 184
Fox, S. 90
French, J. R. P. 142
French, K. 76–7, 83
Fry, R. 6
Fulcher, L. C. 192
Fuller, R. 88
Furniss, 179

G

Garber, L. 190
Garner, H. G. 9, 88
Gawinski, G. 6, 107
Gibbons, J. 179
Goble, R. 186
Goldberg, E. M. 88
Goodstein, L. D. 33
Graessle, L. 6, 107

H

Hadley, R. 176
Hall, A. 88
Handy, C. 82, 86
Harrington-Mackin, D. 34, 66, 88, 151–2, 205–6, 216–17
Harrison, L. 189
Hatch, S. 176
Hatfield, B. 184
Health Advisory Service 185
Hellard, L. 184
Henderson, P. 180
Hendry, E. 187
Hill, S. 34
Hillman, J. 176, 212–13
Hobdell, M. 71–2
Holder, D. 84
Home Office 179, 185, 187
Hornby, S. 113, 126–7
Horwitz, J. J. 8
Houldsworth, N. 10
Hunt, J. G. 203
Huntingdon, J. 182
Hurson, K. 70, 205
Huxley, P. 184

I

Illich, I. 234

J

Jeffreys, M. 182
Jerome, P. J. 163–4
Jones, R. V. H. 186

K

Kagan, C. 158
Kahwajy, J. L. 148–9
Kakabadse, A. 82
Kane, R. A. 6, 43, 88, 147, 181
Kaner, S. 160–2
Katzenbach, J. R. 6
Kearns, C. 184
Keller, S. M. 190
Killilea, M. 16
King, D. 184
Knoke, D. 11
Kuklinski, J. H. 11

L

Leathard, A. 186
Leicestershire Health Authority 239–42
Leigh, A. 35
Lewis, J. W. 71
Lindström, K. 69–70, 159–161
Likert, R. 31, 51–4, 170, 206
Lind, L. 160–2
Lipnack, J. 36
Litwin, D. 190
Lloyd, S. 10, 179
London Borough of Bexley 179
Loxley, A. 27, 28–9
Lundy, J. L. 52–4, 119

M

McCann 123–4, 125, 137
MacDonald, F. 10
McDougall, M. 76
McGeogh, P. 34, 163
McGrath, M. 176
McGregor, D. 30–1, 52–4
McIntosh, J. 181
McIntosh-Fletcher, D. 7
McKenzie, M. 176, 212–13
McLeod, E. 191
Maddux. R. B. 52–3
Maguire, L. 17
Marchington, M. 6, 34

Margerison, 123–4, 125, 137
Marriotti, J. L. 35
Maslow, A. 80
Maynard, M. 35
Mayo, E. 14, 30
Merry, U. 60, 78–80, 103, 106
Metropolitan Police 179
Middleton, L. 180
Mistral, W. 184
Mizrahi, T. 159
Mohamad, H. 184
Morgan Report 10
Morrall, P. A. 183
Mouton, J. 31–2
Mullender, A. 180
Munday, B. 177–8
Murphy, M. 48, 83
Murray, T. 90
Musselwhite, E. 70, 205
Myers, J. 187

N
Nadel, S. F. 14
Newton, C. 183

O
Oakland, J. S. 85, 107–8
O'Neill, P. 48, 83
Onyett, S. 184
Orelove, F. P. 9
O'Sullivan, D. 184
Øvretveit, J. 8, 42, 125–6, 190, 209–10
Owen, H. 52–4

P
Pancoast, D. L. 16
Parker, G. M. 52–4, 88, 123
Parker, J. P. 176

Parsloe, P. 55, 87
Pathmanathan, I. 184
Patmore, C. 184
Paxton, R. 10, 184
Payne, C. 23, 78–9
Payne, M. x, 5, 10, 49–50, 72, 85, 130–2, 152, 188
Pence, D. 7, 179
Peters, T. J. 84, 209
Peterson, M. F. 202–3
Perrin, C. 70, 205
Piepe, R. 119–21
Pietroni, P. C. 38, 42, 157–8, 167
Platt, S. 119–20
Plovnick, M. 6
Poppleton, S. E. 202
Pritchard, J. and P. 7, 182
Pruss, A. 117–18
Pugh, D. 23

Q
Quick, T. L. 52–3, 88, 117

R
Raven, B. H. 142
Rawson, D. 128–9
Ray, D. 35
Rayner, S. R. 211, 213
RCGP 181
Redman, W. 7
Reith, M. 185, 214
Rhodes, R. A. W. 16
Rhodes, V. 88
Robeaux, P. 202
Robertson, S. 190
Robinson, D. 184
Rose, S. R. 7, 155–6
Rushmer, R. 75, 102, 104–5
Ryrie, I. 184

S
Sainsbury, E. 183
Savio, M. 183
Schein, E. H. 31, 93, 95, 114–15
Schindler, R. 176
Schmitter, P. C. 16
Scott, J. 11–15
Scott, T. 78–9
Seed, P. 11, 18–19, 99, 128
Seyd, R. 176
Shaw, I. 69, 186–7
Shepherd, G. 40
Sheppard, M. 182, 183, 198–9
Shonk, J. H. 6, 204–5
Simon, D. 90
Smale, G. 163–5, 176
Smith, D. K. 6
Smith, P. B. 202–4
Smyth, J. 119–22
Sowter, D. 23
Spencer, J. 117–18
SSI 180
Stamps, J. 36
Steinberg, D 94–5
Stogdill, R. M. 202
Stones, C. 180
Storrie, J. 186
Stradling, S. 48, 83
Streek, W. 16
SWSG 179
Syer, J. D. 7, 70, 122

T
Tennant, A. 176
Thistlethwaite, P. 189
Thompson, N. 48, 83
Tibbit, J. E. 190
Tilton-Durfee, D. 10
Toldi, C. 160–2
Trevillion, S. 16, 18–19

Truefitt, T. 88
Tuckman, R. W. 70
Tulle-Winton, E. 88
Tuson, G. 176
Twinn, S. 180

V
Vaughan, P. J. 185
Vellemin, R. 184
Vickery, A. 99
Vroom, V. H. 202–3

W
Walton, R. E. 148
Warburton, R. W. 88
Ward, A. 192–3
Wardle, M. 84, 176
Warren, C. 180
Wasserman, S. 11–15
Waterhouse, L. 179
Waterman, R. H. 84
Weaver, J. 184
Webb, A. L. 71–2
Wells, J. S. G. 185
Welsh Office 10, 187
Wenger, G. C. 17, 99
Werbner, P. 21
West, M. A. 8, 81–2, 156–7, 161–2, 208
Whittington C. 130
Whittington, D. 75
WHO 6, 180
Wilson, C. 7, 179
Wilson, G. 33, 35
Wilson, P. 35
Wolfenden Committee 39
Woodcock, M. 52–3, 69

Y
Yetton, P. H. 202–3

Z
Zenger, J. H. 70, 205

Subject Index

5WH 92, 107, 110, 165

A

accountability 6, 35, 40, 89–90, 168, 170, 176, 186, 194, 202, 209–11, 217
see also: responsibility
action, 'action-sets' 19, 99–100
activities in teambuilding 22, 59, 102, 105, 243–7
advocacy 37–8, 89, 194
affiliation 78
agencies 9, 40, 50, 58, 79, 85, 86, 90, 92, 94, 106–8 134, 145, 147, 149, 176, 194, 196, 203
see also: interagency, multiagency
aim 5, 6–7, 34, 49–50, 52, 54, 56, 81, 90, 100, 115, 123, 149, 155, 168
ambiguity *see* flexibility
ancillary staff *see* paraprofessionals
anthropology 11, 13, 14, 28, 157
appraisal 77, 208
apprenticeship team 72
area team 8, 72, 131–2, 176–8, 204, 212
assertiveness 76
assessment 90, 190
care management 188
child protection 10, 179, 187
learning disability 184
teams/networks 21, 46–67, 93, 97–9, 208, 213
athletics team 8

B

benchmarking 85, 107–8
brainstorming 78, 246–7
briefing *see* team briefing

boundaries 9, 11, 12–13, 68, 72–4, 89, 102–3, 113, 126, 128–30, 132–3, 138–40, 168, 170, 175, 183, 191, 211, 216

C

career planning 76–7, 80
careers guidance 134
care management 17, 188–9
care programme approach 185–6
carers, 16, 36, 62, 78, 80–1, 102, 126–7, 142, 188
case management *see* care management
change, change management 74, 97, 106, 163–5
child protection 7, 16, 38, 41, 176, 178–80, 187, 219, 221–8
Children Act 1989 27, 176, 187
climate 81–2, 208, 218
coaching *see* team coaching
collaboration 5, 11, 16, 36, 40, 50, 52, 68, 74, 82–3, 88, 95–6, 116, 145, 149, 169, 175, 177, 180, 184, 186, 191, 198–200
definition 27
collective responsibility teams 8
collegial team 72
common aim *see* aim
communication 6, 14, 19, 31, 34, 49, 51, 52, 54, 59–62, 70, 82–3, 93, 95, 130, 149, 154, 158–63, 165, 170, 178, 179, 192–3, 211–13
see also: language
community 2, 3, 10, 12, 14, 19, 20, 40, 58, 74, 97, 99, 125, 127–8, 134–5, 144, 169, 172, 176, 220

community care x, 10, 41–2, 88, 186–7, 188–9, 228–34
community health 40–3, 175, 180–6
community justice x, 21, 27, 41
see also: criminal justice, probation
community mental health teams 172, 184, 234–9
community psychiatric nurse (CPN)/nursing 72, 89, 131, 183–4
community social work 176–7
community teams 5, 131
competences 6, 78, 85, 108
complexity 11, 74, 87, 109, 133, 184, 188, 194, 201
complex team 72
conflict 15, 52, 59–62, 87, 88, 90, 93, 96, 122, 133, 148–56, 165, 168, 184, 194, 204, 208, 212, 218
connected 11–12, 128
consultation 16, 32, 74, 77–8, 93–6, 154, 163, 201, 204–5
contingency views of teams/leadership 69, 71–4, 202
cooperation 2, 5, 28, 29, 52, 158, 168
cooperation theory 28–9
coordinate, coordinated professional teams 8
coordination x, 2, 5, 6, 16, 26, 27, 36–41, 68, 76, 179, 186, 204
definition 27, 131
councils for voluntary service (CVS) 39, 73
counselling 1, 73, 181–2, 190, 208
crime prevention 10
criminal justice 2, 21, 38, 239–42
Criminal Justice Act 1991 239

culture 75, 82–4, 86, 157, 185

D

day care 2, 8, 62, 82, 99, 129, 165, 184, 191–4, 213
decision-making, decisions 6, 41, 53–4, 59–62, 93, 97, 125, 138, 147, 149, 150, 157, 192, 211
delayering 35
democratic leadership 31
density 11
development
of services 10
of systems 17
of teams and networks 21, 22, 68–112, 177, 243–7
personal 10, 53–4, 57, 76–81, 192, 208
professional 79
developmental views of team development 69–70
differentiation, *see* task
disability 11, 21, 41, 80, 99, 180, 188, 214
discipline 72–4, 89, 102–3, 157–8
distance 12–13, 18, 96, 115
division of labour 25, 84
doctors *see* general practice, medicine
domain 72–4, 102–3, 149
domestic violence 180
domiciliary care 2
'drawing in' 3, 201

E

early years 10, 180
education x, 1, 21, 38, 42, 89, 134, 157
elderly people 17–18, 29, 42, 80, 88, 100, 181, 188, 193
equal opportunities policies 77, 146
equifinality 28

employee involvement 34
empowerment 4
encounter groups 31
ending 48, 95, 100–1
ethnic issues 21, 35, 51, 80, 83, 95, 113–14, 144, 146–7, 213
European Union 26, 38
evaluation 10, 94, 100, 153, 157, 165, 178, 194, 195–6
  see also: assessment
evidence 49, 54, 56
exchange *see* social exchange
exclusion 59, 76–7, 83, 113, 144, 147
  see also: social exclusion

F
family centres 180
family therapy 17, 47
feedback 92, 152, 159, 162, 192
field theory (Lewin) 13–14, 92
field organisations 74, 169, 175–80
flexibility 86, 88–9, 175
  see also: role blurring
FLIBbers activity 138–40
focal point, focus of networks 12–13, 98–100, 123, 129–30, 138–40, 216
  of tasks 82
  of teambuilding/ work 76, 126, 211
  maintaining 82
followership 22, 202, 212–15
football teams 8
forcefield analysis 92, 110–11, 212
forming 70

G
gender 10, 20, 21, 35, 51, 76–7, 80, 82, 84, 95, 114, 146–7
general practice, general practitioners 1, 8, 38, 39, 40, 41, 99, 132–3, 141, 180–6, 199, 204

gestalt psychology (Köhler) 13–14
goal, *see* aim
'going out' 3, 201
government 25–6, 36–7
GPs, *see* general practice
group dynamics, group relations xi, 3, 13, 31, 53, 59–62, 70, 93, 101, 117–18, 122

H
harassment 147
Hawthorne research 30
health centre 72, 132–3, 180, 83
health visitor 1, 100, 132, 181–2
hierarchy 32, 58, 80, 84, 86, 133, 170–5, 176, 179, 189, 191, 209
high-achieving teams 34, 169
hospital care, hospitals 129, 131, 136, 183–4, 189–91, 204, 212
housing x, 21, 39, 42, 89, 143, 183, 184
human relations management 13, 30–2, 51

I
icebreaking 245
identity, identification 19, 95, 113–15, 124–33, 138–40, 205, 215
individual development *see* development, personal
individuals, individuality 113–140
informal care 16, 185
informality 52, 54, 56, 157, 183, 185, 195, 209
information 15, 19, 40, 52, 58, 61, 84, 92, 125, 134, 138, 145, 149, 154, 157, 186, 196, 201, 212
inspection 10, 194
intake/team 72, 151, 176
integration, role 71–2
integrative teams 8

interaction influence 51–2, 206
interagency 9, 93
  see also: multiagency
interdependence 6, 52, 95, 149, 192
interdisciplinary 9
  see also: multidisciplinary, transdisciplinary
interprofessional 9, 95
interweaving 169, 187
institutional settings 74–5, 189–94
intervention networks 17

J
job enrichment 80–1, 103, 156, 218
Johari window 55, 60–2, 65–6
Joint care planning 184

K
keyworker 39, 90, 193
knowledge, knowledge base 5, 6, 9, 78–9, 85, 89, 113, 115, 145, 156, 165, 206, 209, 217

L
language 82, 95–6, 111–12, 130, 146, 157–8, 160–1, 167
latent characteristics 114–15
law *see* legal
leadership 22, 31, 42, 46, 52–3, 57, 68–9, 75, 83, 93, 104, 122, 158, 201–7, 209, 211, 216–18
  see also: team leader
learning disabilities 40, 143, 184
legal, legislation 85–7, 89, 108, 144, 145, 157, 163
liaison 130, 162, 200
linking pins 31, 170–1, 175, 211
links 53, 55, 56, 97–101, 125, 128, 130–2, 138–40, 184, 194, 211, 212
  see also: relationships
local authorities 26, 40, 73, 170, 175

locality commissioning 2
logistics 78–9

M
management xi, 8, 21, 30–5, 50, 69, 95
  see also: leadership, team leader
managerial grid 31–2
markets 36
mathematics (networking) 10–11, 13, 14
matrix structure/team 172–4, 179, 209
medicine 89, 142, 145, 156, 157, 181
meetings 193–4, 211, 213
members, membership *see* team members
mental health x, 10, 16, 38, 41, 43, 73, 89, 93, 99, 129, 131, 132, 141, 182–3, 183–6, 188, 219, 234–9
Mental Health Act 1983 185, 235
mentally disordered offenders 185
mentoring 20–1, 77
middle managers/being 'in the middle' x, 35, 211–12
minorities 2, 51
mirroring 62, 66–7, 160
mission 7, 81, 107
motivation 34, 54, 75, 78, 84, 103, 104, 106, 116
multiagency 9, 40, 205
  see also: interagency
multidisciplinary 9, 212, 215
  see also: interdisciplinary, multiprofessional, transdisciplinary
multifinality 28
multiprofessional care/teamwork/work 38–43, 77–8, 89, 91, 93, 95, 113, 118–19, 125, 127–8, 133, 142, 147, 169, 178, 180–7, 190, 195, 209–10, 215, 219, 220, 234–5, 242

care management
189
critique 90
definition 4, 9, 21

N
need, needs 80, 81, 115
networking, networks
xi, 3–5, 10–23, 43,
54, 57, 58, 63–4,
72–4, 76, 96–101,
113, 125–35, 158,
176, 189–90, 201,
215
bridge in 12
community 74, 169,
176, 187–9
concentric 13, 126–7
definition of 13,
22–3
diagrams 12, 19, 48,
64–5, 127–9, 131,
135, 166, 175
family 10, 14, 98–9
field of 12–13, 128
as frames of
reference 18–20
interventions 17
issue 16
kinship 14
personal 18–20
policy 10, 24–5,
43–4
points in 11–12, 97,
129–30
sets in 13, 17, 128
social 11, 17, 29, 42,
130
structure of 15
NHS Act 1977 235
NHS and Community
Care Act 1990 27,
176, 184, 185, 235
non-professional *see*
paraprofessional
non-summativity 53–4
norming 70
Northern Ireland 26
nurses, nursing 9,
42–3, 89, 142, 146,
156, 158, 178, 181,
183, 186
see also: community
psychiatric nurse/
health visitor
nursing homes 1, 189

O
objective *see* aim
occupational therapy
146, 165

one-on-one leadership
204
openness 52, 56
open teamwork 3–5,
11, 19–20, 38, 47,
51, 56–7, 59, 73, 76,
78, 81, 88, 101, 116,
123, 124–33, 134–6,
141, 142–3, 144–5,
148, 163, 168–9,
172, 177, 178,
214–16
definition 4–5
manifesto 3–5
operational priority
system (OPS) 88
oppression 2, 90, 141,
148, 199
opted-out schools 1
organisation
development 32
organisations 5, 15–16,
20, 22, 25–6, 28–9,
71, 72–4, 76, 82–3,
86–7, 102–3, 117,
125, 130, 136, 141,
155, 156, 162,
168–76, 183, 187,
202–3, 215
see also: agencies

P
paradoxes in teamwork
1, 168, 215
paraprofessionals 87,
133, 176, 177–8,
181, 213–15
participation 4, 5, 27,
31, 38, 50, 53, 54,
56–7, 75, 83, 100,
105, 113, 126, 142,
148, 150, 156–8,
162, 165, 166–7,
168, 172, 177–8,
180, 187, 201, 204–5
participative leadership
205
partnership x, 2, 27,
35, 36, 37
see also: service
users
'patch' 87, 176
pathways 42
PATIO 213
PAUSE strategy 153
PCGs *see* primary care
groups
performance indicators
(PIs) 87, 100
performing 70
person *see* individual
person culture 82

personal development
see development,
personal
personality 113
planning of services
10, 40
police 21, 39, 41, 89,
175
policy 10, 25–7, 36–8,
50, 85, 87, 163, 165,
178, 185, 192, 196,
203, 211
networks 10, 24–5,
43–4
position 15, 114
power 26, 51, 72, 80,
84, 92, 95–6, 126,
141–9, 156, 158,
163–5, 168, 215
culture 82
principle 92, 144–6,
148, 159, 165, 166
practice nurses 1
preferences 71, 125
pre-school care *see*
early years
presentation (in
linking) 132
prevention 157
conflict 150
crime 10
primary care groups
(PCGs) 2
primary health
care/teams (PHCTs)
41, 129, 180–6, 189
see also: community
health, general
practice
priorities 55–8, 87, 99,
103, 108–9, 163,
205, 212
privatisation 2, 134
probation x, 2, 27,
239–42
see also: criminal
justice
problem assessment/
solving 48, 55, 61
82, 91–3, 110–11,
123, 151, 204
process, process
consultation 32, 50,
60, 70, 93, 149,
162–3, 205, 207, 217
professionals,
professions, 2, 3, 4,
7, 27, 36, 40–1, 43,
44–5, 49–50, 70, 72,
83, 85, 87, 89–90,
95, 97, 113, 116–17,
124–5, 133–5, 145,

147, 159, 169, 176,
181, 183–7, 190,
194, 198–9
see also:
development,
professional
interprofessional,
multiprofessional
projects 34, 77
protection 2, 219
see also: child
protection, public
safety
provocability 28–9
psychiatric care,
psychiatry *see*
mental health
psychology 11, 14, 157
public safety 2, 239–41
purchaser–provider
splits x, 1, 178

Q
quality/management
33–4, 75, 81, 147,
205
questionnaires 49

R
rating scales 49–50,
60, 85, 103–6, 138
rational management
30, 34
see also: Theory X
reciprocity 16, 28–9,
99
reference groups 115
regulation 37, 177
relationships/social
relations 11, 15,
17–19, 20–1, 29, 31,
50, 54, 58, 59–62,
81–2, 84, 99, 104–5,
114, 125, 127–8,
130, 138, 141, 170,
175, 183, 190, 191,
193–5, 203
replacement
(collaboration) 200
representation (in
linking) 132
residential care 2, 8,
10, 18, 38, 41, 59,
62–3, 82, 127, 136,
177, 183, 191–4, 213
resources 2, 15, 16, 34,
40–1, 58, 90, 94,
130, 134, 163, 165,
168, 178, 195, 211
responsibility 7, 9,
34–5, 40, 52, 56, 79,
84–5, 94, 104, 133,
151, 154, 156, 162,

165, 170, 178, 184, 195, 207
  see also: accountability
review 10, 48, 49–51, 53, 54, 57, 74, 91
rhetoric *see* language
RISC strategy 152–3
risk 2, 109, 133
role x, xi, 6–7, 9, 15, 52, 54, 56, 71–2, 75, 79, 82–3, 86–91, 93, 113, 114, 117–24, 128, 130, 134, 149, 158, 178, 191, 201, 211
  blurring 88–91
  clarity 86, 88–91
  culture 82, 86
  integration 71–2, 86–8, 114, 124
  release 9
  subverting 117
  teambuilding 117
  see also: tasks
rotation 80, 88, 205
rounds 245–6
Royal College of General Practitioners (RCGP) 181

S
scientific management *see* rational management
Scotland 26
sector 83, 134
  private 2, 27, 134–5, 188
  public 2, 36–7, 134–5, 155
  state, statutory 36, 134
  voluntary x, 2, 27, 39, 41, 73, 134–5, 184–5, 88
security 78
Seebohm reorganisation 176, 183
self-directed/-managing teams x, 34–5, 74, 86, 169, 206
service development 10, 39–40, 74
service users 1, 2, 4, 17, 18, 36, 37, 48, 49, 53–4, 56–7, 58, 62, 63, 74, 78, 80–1, 86, 87–9, 91, 102, 108–9, 116, 126–30,

141, 142, 144, 147, 148, 169, 170, 172, 187, 188, 194, 206, 213, 215–16
  see also: partnership
shifts 127, 193
situational views teams/leadership 69, 71–4, 202
skills 4, 6, 7, 20, 62, 71, 75, 76–9, 83, 85, 89, 97, 113, 117, 123–4, 156, 159, 163, 191–2, 206, 208, 211, 217–18
snowballing 55, 78, 246
social division 21, 144, 145, 146–8
  see also: ethnic division, exclusion, oppression, social exclusion
social exchange 16, 28–9, 200
social exclusion 2, 20, 38
  see also: ethnic issues, exclusion, oppression, social division
'social loafing' 155–6
social services departments (SSDs) x, 8, 29, 41, 42, 72, 76, 83, 87–9, 129, 143, 165, 175, 183, 188, 196, 204, 212, 240–1
social supervisor 185
social support 17–18, 208
social work/worker 13, 16, 38, 39, 42, 89–90, 131, 143, 146, 156, 158, 181–4, 186, 190, 199
  see also: community social work
sociology, of networks 10
  structural-functional 13
sociometry (Moreno) 13–14
specialisation 71–2, 84, 87–8, 114–15, 176, 177, 183, 209
specialised collegial team 72
sports teams 84

SSDs *see* social services departments
staff development 74, 77–8, 208
storming 70
strategic management/ teambuilding 74–5, 81–4, 203, 215
stress management 76, 79, 106, 150, 212
structure of organisations 22, 74, 141, 170–5, 184, 195, 209, 215
supervision 34, 77–9, 94, 176, 177, 193–4, 204–5, 209, 213–14, 218
support 1, 52, 56, 99, 106, 187, 196, 207–10, 215, 218
SWOT analysis 55
synergy 7, 52–4, 56
systems 7, 14, 17, 28–9, 53, 174–5, 183, 189, 190

T
talk *see* language 95
tasks 6–7, 31, 34, 70, 71–2, 79, 82, 83, 114, 155, 204
  differentiation 71–2, 84–6, 114, 124
  see also: roles
task-focused assessment/teamwork 48–9, 55–9, 123
Taylorism *see* rational management
team
  briefing x, 34, 162–3, 244
  characteristics 6–7, 48, 51–4
  climate 53–4
  coaching x, 34, 77, 204
  definitions 5–8, 22–3
  and network 4
  taxonomy 72
teambuilding 21, 22, 74–112, 204, 243–7
  approaches 74–6
  as circle, cycle 70, 101
  see also: activities, strategic teambuilding
team leader 8, 22, 46–7, 50, 123, 204–8
  see also: leadership

team members/ membership xi, 7, 52, 93, 122, 125–7, 141, 147, 148–56, 170, 193, 196, 204–5, 215
'teamnets' 35
team spirit 70
'teamview' 69–70
teamwork 29–39, 79, 184
  critique 32–3
  definitions 4, 5–8, 27
tennis team 8
tension 177, 185, 196–7
T-groups 31
Theory X and Theory Y 30–1
total quality management (TQM) 33–4
touch 59
traditional teams 3, 5
training 34, 57, 58, 69, 77–9, 81, 85, 88, 89–91, 95, 163–5, 178, 186–7, 193, 206, 211, 218
transdisciplinary 9
transitional teams 5
transport 98–9
trust 52, 70, 116, 183–4, 207

V
values 52, 74, 83, 115, 199, 217
vision 81–2, 107, 211
visits 90
volunteer bureau/ volunteers 3, 39, 80, 177–8, 213–14

W
Wales 26
weight
  network connections 11–13
  factors 110
women 76–7, 82–3
work flow 42, 50, 58
work groups/teams 5, 7, 127, 171
work role 86
work, content/type of 71, 76, 94, 108–9
workloads 50, 55–8, 87–8, 213